I Remember America

THE MACMILLAN COMPANY
NEW YORK · CHICAGO
DALLAS · ATLANTA · SAN FRANCISCO
LONDON · MANILA

IN CANADA
BRETT-MACMILLAN LTD.
GALT, ONTARIO

I Remember America

■ BY WILLIAM E. BOHN

With a Foreword by
CARL SANDBURG

New York   The Macmillan Company   1962
A DIVISION OF THE CROWELL-COLLIER PUBLISHING COMPANY

© WILLIAM E. BOHN 1962

First Printing

The Macmillan Company, New York
Brett-Macmillan Ltd., Galt, Ontario

Printed in the United States of America

Library of Congress catalog card number: 62-13190

TO E. R. B. ■

FOREWORD

William E. Bohn, known to his friends as Bill, is a many-sided man, a writer, an editor, a ball fan, a bird watcher, a bookman, a gardener. He is and has long been a traveler with keen eyes, and among these pages between these covers he takes you to the Grand Canyon with Joseph Wood Krutch as associate interpreter—and you will find him good company among the Maine coast fishermen and the artists and beatniks of Greenwich Village. For many years I have found him good company in his meditations. He learned reading and writing and arithmetic in an old-time pioneer "little red schoolhouse." Later he had the experience of teaching in a city elementary school in which some big, tough lads, now generally known as juvenile delinquents, tried to do him in and got lambasted—he reports the fight amidst these pages. Verily, he has been around the American Scene.

Reading this American citizen, William E. Bohn, you can get with absolute clarity the difference between a Socialist and a Communist. He has been a grade-school teacher, an assistant professor of English at the University of Michigan; and his own story of how he came to leave the University of Michigan for a better-paying position in another institution in the East comes from him as a fascinating narrative. He begins this story with the following paragraph:

"As I enter upon this tale of the events that led to my separation from the academic life, it occurs to me that I owe an explanation to my younger readers. It is now many years since I have heard of anyone who was ousted from a university or college position because of his profession of Socialism. On the contrary, I know a goodly number of men well known to be Socialists who occupy high positions in various institutions of higher learning. There has been a great change in the world of teaching and learning since the days of which I write, away back in 1901–10."

You will find Bill Bohn an extraordinary specimen of a reasonable man, having been a traveler all over America and having been a literary critic, a sportswriter, a geographer, an oceanographer, a smoker of cigars and pipes as against cigarettes, and, as I said before and will now repeat, "a reasonable man." You should find him pleasant company. We could go into the vernacular about him: "He knows his onions," or, rather strictly, "He knows a hawk from a handsaw." Or we might say, "He is a nice guy," but he is one of the nice guys who is also a tough customer in the realm of the reasonable life and how to live it for yourself. My Lords, I have done, save for my final word that high school and college students can learn from these little essays how to be an American citizen who understands the technique of combating Communism.

CARL SANDBURG

Columns by the thousand

Writing a column is like going a-fishing. Sometimes you catch a whopper and sometimes you lose your patience. There are always plenty of lively ideas and events. If you fail to connect with the right ones, the fault lies in your dullness. If you come up week after week with something reasonably racy, ten to one it is your readers who deserve the credit. With all the words and all the paper floating about the world, I cannot give adequate thanks to the men and women who have solemnly assured me: "You know, I always turn first to your column."

During the past twenty years I have written almost exactly a thousand columns. From among this heap we have selected, with a good deal of groaning and gnashing of teeth, just about a hundred. My first little essay went out during the days of Pearl Harbor. The recent ones discuss the possibility of a catastrophe that would make that look like a children's party. At any rate, our old world has not grown dull. These years of my columnar existence are among the most thrilling of my entire life.

If credit is due for the achievement of this millennial series, it should go to Mr. S. M. Levitas, the brilliant creator and manager of the *New Leader*, who has, to our deep regret, now been taken from us, and to the ingenious and resourceful young men he called together on our staff.

W. E. B.

CONTENTS

AROUND THE YEAR

E pluribus unum

■ I am writing this as Red Barber's vivid voice is simultaneously selling Gillette Blue Blades and announcing the last hot game of the hottest World Series in history. More fans have seen these seven games than have ever been drawn together by any other series. The interest centered in them has been more intense; their partisanship has reached a high temperature. In every way, this struggle between the Yankees and the Dodgers has set a record.

But knots of people polarized into unity amid diversity at Ebbets Field or the Yankee Stadium are only the favored few among hundreds of millions scattered far beyond the boundaries of this country. Television, the latest form of magic to enlarge the circle of onlookers, has been only partly responsible. Every office, every school, every barroom, every street corner has practically become an annex of the bleachers. On Friday afternoon I took my regular train from New York to Delaware and my garden. I walked down the street and caught a taxi, fooled about, making some purchases and getting my shoes shined in the station, spent an hour and a half on the train— and at no time was I cut off from Ebbets Field for more than a few minutes. At the corner where I caught my taxi, two television sets kept me and hundreds of others posted right up to the last pitch. In the taxi, the radio took up the tale of mighty deeds. In the station I no sooner left the range of one receiving set than I came within earshot of another. And on the train the passengers in my car divided themselves into two audiences crowded about two portable radio sets. Before we reached Newark, we were pounding one another on the back and shouting exclamations. Common interest and shared knowledge had quickly turned us into boon companions and friendly partisans.

It must have been the same in thousands of far places. I hope that no one will interject a sour remark to the effect that this is an unhealthy and merely symbolic interest in sports. Feeling is so deep,

3

the following of records is so eager, the knowledge and understanding of what goes on are so thorough and so widespread that the millions cannot be accounted mere onlookers and applauders. Intellectually, if not physically, they participate in the fullest sense.

A couple of snooty columnists who shall be nameless slyly express shame at people who can whoop it up for Willie Mays or Mickey Mantle while Africa is starving and the Communists are starting trouble again. Whether we should be ashamed of ourselves is, to say the least, doubtful. Writers who deprecate our lust for crude sports are, of course, always thinking of the cultural superiority of continental Europe. Which reminds me of something.

Some twenty-five years ago a German economist and Socialist, Dr. Alfred Braunthal, fled to this country from Hitlerian Europe, and in the course of time he naturally came to lecture at the Rand School. A point that he made had a bearing on the question of the usefulness of our folkways. The lecturer told a tale that might have been repeated or substantially duplicated by a million migrants from almost any country on the old Continent. He had been born into a Socialist family. He had been educated in Socialist schools, had played on Socialist teams, had spent his spare time at Socialist tasks, had been married in a Socialist wedding, and had found his profession as head of a Socialist school. He remarked dryly that had he remained in Germany, he would certainly have received an orthodox Socialist burial at the end of his Socialist life.

From the cradle to the grave the typical German Socialist lived a segregated life. And not he alone. The German Catholic lived a similar isolated life in his group. The German Lutheran did much the same. And so on. The population was a congeries of separate cells. No one crowd understood or trusted any other crowd. It was taken for granted that all those in one crowd would go on indefinitely hating and fighting everyone in all the other parties and churches and classes. There were at least half a dozen Germanies.

Dr. Braunthal, now a patriotic American and still a loyal Socialist, went on to describe the astonishment with which he viewed life in England after the advent of Hitler had forced him, along with his family, to make a hasty exit from his native land. The English are like us in that they have genuinely national sports.

The German educator viewed a soccer game from the bleachers.

To the stranger's astonishment, there were no Conservative, Liberal, or Labour party teams. No Anglican teams booted balls against the nonconformists. In the bleachers and grandstands men and women of all parties, religions, and factions sat cheek by jowl and applauded their teams. And our astonished onlooker soon discovered that Laborites went to church with Conservatives and Liberals and prayed to the same God.

From here on, you can easily reconstruct Dr. Braunthal's thought. Germany was divided into ideological compartments, and Germany proved to be an easy prey for Hitler. England has a unified population, and the greatest men have to wait for the next election for a chance to unseat the rival party. And in this country, though we have not solved all our problems, we have faith in the common sense and the common decency of our fellow citizens. It's a help. It gives us hope. And the Dodgers and the Yankees are in there pitching for a common understanding.

Red Barber proclaims with well-dramatized excitement that the struggle of titans is ended. The Yanks have won the game by a score of 4 to 3. The Blue Blades, I gather, have carried the day by a much larger margin.   ■

Organized adolescence

■ I used to think it strange that our Negro fellow citizens made such a point of the natural desire to break into professional baseball. The game is, you think, just a sport; the Negroes are getting on in politics, business, the arts—why should they be so hot about playing a game? The answer is that baseball is much more than a game. It is a big sector of American life. If you are out of it, you are only a fractional American.

Many of these fine summer afternoons I have spent with tens of thousands of my coatless fellow enthusiasts at the Yankee Stadium.

There I have shouted, applauded and, occasionally, groaned at the doings of Mantle or Berra. Between crises there was always time to listen to inspired conversation from roundabout. There was, even, time to pursue vagrant thoughts about what my eyes and ears conveyed to me.

I suppose that everyone knows by now that customers are flocking to the games by the million. The morning paper carries the news that 75,000 came out to see the show in Cleveland. The Yankee Stadium frequently serves as host to almost that many. The question is: How has this combination of business and sport managed to polarize the attention of these millions? For many of them it monopolizes leisure time during the spring and summer months. It takes the place of theater, music, personal indulgence in sports and recreation. How come? What is the secret?

The answer must come from the rooter's mouth. And in the long, sunny afternoons of listening, I think I have got it. For the average fan the experience at the Yankee Stadium is a happy regression to his adolescence. For the two tense and coatless hours he is a boy again. He loves and hates with boyish abandon and unreason. He expresses himself with primitive cries of approval and objurgation. All the business, all the moral and political problems of adult life have been rolled off. He lives as superman in the deeds of the highly trained athletes performing before his enchanted eyes.

The performers are admirably fitted to invoke this healing state of mind. Once in a generation there may appear a Christy Mathewson or a Lou Gehrig or some other dignified gentleman player. But the run-of-the-mill heroes are of a different type. All of us frequenters of the ball parks have seen the evidence of this. But, following an old habit, I have done some research. Perhaps you did not know that G. P. Putnam's Sons have published a series of $3 books dealing with teams and a few of the more distinguished players. And they are good. So, with great pleasure I devoted the last weekend to the volume about the Yankees.

If you will follow me in the reading of this history, you will note that the owners of clubs and the managers are very serious gentlemen. They had better be. It was estimated that Colonel Ruppert's baseball empire was worth $7,000,000. But the players who bring in the profit on this enormous investment are nothing but a bunch of kids. Some of them may literally be kids, boys of nineteen or twenty years. But if they play until they are forty, there is usually no diminution in their juvenility.

In 1939 the Yankees trounced the Cincinnati Reds in the World Series. They had beaten all records "by winning four World Series in a row, the last two in four games each." In 1928, at the end of another successful World Series, there had been a convivial celebration on the train bearing the players back to New York. The triumphant heroes had gone through the cars tearing shirts from reluctant backs—even from that of the aristocrat Colonel Ruppert. Now, in 1939, remembering the good old days, the somewhat inebriated celebrants set out to repeat the performance. Joe McCarthy, the manager who had torn his heart out managing this lusty crew, stuck his head out of his drawing room and shouted: "What are you, a lot of amateurs? I thought I was managing a professional club. Why, you're worse than college guys!" In his calmer moments, though, old Joe knew that if these boys had not had the spirit of amateurs and college guys, they never would have won pennants and World Series for him. It is the unbounded, practically unmanageable spirit of youth that makes champions.

Babe Ruth is the top example of all this. I could fill much more than the space allotted to me with tales of his rather crude boyishness. And Tommy Henrich, my favorite player. To see him perform with a ball during batting practice was better than a trip to the circus. To the manager this is business. To the performer it is play.

The fact that a sort of primitive prankishness is one of the sources of success is proved by the history of the Yankees. It is equally well demonstrated by the popularity of the Brooklyn Dodgers. The Brooklyn team and the Brooklyn people have been shamefully maligned. There used to be no better place in the world to pass a sunny afternoon than Ebbets Field. The grandstands were small, accommodating only some 30,000. The spectators were crowded together. There was a warm feeling of community, of participation. The people were like a college crowd or the citizens of a small town. And the players capered about and made good plays and bad with the feeling that they were under the eyes of their neighbors. When Leo Durocher talked back to the umpire, he was merely acting the part of the popular big bad boy of the village.

So you go. I go. Millions go. For an hour or two we shuffle off what we call reality. We live a dream life in a world that is strangely real. Our trip back to our youth and that of our race does us good. The shedding of the complicated pattern of words and actions that has been imposed upon us affords rest for the spirit. So we pay our money, and the profits of the owners roll in.　■

A babe shall lead them

■ I doubt whether we Americans have ever consciously faced graver issues. We stare at the possibilities of a suicidal war. The moral and political choice between freedom and dictatorship is forced upon us. A debate that goes down to the roots of things engages the minds of men around the world. In this country, because of our predominant position among the democracies, even the most heedless and thought-less of us is impelled to take sides in the battle of ideas. We are a more serious nation, a more alert and intelligent nation, than we have been in a long time. But only a few years ago, in the midst of this concern with world affairs, the whole nation—or so it would seem—turned its attention to a man who never went to war, never had an idea, never had any connection with what is regarded as the deeper issues of life. It is easy to see why the writers and radio commentators devoting their time to Babe Ruth feel the need for apology. In our sort of world, it seems somehow improper to pay such homage to a man who was, after all, literally a playboy.

There is something here that requires explanation. The man Ruth drew all eyes and all hearts. The great and the wise, as well as the humble and the foolish, were among his admirers. He had the com-monest touch, the widest appeal. The chubby chap who smote the ball mightily with a stick of wood had admission to every man's heart.

There have been among our great athletes many who were better men. I recall, as millions do, Christy Mathewson and Lou Gehrig. Both of them stood at the very top for brilliant and consistent prowess on the diamond. Both of them were college graduates and, moreover, men of conspicuously fine character. Without being prosy or preachy, both were notable for the good influence they exercised over the young people of their time. In every sense of the word, they had class.

In comparison with these two, Babe Ruth was notable as a rough-neck. He was rough and irresponsible to a really conspicuous degree. How definitely he varied from the Sunday-school, storybook type appears the moment you compare him with the other hero of the batter's box, Ty Cobb. Cobb was no shining knight. So far as I know, he never signed a pledge to abjure liquor, and his language is said to have been more spicy than elegant. He was by no means in the Christy Mathewson–Lou Gehrig class. But he worked harder than Babe Ruth at being a successful athlete. He strained more, paid more heed in order to give a consistent performance. There was lacking the element of careless playfulness that gave the Babe a part of his charm.

Babe Ruth's preeminence was not the result of patient toil. He did not win his way to the top by ceaseless effort. Success was not the result of virtue. He had a gift. That is all there was to it. A fairy may have passed it out to him as he lay in his cradle. Somehow his eyes, arms, legs, and nerves were adjusted so that he could see the ball speeding from the pitcher's hand, meet it squarely, and send it to the far parts of the field or, even, beyond any fence or wall that stood in his way. His reaction was just a little quicker, just a little surer than that of any other player. It was so from the very start. It was not something that he had to learn. It came to him like a golden spoon, a magic touch, a fairy gift. No preacher could point to this man and say to the youth of the land: "See how he has labored and succeeded; go and imitate him."

It was this easy success that gave the Babe his carefree stance. He did not have to try and to train the way others did. He could eat gargantuan meals and wash them down with quarts of drink. He could go gaudily dressed on midnight jaunts when all conscientious athletes were taking their required rest and preparing for the trials of the coming day. He could get drunk now and then and laugh the time away with the friends in every city where his team stopped over for a game. To a fellow with his magic gift, the carefulness required of others was a tiresome and unnecessary virtue. His managers might spend sleepless nights, might swear and warn and fine the Babe. It had no effect. As Fortune's darling, he was above rules and reproofs.

This Falstaffian enjoyment of food and drink and rowdy society fitted in well with Babe Ruth's love of children. A smarter fellow, a more sophisticated man would have restrained the impulse to visit kids in hospitals. He would have been self-conscious. He would have said to himself that the thing would look phony, oversentimental, hypocritical. But this big lumbering fellow never had a doubt. It was the natural thing for him to do and he kept on doing it. He had the impulses of a big and kindly dog. There seemed to him to be no reason for restraint or pretense.

I suspect that the supreme popularity of the great home-run king was largely due to the fact that in this world, which is more and more tightening up on the individual, he achieved a degree of freedom of which the rest of us can only dream. No weight of ideas or duties bore him down. He could talk back to his bosses. He could break all the rules. Common as he was in all his manners, speech, and ways of life, he could stand supreme where tens of thousands of eyes converged and his bat met the ball with a resounding crack. He was the common man's symbol of success and glory. This man batted for all of us. For everyone he knocked home runs and received the plaudits of the multitude.

He received wider homage than other athletes who may have been equally great because of his higher degree of naturalness and spontaneity. He lived continuously at a point where all of us can meet. Especially in a time like this when life seems grim—a man who wore his luck with a careless grace seemed to have achieved the very highest success. ∎

On shooting Santa Claus

∎ I have always been a fall guy for everything connected with Christmas. Both the Christian and the heathen symbols of the season seem to me to be among the best things in our tradition. The

Christ being born of poor parents among gentle cattle in a stable. The Wise Men coming from the East bearing gifts. Santa Claus being whisked gaily across the world in a sleigh to the music of bells, and distributing gifts, theoretically, at least, evenly to rich and poor. Tiny Tim getting a succulent piece of the goose. The transformed Old Scrooge. The carols being sung across the snow and under the stars. . . . The whole celebration is infinitely beautiful and infinitely good. All the crudeness of our commercial stupidity cannot rob it of an iota of its meaning or its charm.

I have, of course, always had to force certain uncomfortable reservations to the back of my mind. Why should there have been such a desperate housing shortage in Bethlehem—or anywhere else? Why, since the war, have so may wives of our veterans been driven to give birth to their babies, not exactly in stables, but in improvised and inadequate homes? Why should Old Scrooge, before his miraculous conversion, keep Bob Cratchit so poor that Tiny Tim was undernourished and undersized up to the moment when he faced the well-advertised and wholly satisfactory Christmas meal? And, finally, how many Old Scrooges never had a dream, and so go on keeping their Bob Cratchits and Tiny Tims on short rations?

All these thoughts about our high holiday coalesced in my mind the other day when someone referred to an immortal remark made by Al Smith. Thinking, I suppose, of FDR's continuing success, the Happy Warrior remarked, "Well, nobody shoots Santa Claus!"

Who is this Santa Claus whom nobody would be inclined to assassinate? Obviously, he doesn't come just once a year. His gifts are more substantial than those that will go into any stocking or adorn any tree. A careless person might say that he is the government— meaning the temporary officials of the United States or of some of the forty-eight states. But a little thought will lead to a different identification.

While we have been looking the other way, a revolution has quietly taken place. The Christmas that Dickens pictured a hundred years ago was a festival of charity. It was good as far as it went. The overflowing feelings of generosity and desire to help, softened hearts that needed softening. But the whole thing was too casual, too fortuitous, to satisfy the conscience of mankind. In Dickens's day the Chartists were marching upon the House of Commons. Since then we have had the Labor party with its Socialism and here we have had our New Deal and Fair Deal. Around the world the trade unions have played their part.

Today Bob Cratchit is probably secretary of the bookkeepers' union. He draws a decent salary and can talk turkey to Old Scrooge, the employer, on Christmas or any other day. As for Tiny Tim, he has had plenty of food and good medical care from babyhood onward. Today he is a husky youngster who doesn't depend on anyone's charity for a good meal. When he says, "God bless us all," it is in no piping or feeble voice. God has blessed him, and he has faith in future blessings. His father has learned that God helps those who help themselves.

What is happening in the world is just the opposite to what ill-intentioned propaganda proclaims. It is loudly proclaimed that people are losing their independence, that they expect handouts from the government. The facts point the other way. In Bob Cratchit's day the poor depended upon charity. From the generosity of the rich came their only relief. And that generosity was but an uncertain and inadequate support. People finally had enough of alms-receiving. They made the great discovery that they themselves are the only satisfactory, reliable, and year-'round Santa Claus.

There are now in this country some 11,000,000 workers who are covered by substantial old-age retirement plans provided for in trade agreements. There are, in addition, all the millions taken care of more or less adequately in our federal and state social security provisions. This has nothing to do with charity or anyone's generosity. There is no handout. The substances divided come from our production week by week. It is our own food and clothing and shelter being divided up among us. Nobody is going to shoot Santa, for that would be committing suicide.   ■

The pleasures of taking a walk

■ Yesterday I did an unusual thing. I took a walk. Here in suburbanite, development-covered northern Delaware where I make my home, everyone has a car. It never occurs to anyone to use anything else. No matter where I am or with whom I am dealing, whenever I have suggested that I could walk home or to any other desired point, I have seen a look of horror come into friendly eyes and I have been buried under multiple offers of cars. One would think I had revealed some proof of dangerous insanity.

But yesterday I was here in my study quite alone. There was no one to interfere and save me from my wild impulse. Beyond my window I could see a clear, clean, and shining world. I needed a haircut, and the barbershop was a couple of miles away. There was no one about to offer transportation by car. I could wander at will through the winding ways of Brandywine Hundred. So off I went.

Pedestrianism offers many advantages over every other sort of locomotion. On my way to the barbershop I made numerous pleasant observations. I was especially pleased by the friendly welcome given me by the dogs as I passed from neighborhood to neighborhood. Many of them followed me as though anxious to make sure I had protection and guidance. For a little way and a short time each one of them was my own pet. And I was interested in the trees and shrubbery planted around the neat new development houses.

Most of the time, however, I was not thinking of the homes and highways of Brandywine Hundred. My mind was far away and concerned with other times, other scenes, and other persons. It was, in fact, picturing other walks with other walkers. My first hikes were with my brother along the Rocky River out there in Ohio, the state where I was born and bred. In or by that lovely, lively stream we could, of course, fish or swim or just loaf. But often we would start upstream or down and just keep on going.

A river is the most lively and altogether satisfactory guide for a couple of boys on a hike. As we went upward it would grow constantly younger, newer, more closely tied in with the land—until, finally, it became a purling brook. As we strode downward, it would become constantly broader, calmer, more dignified and responsible.

Here and there a dam would furnish power for an old-fashioned flour mill and, incidentally, a swimming hole for the boys from miles around. We knew that at the end of its exciting career it would rush foaming into Lake Erie.

Our imaginations were enlivened by the thought that the most intimate countryside stream is a part of that great system that carries the water to the sky, brings it down in the form of rain, and then carries it from the highest mountains, through the widest valleys, and out into the great sea—on its way enlivening and enriching the soil and making possible the life of the human race. What a subject for a couple of boys who were not in the least pressed for time!

In the water, of course, there were myriad sorts of fish, frogs, crabs, and turtles. To a couple of young chaps just getting their first notions of Darwinism, these creatures were a never-ending source of interest. Our discussions may not have been very scholarly, but they were far-ranging and full of bold theories. The chief subject of speculation was the future of mankind. The world would, of course, grow better and better, and we pictured ourselves as taking a not too humble part in this improvement. What a wonderful world and what wonderful lives we foresaw as we lolled on soft banks and listened to the laughing music of the stream!

And then, as I strolled along on my way to the barber's establishment, my mind leaped ahead to the time when, with the most understanding friend I have ever had, I went wandering through the exciting landscapes of northern France. We had started out to spend a year at the Sorbonne, but arrived a couple of months in advance of the opening of the term. My friend suggested that the best way for me to learn French would be for us to turn ourselves loose among the French. So we set out from Rouen and followed our instincts through Normandy and Brittany. Within four weeks I was jabbering French, but this was not the chief result of our method of travel.

In those days—that was in 1903—there were few American students or travelers of any sort in Europe. In our two months on the road we met not a single countryman. We were lost on French roads, in French inns, homes, churches, and cathedrals. We were lost in France. We spoke, ate, drank, and thought as those provincials spoke, ate, drank, and thought. The beauty of the French landscape and the French towns soaked into us. I thrill now when I recall Amiens, Chartres, Beauvais.

My journey to the barber's chair was not so exciting and significant as all this. But it did, at least, give me a chance to call back the richness and goodness of old experience. ∎

Thrushes, larks, and nightingales

∎ If I had nothing else to do, I would write a book about the poets and the birds. I suppose I could begin with Homer, but being fundamentally opposed to labor of any sort, my impulse is to jump to the conclusion that Geoffrey Chaucer would furnish the natural starting point. He was, after all, our first great English poet, and in virtually every way he was tops. He pictured this palpitating world in as lovely a fashion as any other master of words and music. The greater sophistication of later writers seems not to have given them any advantage over him; Chaucer found it perfectly natural to picture men and women living cheerful lives among birds and flowers. His *smale fowles* making melody may not have been bound on a pilgrimage to Canterbury, but they had much to do with cheering up the merry company that set forth from the Tabard Inn.

Shakespeare, too, must have had a sharp ear for the songs of larks, nightingales, and every other sort of tuneful winged creature, for time and again he used them to set his scene or furnish symbols of beauty and cheer. For him the lark forever sang at heaven's gate. And Shelley, the most melodious and inspiring of our later poets, thought of our aerial songsters as his chief teachers and inspiration. He called on the skylark to inspire him with gladness and harmonious madness. Keats thought of his nightingale as instructor: "No hungry generations tread thee down." All these supreme lyricists considered birds chiefly as musicmakers, and did most to celebrate their part in the lives of us comparatively earthbound humans.

I have no skylark and no nightingale in my garden, but there are tuneful songsters aplenty. Our white-throated sparrow surely sings one of the sweetest, most heart-searching lyrics. This year he remained with us practically all winter long and began to sing in the deep cold of February. Now that spring has really come, he starts his roundelay before the dark has been scattered. Our richest and most varied musician is the thrush, who has not yet arrived for his 1960 concert season. But any evening now his notes will rise from the deep woods, and I shall continue my old argument: "Yes, you are quite right: we Americans have no skylark and no nightingale. But we need not envy anyone; we have our thrushes."

It is exasperating to be so close to all these different birds and have so little real knowledge of them and so little satisfactory contact with them. Now and then I read an article about bird migrations. Even the tiniest of them, the hummingbirds, make the long flight over the Gulf of Mexico to their winter home in Brazil. What an engine they must have! I have had explained to me various theories about how they find their way for thousands of miles. Even the fledglings, only recent masters of flight, find their way over land and sea without assistance from their elders.

One observation about this migration business I can make on my own authority. Within my time there have been considerable changes in bird tourism. Birds are not so unvariable and automatic as people have thought. Robins and cardinals go farther north in summer and stay farther north in winter than they used to do. We now have these handsome and lively visitors with us well north during the summer in Ohio and Delaware.

The thing about birds that chiefly fascinates me is the problem about their memories. As I dig in my garden, I am often accompanied by a pair of busty robins. Now and then I turn up a fat worm or some other inviting morsel, and my winged friends, keeping as near as they dare and never missing a trick, manage to gobble up a substantial meal. What puzzles me is the identity of these sharp little operators. For years I have been followed up and down the garden rows by two hearty feeders who look forever the same. They may well be the very same birds year after year. Perhaps they recall this little patch of ground where they fared well in the past and have every reason to believe they will be treated well in the future. Often they seem to be eyeing me with a knowing look. From time to time they chirp little remarks which I, never having learned robin language, fail to understand. So there we are, the robins and I, day after day, year after year—all of us talking and no one understanding a word.

Keats imagined his nightingale was heard in ancient times by emperor and clown, or by Ruth amid the alien corn. I think of my eight or ten sorts of birds and of my squirrels and rabbits as going back much further than that. Their ancestors occupied this wide continent long before any Indians, or any sort of humans, came this way. It was their place long before it was ours. But they have no cause to object to us as impudent intruders. There are many more of them now than there were in more primitive days. Our advance has greatly increased their supply of food. Their songs may be in the nature of payment. ∎

The not so silent night

∎ This is written as bells are ringing, horns are blowing, and every radio station in the country is dreaming of a white Christmas. George Bernard Shaw, who was at once our greatest wit and our greatest puritan, used to writhe in frustration. On the occasion of his ninetieth Yuletide he sent word to the papers: "Fifty years ago I invented a society for the abolition of Christmas. So far I am the only member." Human beings are a contradictory lot. In the 1960's they seem more cynically selfish and cruel than at any other time in their long history. Yet never has there been such celebration of the birth of the prince of peace and brotherhood.

This gorgeous holiday of generosity is a tribute to the spontaneous hopefulness of the young. It is a disguised assuagement of the guilt feeling of the elders. We know that we have made the world a dirty and dangerous place where people have just lately been slaughtered by the millions and where even now great nations are struggling in underhanded and nefarious ways to increase their power and their holdings without the slightest regard for human welfare. Because we have made it such a place, we dare not look into the innocent faces of our children and confess what we have done. So we invent Santa Claus; so we turn on the lights and ring the bells; so we have this time of glee and giving. I am not against it. I am, indeed, very much for it. It is the tribute that vice and failure pay to virtue. It is better to have the spirit of love dominate limited areas for a limited time than to have no love at all. But anyone hearing the songs and the bells must have long, long thoughts about what is going on within the sound of them. The stretch between ideals and reality is as far as ever, and the connection is of the most tenuous.

I was talking last week about the sessions of the United Nations. The General Assembly and most of the committees and commissions hastened their labors in order that their members might hurry away to their homes for the Christmas season. It would have been better had they remained. A little of the spirit of Christmas would not have come amiss at Lake Success.

When Liston Oak proclaimed that he finds the United Nations a bore, what he meant was that he failed to find in its proceedings the warmth and beauty of human idealism. Since the first caveman went out with a club to get what he wanted, there have been people who yearned for a different sort of world. No philosophers or economists were needed to arrive at the conclusion that life would be better if warclubs were turned into firewood to warm the domestic hearth. Each club wielder probably honestly believed that he would prefer a life of peace if only the other fellow could be trusted not to take advantage of him. The idea has been practically universal at least as far back as we have any written record of human thoughts.

Peace, justice, love have been the master themes of all the prophets. When the angels sang "Peace on earth, goodwill to men," they were summing up the message of all religious leaders and of all idealists. Though most of the churches are nationalistic and racialistic, the humanitarian dreams of their founders have continued to echo in the homilies of their priests and preachers. As I have listened to the radio programs during the past few days, I have been amused by the frequency with which Tennyson's resounding lines about "the Parliament of man, the Federation of the world" were repeated over and over again.

The labor movements of the world have always been for peace. International Socialism has always had it at the head of its program.

It had a theory about the causes of war and the way in which they could be removed. At all the great gatherings of the Socialists or trade unionists—no matter what their country or their race or their language—they have spoken longingly of the time when peoples would cease fighting and when they would increase their wealth and happiness by free interchange of goods and services.

And this is far from being the end of the story. Think of the makers of the atom bomb and their stern warnings that we must lay aside our arms. They are fairly representative of the scientists from the beginning down. Then think of all of the artists, the musicians, the writers. There is hardly one among them who has reached any high degree of distinction who has not somehow voiced the mood in which Beethoven finished the Ninth Symphony. And as to the voiceless and ordinary people throughout the world, there can be no doubt about their deep longing.

The plain truth is that this is not a Christmasy world. It is still a brutal, selfish, and bloody world. All the dreams of prophets, preachers, scientists, artists have failed to affect the course of events in Turtle Bay or in the war departments and parliaments of the world. We talk about peace and prepare for war.

I confess that the UN has given us the closest approach we have ever had to Tennyson's vision. The colored nations and races are at least on hand to speak for themselves. They are no longer dependent on the so-called whites. It is notable that when fifteen years ago Madame Vijaya Lakshmi Pandit rose to speak for the Indians who were being discriminated against in South Africa, she was received with warm applause by the delegates of the General Assembly as well as by the large audience. There was general recognition of the fact that here were something new and something fine. Helpless and suffering people had found a voice to speak for them. It was something, regardless of what the Assembly did or didn't do.

And there have been two American delegates who have spoken and worked effectively for humanity. One of them, of course, is Eleanor Roosevelt. What she did for the displaced people of Europe is a notable humanitarian achievement. It was due largely to her persistent efforts that nearly a million men, women, and children may not be sent back to countries where they would face death and imprisonment.

The other American who voiced, at the very beginning of the

UN, the age-old dream of humanity among the crackling of the dry bones of legality was Bernard Baruch. When he made his address before the Atomic Energy Commission, all the humanitarians of the ages were speaking in the words of an American businessman: "We must have wholehearted and not halfway measures. . . . I believe that the finest epitaph would be: He helped to bring lasting peace to the world. . . . I beg you to remember that to delay may be to die. I beg you to hold fast to the principle of seeking the good of all and not the advantage of one." These words were spoken, not in a church, but before the official delegates of the governments of the world. The spirit of peace had found a voice in a place of power.

But such voices were merely harbingers of a better time. And that time is not yet. The most dangerous thing for civilized people to do is to kid themselves. The dream of peace is symbolized by the United Nations. The plea for peace has found a voice in a place of authority. But we do not have peace and, thus far, do not even know how it may be created. The plain truth is that the ancient dream is still a dream.   ■

Astronauts and the human spirit

■ Seven good-looking young married men, each with a high IQ, have been chosen to furnish the first of our Mercury astronauts. A smarter-than-average old man exclaimed, "What idiocy! to go gallivanting off to the moon when we haven't even learned how to run things here on earth!" What my friend had failed to recognize was that this is all part of a process that has been going on for thousands of years. When Marco Polo started toward the East and Christopher Columbus set out for the West, they were responding to a human impulse that will go on as long as the human race remains human.

As far back as we know anything about them, our ancestors have always been restless critters. No matter where it was that they started, they have not been content to stay there. By land and by sea—and now by air—they have pushed out and away. Thousands of years ago they were curiously peering into the secrets of the planets and stars. The development of improved sailing vessels and the increased use of beasts of burden for purposes of transportation made possible the exploration of the central land mass of Asia, Europe, and Africa. By way of the Aleutian Islands and Alaska, the Western Hemisphere was made a part of the human base much earlier than we used to think. And the farthest islands of the Pacific were not left uninhabited.

Means of travel and of communication depended, of course, on invention and discovery. The telescope and the compass increased the safety with which seas could be searched. By the end of the fifteenth century the whole process had advanced to a point that made the initial organized journey to the New World imperative. Had Columbus and his Spaniards not dared to make the great experiment, others would certainly have ventured the trial run. The endless chain could not have been broken.

The period of very little less than five hundred years from the crossing of the Atlantic to the present has been the most active time in human history. Discoveries, inventions, explorations have gone on in every direction and by every medium. For the most part, the little peninsular continent of Europe has been at the heart of this ceaseless activity. During the nineteenth century an astonishing number of advances were made in the United States, which is, after all, in many ways a projection of Europe. And an extraordinary amount of physical and intellectual progress has been made here in recent decades.

As time has gone on, the part played by expert scientists has constantly increased. There have been dozens of Einsteins. Modern physics and chemistry have led to the piercing of secrets of nature that were complete mysteries until recent times. The availability of atomic power has aided our nudging about under and over the ice of the earth's polar regions. Today this new source of energy powers the rockets that send the various sorts of capsules out beyond the air and into orbit about the earth and that, in the end, may carry one of our tiny human beings out to the moon or far and away beyond.

There is something tremendously impressive about the competition now going on between Russia and the United States. These are great, powerful, and ambitious nations. The Russians pushed eastward across the wide reaches of Siberia. We, with our friends the Canadians, rolled on toward the west until we drew up at last at the farthest outstretched finger of Alaska.

But our contest is not merely geographical. We are struggling mightily in the field of ideas, of invention, of discovery. It is a thousand pities that this noble conflict should be debased by association with what is very appropriately called the cold war. We in the free world, who are perpetuating the ancient traditions of learning, ought to remind ourselves that the great achievements of Russian science will remain for a long time after the Soviet tyrants are gone.

I think of all the ships that have sailed, of all the airplanes that have taken off, of all the inventions and discoveries that have been made since Columbus put out from the little harbor of Palos. Inevitably my mind reverts to the thousands who have died in the many perilous adventures by land, sea, and air. And then I look at the pictures of these seven handsome young men, one of whom is to be crowded into a Mercury capsule and sent off and away, not into the upper air, but beyond the air, away from both the earth and the air. I naturally have had the thought that it would be better to send an old fellow like me, a man who has lived his life and had his chance. But the more I consider the matter, the more evident it becomes that this is a foolish notion.

The man who makes this perilous journey must be tiptop. He must make observations, keep records, make decisions. So he must be selected from a group who have the highest IQs and have stood the most rigorous physical and psychological tests. And all that we envious oldsters can do as we wave our goodbyes is to wish this new Columbus a journey with none but the inevitable pains and hardships and, if at all possible, a safe return to the proud and anxious wife and children.   ■

Nikita Khrushchev in my garden

■ Nikita Khrushchev reached down into my house in Delaware the other morning and made me get up at 4:50 o'clock. And, out in the unbelievable loveliness of my moonlit garden, I actually saw Sputnik II bearing its Bolshevik pooch Laika shoot like a brilliant star across the soft and spotless blue of the sky.

To be sure, Khrushchev had an ally in the person of my very effective and efficient wife, Edith, who cannot by any stretch of the imagination be counted among the Communists, though she may have a touch of the dictator. It had been foretold that Sputnik II would burst upon us at 5:07. But the undisciplined alarm clock exploded at 4:30. Theoretically, that is a terrible time at which to be called out of the warm nest of sheets and blankets. But actually, when I came wonderingly into the world of consciousness, my sensation was one of delight.

Even while I was fumbling about in search of winter clothes, I became conscious of the great moon slanting down toward the west and of the magic pattern of shadows on the lawns. When we emerged out of doors, I forgot all about Sputnik and Russia and the poor little dog 'way up there in the sky by herself.

This world right here, in Delaware, in America, in my own garden, was so lovely as to demand all my attention. The full moon was low and bright in the west, and seemed closer than I had ever seen it before. It was easy to imagine why spacemen think that a quick jump will bring them down on its gleaming surface. And then suddenly it occurred to me that the Bolsheviks are not the right ones to make the first contact with a satellite so closely linked with our most romantic experiences and imaginings. They have given a bitter meaning to our very word "satellite." Then came a wild and foolish thought. Suppose that the moon should actually be in danger of Muscovite conquest—imagine the hosts that would volunteer for its defense. The poets and song writers alone would make up a formidable army.

But the garden immediately about me was being transformed by this nocturnal illumination into a landscape quite different from the common scenery of daytime. The shadows of the trees that had shed their leaves were utterly fantastic. Maples, which still flaunted their golden glory, looked like giant bouquets of brilliant blossoms. And flowers on the garden plants that we had tended for years, with which we were intimately familiar, seemed astonishingly large and bright. I am sure that if I had looked the next day I should have seen no such roses and chrysanthemums as bloomed on every side there under that magic light at five in the morning.

It was Edith who called me back to the business of our expedition. She drew me along the driveway. In the soft stillness of the early morning, the crunching of my shoes on the gravel gave out a really thunderous sound. We spoke in whispers—as if there were fairies about who might be disturbed. Soon we reached an open space, away from the trees, where we had a clear view of the south and east. Sputnik I had come from the northeast and flashed off toward the southwest. But Sputnik II was supposed to reverse this course. We were looking away from the moon and up into the soft, deep sky. Just one great planet—it must have been Jupiter—burned low on the horizon. For the rest, the blue was patterned only by the faintest of distant stars. And here were we, alone in the stillness, searching the far spaces for a strange intruder.

And then it happened. It was really an astonishing experience. Everything else up there in the sky was as we have always known it. The Hebrew prophets, the Egyptian astronomers, the Greek philosophers saw the great galaxies slowly turning precisely as they are turning now. But then suddenly, as we looked, there appeared a brilliantly flashing body moving swiftly across the sky past all the ancient configurations with restless and unbelievable speed. In a moment it was gone—and Orion, the Big Dipper, Cassiopeia, and the others remained as they have forever been, outlined in soft points of light.

But the sky for us will never be the same again. Our relations to it, at least, have been forever altered. We human beings have shouldered our way out from our little planet. And when we stand and look, as Edith and I did on that moonlit morning, it seems as if there were a new star up there, a quick, nervous, restless star. It is something new in the universe, a man-made creation with human limitations and peculiarities but astral magnificence.

From the beginning, men have gazed and wondered. Through long ages, the secrets of the heavens have slowly been revealed. But now we begin to see the possibility of flying out and shaking hands with the stars and planets. When we said good night to Khrushchev and Sputnik II, it was comforting to turn back through the garden, which was still homelike and familiar though so strangely transformed. I wondered what the Russians were thinking when they looked up from their gardens to see Sputnik II flashing across the sky. Perhaps that is the most important point of this whole matter.

∎

The continuous incarnation

∎ This is an age of impenetrable pessimism. There is much talk of a failure of nerve. The preachers advertise sermons on the failure of faith. Sometimes I think that what we really suffer from is a failure of memory. In the face of the mysteries of life, men have always been in precisely the same situation. The one thing certain in this uncertain world is that no important change in this relation will ever take place. When we say—as so many do nowadays—that things are worse, that men are harder, that life offers less of hope, our talk is meaningless.

The atom bomb can kill more living creatures in a minute or an hour than could a medieval catapult or a Renaissance blunderbuss. But as far as man's spirit is concerned, the difference is insignificant. Hitler killed human beings by the millions. In previous ages murderers were content with the destruction of hundreds of thousands. But our population is now greatly increased. Everything is done on a greater scale. That there has been a worsening of human thought or feeling no one can prove. No one even tries to prove it.

I have a notion that our blank consternation actually arises from the fact that we are better than our ancestors rather than worse. Perhaps we are more honest in facing up to human cruelty and ignorance. At least among those who do the talking for us there is less tendency than there used to be to gloss over our shortcomings.

We have a horror of hypocrites who try to conceal the ugliness of the present with fine words about the beauties of the future. Our minds are on the heavens and the hells right about us rather than on those of imagination. And it is a part of our ethic—the best part —to insist on talking straight out about what we see.

These considerations may seem far from the bells and wreaths and gifts of Christmas. But they are actually right on the beam. When Christians speak of the incarnation, they refer to the manifestation of spiritual perfection as it took place in the person of Jesus. The most significant statement of this idea is in the first sentence of the Gospel of St. John. We are told that "The word was made flesh." That is, the ideal was made flesh, was made visible, palpable. Goodness, greatness, beauty were made flesh.

The significant thing about man—the very thing that makes him man rather than beast—is his eternal struggle for this sort of incarnation. Looked at in one way, his whole history has been an endless effort toward this sort of transformation. It has been a tireless attempt followed by endless failure. The Christmas chapter of this epic is far from being the only one. And I am not thinking especially of other religions. I have in mind such things as the art of the Renaissance, as the English struggle for liberty, as the American Declaration of Independence, as Abraham Lincoln's devoted life and death. There have been many men in many lands who have struggled to bring heaven down to earth. All of them succeeded in a measure. All of them failed.

Our Bill of Rights was a fine effort to make the real jibe with the ideal. Truman's Civil Rights Commission spelled out for us the degree of its failure. The Assembly of the United Nations has long had an International Bill of Rights. There are many to say that such a step is silly. Russia and all the countries under Russia's leadership will flout such a set of rules. Of course they will. Every fine statement of human ideals has been opposed or disregarded or simply ignored by a large part of the population of the globe. But as long as the fine words are set down where they will be remembered, they are not silly or pointless or useless. They will never let men rest.

In the Christmas story the angels are reported to have sung from the upper air, "Peace on earth, goodwill toward men." This human aspiration, expressed with such brevity and beauty, has never been realized. The Christian churches—as well as all other churches—have failed. We do not have peace. With regard to this ideal—as well as many others—we have continuously fallen short. For a long time our descendants may not do much better than we have done. But if they keep their flag aflying, life will be enriched—and each generation can experience the thrill of inching forward toward the wider, nobler future.

In one respect we are, I think, better than our ancestors. We are more honest. We expect bleak frankness among social workers, psychologists, political reformers, and people of that sort. But I am not thinking of them. I have in mind expressions of opinion that are coming from all kinds of religious circles, both Catholic and Protestant. There is an increase in realism. Church people are no longer content with a purely personal religion. They insist on putting their ideas to work here and now. They have less tendency than folks used to have to grow ecstatic about heaven and the Bible and their own internal experience. It is becoming a matter of duty to stare this tough and unpromising old world straight in the face. That is not bad, but it leads to pessimistic speaking and writing.

But those angels are still singing. The Declaration is still gloriously up there ahead of us. The Fourteenth Amendment of the Constitution of the United States still stands and, by the way, has an interesting chance to be turned from words to reality. The change that has come over us is, in part at least, a lessening of credulity. This great world is like a child that has just discovered that there is no Santa Claus. Whatever good is to come must be of our own creation. Things have not changed. We are just closer to seeing them as they are.   ∎

Winter solstice of our world

∎ It is well for us to remind ourselves that Christmas comes to us from times away back beyond Christianity. The thought is a broadening one, and makes for inclusiveness and toleration. In all parts of our northern world celebrations of the winter solstice were among the high feast days of the year. It is easy to imagine how, in the slow course of centuries, this sort of thing came about. Imagine our ancestors in the forests of Europe. They lived in caves or huts without windows. No Edison had, as yet, invented electric bulbs or kerosene lamps or tallow candles. When the sun went down it was dark—and that was that.

It is difficult for us to re-create the state of mind of folks in those days as the season advanced and the periods of illumination relentlessly contracted. With the long darkness came the unconquerable cold. Men and women were more and more thrown back upon their own resources for comfort and sustenance. The outside world grew daily more savage and inimical. As the season of maximum dark and cold approached—in what we call December—spring and revival must have seemed so far away as to be practically no part of life.

And so—to cheer themselves up in the dark, to fortify themselves against the cruel cold—our faraway forefathers gathered what food and drink they could in so unfavorable a season and had a rollicking feast on or about the time of the winter solstice. The celebration had many names in the myriad dialects, but it was everywhere a very heathen and human affair. Whatever religious meaning it had was very different from anything within our experience. Human creatures in a bleak world found what comfort they could in whatever companionship or gaiety they were able to devise. It was a brave effort to oppose human warmth to Nature's encompassing cold, but of high moral meaning there was a minimum.

And then came the Christian missionaries. Devout fellows they were, and resourceful. No one had any record of the birthday of Jesus Christ. I have never heard that either Joseph or Mary kept a diary. But here was this ancient feast celebrated by all the tribes throughout the wide stretches of forest and plain. By making that occasion the natal day of the Savior, they would ensure its festive celebration and ease the transition from heathendom to Christianity. All that was required was an extension of the ancient symbolism. Originally, the savage heathen had merely prayed to his gods for spring, for warmth, for the return of sustaining vegetation. Under Christian tutelage, they could add the longing for peace and love and the joys of human harmony. It was a happy idea—and it worked like a charm.

This decade of the 1960's seems to be a winter solstice of human history. We have had other bad times, but none so dangerous. There has usually been a leisurely rhythm about both our wars and our depressions. In between there have always been periods when humanity could catch its breath and brace its spirit for the next onslaught of misfortune. All that has now been changed. One reason for the depth of our present distress is the fact that World War II came before the debris of World War I had been cleared away. When my nephew, Dick, came back from his term of service in the Army of Korea, I said to him: "Well, boy, here you are. You've served your time." He answered with his subtle, boyish grin: "That's what you think, Uncle Bill. In five years I'll be going back for the real thing."

The horrors of the atom bomb and chemical and biological warfare have been dwelt on by every lay and clerical preacher using every possible vehicle of expression. Not only are we threatened with more frequent wars. The forms of destruction that loom before us surpass everything imagined by the most unbridled fanaticist. The political structure of the world is more gigantic, less amenable to humanitarian appeals than ever before. Nice people plead for a pacifist policy on the part of the United States. Little do they seem to realize that heading off the looming cataclysm lies outside our power. Our being nice, gentle, understanding, humanitarian has nothing to do with the case. We sing, "May all your Christmases be white," knowing well that some of them are liable to turn lurid red.

A close friend of mine used to say, "The only way to be an optimist is to take a long-range view." Our heathen ancestors heaped wood on their fires and cheered themselves with food and drink when spring seemed far off. When Christ was born and the angels, according to the tale, sang "Peace on earth," the world was an unhappy and war-haunted place. Christmas in its beginning was not a season of carefree rejoicing. It was, rather, a time for men and women to gather their strength and hope for the long pull. In a dark world a candle was lighted. In a tough old place human love was kept glowing. There was the stubborn hope that in time the candle would light all the world and that love would include all humanity.

The Workers Defense League estimates that there are 20,000,000 slaves in this twentieth century world. There are more injustice, more indecency, more cruelty than ever before. For people who believe in Christian—or any other—ethics, the main business is to keep justice, decency, and kindness alive and to widen their scope. Such people must never give up or give in. They must be eternally sensitive to evil wherever it shows its head.

We are persistently being told that people in other parts of the world are so different from us that they do not care for our sort of liberty or justice. Don't believe it. The languages and social patterns of these far people may be myriad and may seem strange, but in their hearts are the same longings as in our own. Some day human love and understanding will penetrate the iron curtains that separate us. If the day were nearer or the obstacles easy to overcome, there would be less need of the Christmas spirit. In the depth of this winter of our world we need it most.   ■

It was fun

■ At last we have had a couple of inches of clean snow on this dirty old town. The window at which I do my writing looks out upon a fine old church. The day the snow fell, I viewed a fantastically beautiful sight. The dark old spire and the dainty finials, even the windows and the doors, were outlined in clean and shining white. The trees were transformed into the daintiest of etchings against the old church wall. While I read in the morning papers how many millions it would cost the city to clear these few inches of shining crystals from the pavements, my mind kept running back to snow in my boyhood, snow in the country—to what snow used to mean when we lived closer to it and entered more intimately into its nature.

The miraculous thing about this shimmering blanket of white is that it creates a new world. At least, that is what it used to do. At night we would say farewell to a universe of familiar greens and browns and grays. Its colors and outlines had changed but slowly through spring, summer, and autumn. Everything about it was usual and expected. And then—suddenly, surprisingly—we would awake on one astonishing morning to an entirely new world. Every familiar object would be transformed into something strangely beautiful. A pump handle or a barn roof or a brook curling through a meadow would be so disguised that one almost refused to believe that down underneath the snow was the same old thing. The entire scene was so new and strange that it furnished a powerful incitement to the fancy.

And somehow the cutting away from routine seemed, for the time, at least, to justify the expectations that had been aroused. My father was a very tough and calculable part of life. He had rigid ideas about when boys should arise in the morning and about how they should spend their time between bed and school. But the change that could be wrought in him by no other influence could be brought about by those millions of tiny crystals that disguised the workaday outlines of life.

When the first great snow came, some fairy or devil or witch possessed that rigid and practical man. From the moment of his awakening and his tasting the tingle in the air, he would be different. There was, in fact, a playful mood about our whole establishment. The shoveling of paths, the feeding of cattle, the carrying in of the wood for cooking and heating—all the routine of life was carried on with a zest that could not be exceeded in any game.

But the climax of the morning came when it was time, finally, to start for school. We had a mile to travel in search of the delights of readin', writin', and 'rithmetic. Even the youngest of us, the six-year-olds, had walked this distance so many times that the journey on foot was not regarded as any hardship. But on the morning of the first snow no such prosaic method of transportation would satisfy my pixilated father. This once his children must go to school in style. No one else in our entire part of the country ever took children to school in a horse-drawn vehicle. But what of that? It had snowed. This was a special occasion. Father was full of life. It was a time to celebrate.

So the cutter was pulled out of the wagon shed. Why it was called a cutter I have never discovered. It was a one-horse sleigh. But what a sleigh! What beautiful curving lines! What a brilliantly shining coat of red! What gay decorative flowers painted in brilliant gold! And into the shafts would be backed old Frank. Now, I suppose Frank would have seemed to an outsider an ordinary farm horse. But on this morning he was far from ordinary. Perhaps it was the great string of bells looped about his middle. Perhaps it was the unfamiliar tang in the air. The very devil had got into that animal. Father had hard work to hold him until we were all packed snugly under the buffalo robe. And the moment he got the go-ahead signal, off he would go, head and tail in the air, the snow from his heels flying over our heads.

The first house we would come to would be the home of the Joneses—and out would come the Jones kids with their sleds. The bells had been their summons. With a belly-bumping dash each one would hitch on behind. Next we would come to the Clarks', then to the Merritts'—and so on. At each house a new contingent would attach itself to the lengthening train. Frank didn't seem to mind. Each new weight was merely a new challenge to his strength and speed. Louder sounded the bells; higher sprayed the snow from his flying heels.

And at last when we swerved triumphantly into the schoolyard, we would unload from our cutter and its pendant sleds fifteen or twenty of the thirty or forty children who sought in this little red schoolhouse all the things that John Dewey talks about.　　　■

BOOKS AND IDEAS

Of youth and age

■ In November, 1950, good King Gustavus and bad Bernard Shaw died at about the same age. Gustavus was called good because, throughout his ninety-two years, he was a perfect example of protective coloration. His contemporary Hohenzollerns and Habsburgs disappeared as wars and revolutions rolled over them. But not the "good," smart, adaptive Gustavus. He had the sense and skill necessary to fit himself into the changing ways of a democratic world—like those arctic birds and beasts that turn pure white for safety against the blinding snows of winter. So he shoved off into the great beyond amidst a chorus of praise from progressive republicans.

Dramatist Shaw made his mark by another technique. He sought distinction by contrasts. Against white, he stood out red. Against black, white was the only hue for him. In a capitalist world, he was for Socialism or Communism. In a meat-eating world, he was a vegetarian. In an alcoholic world he was a teetotaler. In London he blackguarded the British. In New York he heaped abuse upon the Americans. Only once did he fail to run true to form. I do not recall that ever while he was in Moscow did he direct his barbs against the Bolsheviks.

The week this pair died, the public mind was much concerned with the matter of age. Everywhere people were praising the old. Editorials furnished lists of distinguished ancients and recounted their achievements. The statistics were said to prove that we are being shoved ruthlessly into the century of the senile. We are, apparently, preparing ourselves to make the best of it. Everywhere I went people were discussing longevity as if it were as important as the invasion of Laos.

"Look," I was told, "a little while ago people lived on the average about thirty-five years. Now we have a fair chance of hanging around twice that long. If the average is away up there, we are bound to have a lot of individuals who postpone their leavetaking beyond eighty or

35

ninety. What are we going to do with them? We talk about conserving our natural resources. But our Social Security system retires at sixty-five people who may be efficient for ten or fifteen years beyond that age. We utilize every by-product except our fathers and mothers."

I still prefer young people to old ones. What I dislike about the usual sort of aged person is his conceit, his narrow-mindedness, his unwillingness to listen. Old folks are forever talking about good manners, although most of them can learn manners from any boy or girl in the street. But never mind about all that. You can't shoot your grandfather even if you don't like him. So the reasonable thing to do is to figure out some way of making use of him.

Perhaps I can clear the ground by rejecting one distinguished proposal. Away back in 1920 Bernard Shaw suggested that the task of governing the world be handed over to the ancients. He brilliantly outlined this mistaken notion in his *Back to Methuselah*, which was written when the author was sixty-four. In his preface he confessed: "My sands are running out . . . my powers are waning." Despite this surprising show of modesty, however, he felt capable of taking on nothing less than the fate of the human race. The basic theory was that greater longevity would lead to greater wisdom and, thus, to the discovery of the vital secrets of human existence.

Man, GBS argued, is in danger of being proved a failure. He may be scrapped along with the megatherium. The reason is that he lacks the sense necessary to the running of his world. And why does he lack sense? Because he is given too little time to develop it. He is shuffled off two hundred years too soon. If he could go on for three hundred years or more, he might have time for some effective adult education.

It all sounds fine at the start. The act in which the idiocies of the present are pictured gives us a chuckle in every line. But the last act shows us the world in which the thing has happened. People are living hundreds of years. All wisdom is theirs . . . and they are the silliest, dopiest, goofiest gumps that you could possibly imagine.

We all make mistakes. Young people make mistakes. Middle-aged people make mistakes. But we have fun making them. In Shaw's perfect world of the multicentenarians, life has been reduced to a blank. There are no sex, no dancing, no business, no poetry. The only suggestion of a content for existence is supplied when a young lady about to graduate into adulthood coldly remarks to a lover whom she is leaving: "Have you ever thought of the properties of numbers?" The reduction of life to this vacuum is the perfect product of government by the ancients.   ■

The great books of yesteryear

■ The day we moved was really not so bad. The only injunction impressed upon me was that I keep out of the way. Before the day arrived when the great moving van backed up to our door and the cheerful giants began to make a desert of the house where life had been so warm and gay, I had gone through my Gethsemane. I had been sternly told: "There are too many books. You must throw away at least a couple of thousand." Throw away two thousand books! Just mechanically select them, coldly throw them into boxes for the junkman. It seemed too much to ask of any man.

But once I had steeled myself for the sacrifice and set myself to the task of selection, I found the process interesting and even amusing. With rows of boxes ranged on both sides of the library, I went at it. Books to be banished went to the left. Those to be treasured in the bright new home, to the right. Many a time I halted and hesitated. Many a cover roused fond recollection that made a just decision hard to make. But during the long afternoon certain broad principles began to emerge from my activities.

The great mass of discarded volumes came from two periods and had entered our library by two different routes. First, there were the "sets"—at least a dozen of them, with twenty or thirty handsome volumes in each. There was the *Universal, Self-Pronouncing Encyclopedia*. Close by stood *Real America in Romance*, which, an inscription informed me, had cost $65.00 back in 1909. *The Library of Oratory*, edited by the shining Chauncey M. Depew, dated from 1902 and was even more imposing. *The Messages of the Presidents* dated from 1897 and contained all the important documents produced by our chief executives from Washington to Garfield.

As I consigned to the junkman these formidable volumes, most of which had obviously never been read, pictures crowded into my mind of the old days and the old ways. The twenty years from 1890 to 1910 were the period of the traveling book agent. Over most of this continent he antedated the bookstore by many a decade. Bright, gay, well coached, he drove up to the doors of his victims in a "buggy" drawn by a spirited horse. The tired housewife was glad enough to accept this excuse for a respite from her back-breaking toil. Her yearning for refinement—often set over against the blustering crudeness of her husband—prepared her in advance for the glib patter of the ambassador of the books. By paying two dollars a month for two years —or some such time—she could have this bright symbol of the higher life in her own living room. It would definitely set her above the women next door. And so culture was sown across this broad land of ours.

But most of my boxes of books for the secondhand man were filled by the crop from a far different literary inundation. The members of our household for generations past had been devoted to popular fiction. If just everybody was reading a novel, that was the novel to be read. The literary sections of the *New York Times* and the *Herald Tribune* were searched chiefly to discover which works of fiction stood momentarily at the heads of the best-seller lists. Popularity was accepted as the proof of quality. No matter what country or language had produced the widely read work or what its character or style, if people were reading it that was the book to buy. At least, that used to be the way of it.

As I sat there among the books on their way to the junkman, I felt like proposing a day of mourning for outdated novels. An old shoe or a funny ancient hat is a marvel of usefulness in comparison. I saw there dozens of novels that, obviously, had once been shiningly popular but were in this later day completely forgotten. Their titles and exuberant blurbs roused not the slightest glimmer in my mind. I wondered what combination of circumstances had led well-known literary men to write such warm commendations. Their extravagant words now looked rather forlorn in their faded splendor. I naturally fell to wondering whether such of them as were still alive ever feel a twinge of conscience or an impulse to right whatever wrong may have been done.

In the end I came to an important conclusion. To my new library in my new home will go the books that have stood the test of time—those sold neither by a glib book agent nor by a Sanhedrin of literary logrollers. They will be books that were bought by someone who did not have to be told what he wanted. In the new bookcases, there will be no long and dreary stretches of works that are never opened.

Let us reserve our supersalesmanship for coffee or soap or beer. Applied to literature it yields nothing but disappointment. The books we really want are the books that, through the years, sell themselves.

■

Ten books most likely to recede

■ In 1950 the persistently enterprising and provocative editors of the Columbia University Press kicked up some sizable ripples in the quiet pool of academic publishing by conducting a literary-opinion poll. What the Columbia editors conducted was an unpopularity contest. The best-seller lists are constantly showing us which books have the most readers and admirers. These editors took the opposite tack. They asked their readers to report which books have bored them the most painfully. The answers have been carefully counted and classified—with rather astonishing results.

Here are the ten books that stood at the top of the boresome list, arranged in the order of their unpopularity: Bunyan's *The Pilgrim's Progress*, Melville's *Moby-Dick*, Milton's *Paradise Lost*, Spenser's *Faerie Queene*, Boswell's *Life of Samuel Johnson*, Richardson's *Pamela*, Eliot's *Silas Marner*, Scott's *Ivanhoe*, Cervantes' *Don Quixote*, Goethe's *Faust*. Just after these monuments to Morpheus come such historic works as Tolstoy's *War and Peace*, Joyce's *Ulysses* and, to prove the bourgeois character of the entire enterprise, Marx's *Das*

Kapital. Even Fielding's *Tom Jones* and Thoreau's *Walden* are mentioned, which goes to show that some persons can be wearied by anything.

In order to make an intelligent comment on this exhibit, one should really have a breakdown of those sampled in the poll, IQ rating, academic standing, and so on. For these lists tell a lot more about the reporting readers than they do about the books. Among the first ten volumes, for example, only *Pamela* seems to me sufficiently remote from our contemporary manners and interests so that a reasonably alert modern might be expected to find it dull. If a great many representatives of the Columbia intelligentsia found the other volumes sleep-producing, the reason must be within the readers' own minds rather than between the covers of the books.

This thought opens up a wide field for speculation. You will note that the polling operation did not include the young and the irresponsible. The persons referred to in *The Pleasures of Publishing* were mostly librarians and college professors. Poor tired souls! They are weary—and since they have spent their lives with these books they deduce that their weariness results from this association. If they were younger, or if they could have a good rest, or if they had come upon *Silas Marner* and *Moby-Dick* in the back room of a saloon without knowing who wrote them, they would find them exciting.

The saddening feature of this affair is that practically all these books are on the required reading lists of high schools and colleges. The horrid thought intrudes that the yawns they now produce had their start many years ago and that uninspired teaching served as their original cause. That some of the correspondents number Shakespeare and Dickens among their soporifics is enough to prove that the classification has little to do with native liveliness, interest, or charm of the volumes under discussion. Anyone who found these volumes dull must have been abundantly endowed with dullness inside or have been unfortunate enough to have them presented to him in a way that robbed them of their innate liveliness.

It seems to me that our school system must accept most of the blame for what is a record of cultural failure. The librarians and college professors whose reactions to literature make up the Columbia survey just didn't get out of their high school and college courses what people are supposed to get. They came away deadened instead of enlivened. And now, in the full flush of professional life, they flunk a simple examination.

I used to think that I knew just how to remedy this situation. I was myself numbered among those who are strangely called "English teachers," and it was at that time that I reached the conviction that the summary execution of the entire cult would be conducive to human welfare.

In recent years I have become skeptical of my prescription. If you were to shoot the present teachers, our system of selecting and training the coaches who are to teach our youngsters the racy arts of reading and writing would raise up others just as stultifying as their predecessors. What we need is new people at the head of our schools and new ways of selecting teachers. If the so-called "English teachers" were as good at their jobs as the football coaches, what a happy change that would be! ∎

Strictly for the sailors

∎ Charitable ladies are constantly assuring us that members of the International Seamen's Union are hungry and thirsty for literature. They have boxes, barrels, and bags placed at conveniently located spots for the reception of any volumes that citizens wish to contribute to sweeten the lonesome hours of the men whose lives are spent crisscrossing salt water. For years we have designated surplus novels in our house as "strictly for sailors." This is to announce that the men of the boundless deep are about to have their lives enriched by a gift of fat and famous volumes.

Perhaps it is due to my interest in best-sellers. Or it may have resulted from the addiction of our family to the book clubs. At any rate, bookcases, tables, chairs, even the floor, are forever loaded with gaudily jacketed products of the author's, printer's, and binder's art. No one can read them all. They pile up until they are in everyone's way—and then off they go to sea.

Last August I had a vacation. It was that period of perfect sunny weather. I was ordered not to work in the garden. The reading of "heavy" books or articles was forbidden. The ladies of the household set up a bar under the walnut tree. There were all sorts of comfortable chairs, couches, benches, and *chaises longues.* Any sort of drink was available at any hour from shortly after breakfast onward. And, of course, there were books, books not for instruction but for delight, strictly useless and—theoretically—pleasurable books. The object of all these elaborate arrangements was to produce for me a period of utter relaxation and agreeable rebuilding.

The idea was excellent, but it didn't work out. The effect upon my temper was distinctly bad. I never quite got to the point of biting my friends and relatives, but I felt myself well on the way toward it. The books looked handsome. The jackets bore exuberant praise signed by the most distinguished critics and novelists of the land. I began to lick my lips in anticipation. I took up the volumes one after another—and it was like taking bites of nothing. You have had melons like that—without flavor.

Before I turned to other fare, I read as much as I could stand of three volumes which, in a sense, belong to the same class: *The Bishop's Mantle, The Angelic Avengers,* and *Red Plush.* All these have stood high on the best-seller lists. When it first came out, the first one hung 'round so long near the top that it seemed to have established a right to permanent residence. So—whether they are good or bad—they are worth talking about.

In reference to one of these volumes the publisher's blurb-artist committed the following piece of asininity—which certainly should take a prize for being the height of something or other: "To the reader a little wearied by his travels through today's world of realistic and hard-boiled books, *The Angelic Avengers* seems to offer the solace of a cool spring in a breathless wood."

The "cool spring" is a tale that the author makes as hot as his stylistic resources will permit about beauty betrayed, deserted and, at last, winning through to true love and aristocratic marriage. All this is placed in the postrevolutionary England and France of the mid-

1900's. The rather uncertain light of postrevolutionary Bourbons sheds what feeble rays of romance it can muster. *Red Plush* deals with the rising bourgeoisie of Scotland as they palpitated under the attack of romantic passion at about the same period.

Now the authors of the last two of these books were talented writers and conscientious craftsmen. Both tales were worked out with careful attention to detail. Each writer was master of an adequate style. If their tales had been written a hundred years ago, they would have made sense. They would have had meaning as a part of the intellectual flow of life in the America and Britain of the time. They belong to the romantic mode that a hundred and fifty years ago was on its way out but lingered on in examples of increasing feebleness. If Walter Scott had written *The Angelic Avengers*, if Charles Dickens or George Eliot had produced *Red Plush*, both books would have been more pungently written and both would have fitted into their places.

But what sense is there in a talented writer sitting down in the middle of the twentieth century and writing books that would have meant something to people in the first half of the nineteenth? The truth is that in the world of reading and writing we never leave anything behind. A large part of our population—the best-selling lists furnish the proofs—are still in the nineteenth century or the eighteenth or the Middle Ages or God knows where.

I am not complaining about any of this. I find it rather amusing. I might set out to reform the world by proving that the critics are not doing their duty. They are supposed to clarify people's minds about things literary. They ought to tag the products that vie for popularity in the market place. They should do at least as well as the Consumers Union does in its field. But you can read the reviews that appear in the New York *Times, Herald Tribune,* and *Saturday Review* without coming upon a clear statement of fact about any of these books.

I have not done justice to *The Bishop's Mantle.* That this book was read by hundreds of thousands is a disgrace to America, a proof of our cultural primitiveness, and a demonstration of the failure of our educational system. The author was advertised as a former teacher of English. But not only was she laggard and feeble in her picture of life; her style was atrocious, crude, and vulgar. If I were to reproduce some of her purple patches, everyone would think them stolen from some satirist. I have not the time or the patience to examine all the reviews, but I am willing to bet that few critics wrote any adequate and honest description of this horrible creation. I hope that the sailormen have stronger stomachs than I. At any rate, off they go, the lot of them—with *The Bishop's Mantle* at the very top.

■

The shmoo reaches upper air

■ The funnies are the American folklore. It is amazing how many features of the standard fairy tale you can find in them. There is, of course, the beautiful princess—who may, naturally, in this blessed republic, be of proletarian origin. There is the fairy godmother or godfather. The friendly giant is known to all of us. The smart dwarf is also familiar in every compartment of this imaginary world.

This universe with its marvelous events taking place according to their own laws, belongs not exclusively to the junior part of humanity. We who live in New York and watch the devotion lavished upon it by the readers of the *Daily News* and *Mirror* are inclined to say that it belongs—if not to the pure in heart at least to the simple in mind. I suppose that in book form the "comics"—which are far from comical—belong chiefly to those below the age of fifteen. But served up daily in the form of newspaper strips they belong to the seven ages of man. It is not unusual in the subway or a bus to see graybeards dipped low to follow the fortunes of the Gumps or of Alley Oop. There are, in fact, men who have grown old without losing interest in fabulous characters who, for their part, have remained miraculously fixed and firm both as to age and to character.

An intelligent and sensitive mother of my acquaintance was surprised and somewhat distressed the other day to have her darling child say to her: "Look, Mummy, when I get old I won't have to spend all of my time reading as you and Daddy do. I am reading all of your grown-up books now in the funnies. I can read Dickens and Mark Twain and all of the others. I can do it fast. And the pictures make it so much more interesting than just the dull print, print, print."

Things like this bother me very little. Even the notions spread by judges and preachers that crime grows from ideas put into junior's head by Little Mary Mixup I can take with antedotal skepticism. I remember when crime was caused by alcoholic liquor. Then we passed laws to abolish liquor—and we soon had more crime than ever. These fashions in the causes of crime are more amusing than alarming.

This brings me back to the fairy tale—which, in its turn, was put on the carpet not so long ago as one of the sources of criminal tendencies. My mother used to tell them without benefit of print—tell them as she had heard them from her mother. They were, with slight and interesting variations, the same as those recorded by Hans Christian Andersen. But to me now the important point is that Mother told them with obvious distaste. She, having been exposed to the literary and moral standards of her adult life, was ashamed of her childhood entertainment. Even in her youth they had been scorned by the authorities of the upper world. They were something low, simple, boorish, something to be whispered by children or by servants in kitchens.

But out of this lower world of Snow White and Sakuntala and Merlin has come much of the poetry and music of our oh-so-cultivated upper world. Any reader can make his own list of masterpieces to verify the thought. The very symbolism of our intellectual life goes back to the imaginations of the primitive unintellectuals.

Now, if all this is more or less true—if the creations of the upper world come out of the dim imaginings of the lower—perhaps we had better treat with more respect the prodigious accomplishments of Alley Oop and Superman. Soon they may be transformed by poet or composer into something priceless and deathless.

A beginning of this transformation has been made by Al Capp. His *Life and Times of the Shmoo* has been reviewed and advertised in all the regular journals and by all the right people. It is sold on all book counters at the respectable price of one dollar. The people, the scenery, the rules of life are those that have long been familiar to followers of Al's comic strip *L'il Abner*. The combination of pictures and captions produces a hilarious story. It has line, it has style, it has surprise, it has sentiment. And it is in a great tradition, that of the utopians.

Half satire on our profit-making system, half take-off on the picture presented by our reformers, it gets full-throated fun out of the setup of this old world. Because the shmoos furnish meat and drink with no penalties of price or labor, softhearted John, the merchant, has conniptions at the thought of his approaching bankruptcy. "If ev'rybody has ev'rything they need," he mourns, "Ah cain't make any money!" To which Li'l Abner ringingly replies, "Nobody needs money no more!"

This end of capitalism even ends the harassment of Choo-choo, the Show Girl. Having plenty of the liberating shmoos, she is free to tell her fat tempter in the checked suit to slap his steak over his own fat face. What happens to Fatback J. Roaringham, of Porkland, Oregon, and how the carefree world liberated by the shmoos was brought back to the bondage to money and work—all this you had better find out from Al Capp's pictures and print. Incidentally, you may learn how to deal with inflation. At any rate, this first penetration of low-life literature into the shops and journals and minds of the upper world was and is an occasion for congratulation.   ■

American dream and American reality

■ On Sunday, March 7, 1948, the literary supplements announced that Ross F. Lockridge's novel *Raintree County* had topped the best-seller lists. On that same day the thirty-three-year-old author committed suicide. The connection between the two facts will probably never be known. Another thing that will doubtless remain forever hidden is the extent of Hollywood's responsibility for this tragedy.

When he locked the door of his garage and died of the gas from the exhaust of his car, this successful young man had just returned from California where he had conferred with MGM about the movie version of his book.

The mere brute facts of this tale are as strange as anything that could be concocted by a fiction writer. Here was an aspiring young man who seemed to have everything on his side. His father was a university teacher of history. There is evidence that young Mr. Lockridge had learned much from his father. Unlike the authors of the conventional "historical" novels, he had a deep understanding of America's past. He had taught at the University of Indiana and had gone on from there to Harvard. There he worked for seven years on his 1,060-page tale. He had a wife and children. He had to teach to make a living. But for the seven years he worked on and on, apparently happy.

The book received the $150,000 MGM award. It was accepted by the Book-of-the-Month Club for its January distribution. Thus it was assured of a circulation up toward the million mark. What the movie rights would produce by way of income is left to the imagination. Money and reputation were being rained down on this aspiring author. The typically ambitious young American seemed to have achieved a typically American success. All he would have to do to make his place secure would be to produce a new book of the expected sort every year or two. They would probably decrease in quality as he went along, but he was definitely in. In the money. In the reputation.

Here is the paradox of the tragedy. The young man had been happy and hopeful as he labored year after year in obscurity. But when money and reputation came piling down on him, he locked the garage door and left the motor running.

To me this tragedy is especially poignant. *Raintree County* is a strange book but a deeply serious one. Whatever one may think of it as a novel, its appearance heralded a new writer of importance. As I closed the book I said to myself: "Before this boy gets through he may be better than Thomas Wolfe. He has ambition, sweep, ideas. He may be better in the end than any of our other writing men." Just then the papers were brought in and I saw the *Times* headline: "Lockridge Suicide at 33."

Raintree County is not exclusively about America. Mr. Lockridge was not the sort of isolationist who asserts a monopoly of dreams for this country. The book is about men facing life—and death. Placing the story in Midwest America at the time of the Civil War gives opportunity to combine the mythology of our Protestant frontier with that of the Old Testament and of ancient Greece. The raintree is the tree of life found in the primeval swamp. The hero of the story, Johnnie Shawnessy, caught a glimpse of it in his youth. The American dream as embodied in the Declaration of Independence and the faith of Jefferson and Lincoln was somehow symbolized by this tree, the golden pollen from which drifted over the land and was, for the most part, lost.

The history of this country during the crucial years from the Civil War till 1892 is pictured in the lives and thoughts of four men. There are Johnnie the dreamer, Professor Styles the thinker, Garwood Jones the politician, and Cash Carney the capitalist. There are women, of course—and what women! Certainly the livest, realest women in any recent American fiction. But these four men represent the drives that make this country—and the world—what it is.

I don't want to give the notion that this book was a theoretical and abstract sort of thing. It is, actually, a lusty tale. Take, for example, the events wherein the professor is driven out of town by the Ku Kluxers and the charmingly appropriate incidents whereby he is enabled to turn the tables on the bigots and hypocrites toward the end of the book. Or, as a piece of absorbing narrative, take the return of Johnnie to the old home town where for six months he has been supposed dead and where an appropriately inscribed tombstone has been erected.

But the meaning of it all lies beyond the reach of these individual lives. In the light from the burning boxcars destroyed in the Pittsburgh strike of 1877, Johnnie, the professor, and Cash Carney discussed the tragedy of American realities. The year before, they had all attended the Centennial Exhibition at Philadelphia. There they had seen what this country boasts of, "the biggest steam engine," "the biggest ear of corn," and, as the professor remarked, the biggest lies and the biggest blondes. In Pittsburgh they saw desperate American workers destroying the biggest and best railway, the biggest and best system of production.

The dream of the golden raintree is an endless inspiration. The young always have their hopes. Every war begins with them. Every educational system has them at the base of it. But the dreams are constantly being destroyed. The author's hero, Johnnie Shawnessy, is the eternal hoper and dreamer. At the end of the 1,060 pages he is ready to rebuild his world all over again.

Ross Lockridge worked long, and produced this book. Instead of understanding what he had set down, America gave him $150,000 and promised him millions more. Somehow that wasn't what he had dreamed.   ∎

It is earlier than you think

∎ It all began with the reading of Thoreau's *Cape Cod*. He is a deceptive fellow, this Thoreau. I selected the book to go to sleep by. A little dull, you know. One thing after another that Henry looked at with his sharp eyes and set down in print. Nothing exciting. No murders and not a word about the atom bomb or the Third World War. That's where I went wrong. I would be sliding along on a little note about the tide or the sand or the fishermen when all of a sudden old Henry would slip in an idea so exciting that I would sit straight up and forget all about sleep.

Then I went to a party on the North Shore of Long Island. It lasted from Wednesday night to Sunday. It was a good party. Sometimes it would be night and sometimes it would be day. Usually you could tell the difference by the fact that the sun shone in the daytime. But now and then it didn't shine according to program and you got all mixed up. This confusion bothered me only once. I took a long walk down the beach, and after having gone for hours without meeting anyone but a couple of gulls and an old crow, I came on human footprints. What worried me is that, not knowing the day of the week, if I should happen to meet the man who owned the feet that made the footprints on the sand I should not know what to name him.

One pleasant thing about the party was that among the dozen participants there was not one who liked Max Lerner's columns. As the periods of darkness and light succeeded one another, various members of the company would develop an unaccountable interest in the time of day or night. Having taken care to conceal my watch, I sabotaged the effort to secure accurate information on this point. Some day I shall start a campaign against timepieces—all watches and clocks, including alarm and grandfather's. Sundials I may tolerate. They don't work at night or on rainy days. For those three days we lived happily without reference to the hands that so rapidly hurry 'round their appointed dials. And when anyone would demand the time, I would answer cheerfully with my amendment to Max's title: "It's earlier than you think."

That worked first rate. Lateness implies shortness of time, desperation, facing of finalities. Earliness suggests plenty of time to look things over, try things out, have a good time and—as the saying goes— do what comes naturally. At a party it is obviously good policy to spread the notion that things are just starting, that all the most exciting acts are still to come.

With Thoreau and *Cape Cod* I had less success. Every now and then during a lull in the conversational orchestration I would suggest: "Now, just about a century ago Henry D. Thoreau was sitting, as we are now, listening to the surge of the sea, and he had an interesting idea." That was as far as I ever got. Perhaps my approach was not right. It may have sounded too much like the introduction to a speech. At any rate, my mention of Henry was always the prelude to a new swell of the conversation piece.

At one point one of the young ladies gave me an exceptional opening. She suggested the abolition of Long Island. Her argument had a purely literary basis. She had been commenting on the effect of this elongated strip of land on current novels. You may have noted that when a novelist takes his characters to Long Island they rapidly deteriorate and the narrative goes to pieces. Her geographical sacrifice was designed to prevent this sort of thing.

Now, the startling fact is that what my young revolutionary friend proposed to do at one fell stroke Nature is accomplishing in her own patient and perennial way. As I walked along the beach under the high bluff of that North Shore, I could see where great clumps of the good soil had been undermined and had come skidding down to sea level, bearing with them trees and shrubbery. One of the oldest inhabitants relates that a rock now some yards out to sea in her girlhood rested cozily on shore. According to her calculations, the sea is devouring the land at the rate of about one foot per year. I will leave it to someone else to calculate how long the island will last at that rate.

My friend Henry discovered the same process under way on Cape Cod. With the passage of time there was less soil, trees and shrubbery gave less coverage, wind was blowing away the sand. But he was far from discouraged. The process was so leisurely that it would require practically forever for its completion, and who could know that it would not be reversed in the course of ages? Nature is like that. And the prophet's feeling has been justified by the fact that a century later the Provincetown Players found enough of dune and beach left in place to serve as the launching place for their descent upon New York.

Henry found comfort, too, in the fact that the sea remained unchanged from age to age. The transformations on land, which seemed revolutionary to many even at that early date, were disturbing to him. The railways, the factories, the big towns, the smoke, the hurry and worry—it seemed to him that all of them were a threat to whatever was good on earth. But the sea had not been conquered. The tides rolled in and out as they always had, and underneath the waves life was as wild as ever it had been. In the deeps remained mysteries that man would probably never penetrate. Some reservoirs of Nature were unconquerable, and the sage of little Walden Pond took comfort in the thought. He shared the feeling of Isaac Newton that great seas of knowledge lay undiscovered before him.

Suppose that another Thoreau were to walk the shores of Cape Cod or Long Island in the year 2046. With his careful eye he would note the slow inroads of the water upon the land. His sensitive mind would be troubled by the increasing mechanizing of life. And it is possible that he would be disturbed by the thought that few of the moral values he knew in his youth would bid fair to resist the pressures of the heathenish life that threaten to tread them down. But, like his forerunner of 1846, he can find comfort in the great untamed seas, vast depths of still-undiscovered truth.

When I listen to my learned friends I have the notion that we are just at the beginning of intelligence. The mechanisms of our own bodies we are just beginning to fathom. Human psychology is just as mysterious as Thoreau's ocean. When hot little men scream that we must do this or that by tomorrow morning or this or that will happen, they may have full faith in their turgid evangelism, but out there on the beach they would sound rather silly.

The progress of civilization is not unlike the slow retirement of icecaps or the crumbling of shores. From Magna Carta to now has been a long time. Intelligence, mercy, the will to cooperate, mutual understanding, democracy—they grow by slow accretion. Revolutions are apparent only to the unschooled eye. The growth of liberty, intelligence, decency takes time. But human nature has the persistent quality of seas and continents. The things that happen to it are never so decisive as they seem. It is only in the long view that we can be sure either of progress or of decay. And no one can tell how far up or how far off we must take our stand to secure a view that is long enough. Of one thing we may be sure. A thousand years from now our descendants will look back on this as a dark—or at least a twilight —age.   ∎

Krutch, Thoreau, and company

∎ I have long cherished the idea of doing a piece on the ecology of Joseph Wood Krutch—with side glances at the American St. Francis who has been his guide and counselor throughout a career of distinguished authorship. When his book *Grand Canyon* arrived, I said to myself: "This is my chance; no man can write a volume about a big hole in the ground that will deserve attention for the entire length of my column." So I just naturally expected to use the wonders of Krutch's career in substitution for the soon-to-be-exhausted delights of the mile-deep, ten-mile-wide amazing crevasse.

But this ecological study must be postponed. This book deserves much more attention than I can give it in my small space. I hate fellows who go gaping about the world exclaiming that Niagara Falls or the Grand Canyon is wonderful. Krutch does no gasping and no gaping. What he does to that big hole is pretty close to magic. He neither rants nor raves. He just quietly explains.

Incidentally, he gives himself a new degree: "Amateur of Things in General." Had I written this column about him rather than about his book, I would have stressed the variety of sciences and arts from which Krutch has drawn sustenance. He has not only exploited all longitudes and latitudes, all climates, temperatures, and elevations. He has moved in on astronomy, biology, geology, physics, anthropology, religion, history, music, and so on and on. He explains the Grand Canyon by utilizing all his arts and learnings.

His muleback journey down into the breath-taking abyss gives the reader a feeling that he is covering the world—including the tiny postscript devoted to the creature known as man. The wild and rugged Arizona wilderness comes out of this book enriched and beautified by having been made the source of knowledge and understanding. The canyon is deeper, the shadows are darker, the great piled-up strata are more solid and colorful, and everything is livelier and lovelier because we are seeing it through Krutch's imagination.

I should record, however, that there were moments when I was inclined to be turned against both Krutch and the idealized pencil maker of Concord. Within pretty definite limits, I will go along with the pair of them. The world of nature is helpful and health-giving. Our crowding populations have destroyed much that was beautiful and valuable. Krutch's account of destruction in this book is horrifying. "More than a hundred species and subspecies of mammals have been known to have disappeared from the face of the earth since the beginning of the Christian era. Along with them have gone perhaps as many birds and an unknown number of humbler creatures. How many plants have suffered extinction has not, so far as I am aware, been guessed at."

Some plants and animals we can very well do without—mosquitoes and poison ivy, for example. And it should be remembered, as a part of the equation, that countless plants and animals have been preserved and spread over the world as population has gained on wilderness. But Krutch's main point will withstand any honest analysis. We have destroyed much, and it is only lately that we have set our minds to preserving and developing.

But there is in both Thoreau and Krutch an attitude toward human beings that I find unpleasant and dangerous. Both of them are afraid of people. Our versatile Amateur of Things in General gives himself away in his discussion of the crowds in our national parks. There are, he explains, three sorts of nature spots, "the wilderness area, the protected nature reserve and the recreation resort." The first is for the small minority, the second for a larger group of the partially civilized, the third for the poor dumb dopes who have never been taught to take care of things. Our author views with dread the onward tramp of this mob.

The hundreds of thousands whom the author saw in our national parks were there because they were hungry and thirsty for the healing that only the wilderness can give. It is inevitable that they should tramp down some dainty plants and endanger the lives of some tiny animals. But whenever I have visited these parks I have been impressed by the awe with which the myriads of common people have viewed the wonders of nature and by the real interest with which they have listened to the talks on scientific topics provided for them.

The millions of people who suddenly have automobiles and the yearning for the woods do create problems, but we cannot solve the problems by being afraid of the people. We need more parks, more guards and guides, more scientists, and greater provision for the comfort of more people. Congress has not created the national parks for the delight of the elite. When I think of these things I always recall a freckled-faced boy who shouted to me as we ended a tour of Mesa Verde: "I learned more today than I ever learned in a day at school." That boy is worth a good many small animals.   ∎

First, second, third, and —ⁿ— class citizens

■ When some Negro objects to being treated as a second-class citizen, I am always fascinated by the phrases he uses to describe his status. If you once start to grade the inhabitants of a state or a town on the basis of any set of standards you can devise, there will be no end to the number of classes you will reveal. And it may be some comfort to the Negroes to discover that not all their people would be in the lower groups, and by no means all those who are called whites would make the upper grades. In a country where about half the citizens habitually remain away from the polls, we are obviously not all first class. And the distinctions may be worth talking and thinking about.

Years ago one of the boys handed me a clipping about newspaper circulation. It seems that the *Editor & Publisher* is feeling happy about an increase in the number of dailies. We have about one daily paper for each family in the country. If they were evenly distributed, every little domestic group would have its own little herald of domestic and world events. It would be a pleasant picture. Each citizen would go to the polls duly instructed on the issues. Each boy or girl would grow up in a home where the doings of the United Nations or of Congress are daily discussed and evaluated. But this is all a dream. Actually, there is no such distribution of newspapers, or of anything else.

I am told that in New York City there are printed seventeen dailies. That is just about one-hundredth of the journals published in the country. In this town the average family reads three or four papers every day. Many persons read far more than that. What we have, then, is some sections where people read the same news over and over again until it fairly swims before their eyes, and other great sections where the citizens practically have no papers at all. The trouble is not that there is lack of papers but that there is gross maldistribution.

When you look at the quality of the daily journals, the situation looks worse. I am not one of those stultified highbrows who sneers at baseball or the funnies. I would not want a paper without either one.

But the doings of Congress are important to all of us. Every daily should carry good Washington reports. The fates of all of us are tied in with what takes place among the nations. A paper that fails to report foreign affairs is not serving its purpose. There are fewer than a dozen journals in this country that fairly cover these two fields, and all of these are in a few great metropolitan centers.

I realize that papers like the *New York Times* and the *Christian Science Monitor* have subscribers in the far reaches of Arkansas and Arizona. But these are the exceptions, the intellectual aristocrats. Most of the folks living outside the few big-city centers get in print very inadequate reports of the things they need most to know. The education for citizenship furnished by our dailies is ludicrously inadequate.

We have, as I said, 1,763 daily papers. We have more than 5,000 broadcasting stations—radio and TV. And in the nature of things— thank God—these stations cannot be concentrated in New York or Chicago. Nature has decreed that they must be scattered, like earth, water, and air, all across the land. Already the chains bring the Metropolitan Opera and the Philharmonic-Symphony to the isolated homes in the far places. And the daily newscasts and commentaries, too, are to be heard everywhere.

What the newspapers have failed to do the radio and television may succeed in accomplishing. They may, in the end, make the world's news, some of the world's thinking and, even, some of the world's art available to everyone everywhere. When President Roosevelt talked into the microphone he had 20 million or 25 million citizens listening to the same words at the same moment. It is probably the nearest we ever came to national unity. Even if it is Steve Allen or Jack Paar who calls us into a circle that stretches across the continent, it is all to the good.

There is, of course, the little matter of owning a receiving set. There are now tens of millions of such gadgets in the country. There are millions of persons without them. But this is a deficiency that can be made up. And once every family has a radio or TV set, much will have been done to iron out inequalities in the matter of access to news and amusements.

Both the newspapers and the radio are dependent on the drives of what we call private enterprise. The difference in the results achieved gives food for thought. Papers are run to make money without any regard to the service they render. The results are far from satisfactory. Most of our people get practically no service. If the papers were run on a service basis rather than just to make money for their owners, they would be distributed in some quite different way.

The broadcasting systems, too, are run to make money. And they make money—lots of money. Owing to the nature of the mechanism through which they serve their public, the distribution of their wares is far more satisfactory. Newspapers are not at all controlled by the government. Broadcasters, again on account of the nature of their medium, with regard to some points, are pretty rigidly held in check. And it is the system that is controlled that responds most fully to public demand, and gives the most widely distributed service. It is in connection with the enjoyment of the products of this system that we reach the highest degree of egalitarianism we have yet attained. As listeners to the radio, we all come closest to being first-class citizens.

I read the other day that out in New Mexico one of those wide-stretched and thinly populated counties had, with the help of the federal government, given health and hospital service to every citizen. It means nothing at all to others whose homes are just over the line. Think of it! Those simple peasant people who have practically nothing and know very little. Yet they have all the advantages, as far as health is concerned, of the wealthiest citizens of New York. It seems strange—yet it should not seem so. Both are American citizens. I suppose those Spanish-speaking Mexicans out there in the Southwest are third- or fourth- or fifth-class citizens.

I suspect that if we could make a careful evaluation, we should find that the further civilization has advanced, the greater has become the distance between those who enjoy the most and those who have access to the least of its benefits. We hear a lot about the millions going into high school buildings or colleges, about the millions who have the use of all the gadgets. We do not hear about all the other millions who hardly go to school at all or whose gadgets are limited to a hoe or a washboard. As is often said, distribution is our problem.

The conquering plant

■ It is strange that I have written so little about Cuba. Now, don't tell me that it is outside my realm. Technically that redolent island may be foreign affairs, but psychologically, economically, and practically every other way it is a part of our home-front business. Time and again, in fact, Cuba has narrowly escaped being one of our southern states. And the events of 1961 brought it almost *too* close to our doorstep.

One thing that has always impressed me is the wide range of Cuba's culture. On any plantation down there or in any village you can see things that are essentially primitive. But in any town you can meet men who are among the most civilized in the world. One day some years ago this was brought home to me in an unforgettable way. Within a few hours I saw a group of workers who looked and acted very much as their ancestors may have looked and acted a hundred years ago—or two hundred—and had the pleasure, too, of conversing with one of the finest scholars and most finished gentlemen whom it has been my fortune to meet, Dr. Fernando Ortiz, the distinguished historian and sociologist.

All of this is a build-up to introduce the *magnum opus* of this man, *Cuban Counterpoint: Tobacco and Sugar*. It is a grand book, and I hope a lot of people on this North American mainland will take a good look at it. It is, above all, a civilized book, the book of a philosopher thinking, but with all of the advantages of scholarship and none of the hampering disadvantages. In the treatment that Dr. Ortiz gives it, history has been absorbed and is imparted with the refinement and good taste of racy conversation.

The author has a challenging theory about how the life of Cuba has developed about the two enchanting products that the island furnishes to mankind in greatest abundance and highest perfection, sugar and tobacco. The two are alike in that they furnish infinite pleasure, but are different in all else. The sweet stuff that enters so largely in cookery and candy and ice cream has from the start been a product of the great plantation, the inhuman mill, the gigantic financing and marketing apparatus. Tobacco, on the other hand, has been brought into existence by the little, lovingly cared-for field, the tiny shop where sensitive fingers have fashioned each cigar or cigarette. So sugar has been at the heart of an industry that depended on slavery or near slavery. Tobacco, on the contrary, has in the very nature of things developed about it little communities of comparatively free gardeners and craftsmen. The contrasts between the two sorts of civilization developing side by side practically from the time of Columbus down to now has given us the counterpoint about which Dr. Ortiz writes with such clarifying eloquence.

I recall that long ago I wrote of the symbolism of the pipe and the cigarette as they are exhibited in the movies. The pipe is regularly the sign of settled character, mildness of disposition, general sturdiness and reliability. The cigarette, on the contrary, marks the flashy will-o'-the-wisp fellow who fascinates today but is gone tomorrow. It is the fellow who toys gracefully with the little tube of tobacco who first attracts the heroine's eye. But when she is in trouble and the chap smoking the heavy-bowled briar appears, you know that he will take over and there will be a happy ending. On the basis of this well-established piece of folklore, I have long advised my juvenile female friends to have fun with the cigarette twiddler, but when they begin to think about settling down to select their mates from among the patrons of Dunhill or Kawoodie. I might even suggest a commercial: "For lasting satisfaction, take a man who smokes a pipe."

All this I wrote in my days of simplicity before I had had the privilege of perusing the fascinating pages of Dr. Ortiz. I must confess that the learned poet of nicotine rather slights the pipe as the instrument through which his favorite weed is to be enjoyed. This straight or curved object of beauty, it turns out, was never popular in Cuba. The natives of Cuba devised the cigar. The peace pipe was characteristic of the cultures of the neighboring continent.

But since he is historically forced to defend the dignity and charm of tobacco rolled elegantly in its own leaf, our author pays his respects to the cigarette in a way that does my heart good. He complains that the trifling and fleeting paper tube is now produced in a great automatic factory that increases capitalization, exalts machinery, and reduces humanity to the point at which the tobacco industry joins sugar as soul-destroying big business.

But it is time to quote: "The paper-covered cigarette seems to have originated in Seville, thanks to the ingeniousness of some guttersnipe who like the sage of the fable was happy to gather up the leaves which another threw away. The cigarette was the invention of the stub-collector. Thus a symbiosis developed between rich tobacco and the poverty of the lower depths. Every cigarette seems to smack a little of fraud and contraband. In Turkey it was flavored and seasoned until it lost its masculine Indian flavor and sallied forth like a eunuch, to find its fortune in the harems of the world."

But the chief objection to the tiny and momentary smokes is the psychological one. Tobacco has been hailed all over the world as the symbol of thoughtful leisure. There are those who, on this score, are willing to give it credit for the advances in philosophy and science made in the modern world. But, remarks Dr. Ortiz, these are degenerate times. "A good cigar is expensive, it is big and it lasts a long time. Today there is no time to smoke it with the relaxation it demands; in the feverish haste of everyday life it would often have to be thrown away almost as soon as it was lighted . . . the cigarette is small and burns fast and, when necessary, can be tossed aside without loss or regret." All that has been lost, in fact, is the satisfaction that might have been gained from smoking tobacco in a more dignified form.

One passage of this book should be picked up by all societies plugging for better race relations. Just at the turn from the Middle Ages into the Renaissance, civilization received four gorgeous gifts: tobacco, chocolate, coffee, and tea. Perhaps these pleasant stimulants did not cause the rise of modern culture, but they certainly added greatly to its charm. And whence came these gifts? Let all our mean little racist puritans ponder the answer.

These precious additions to the joys of living were given to the whites by the colored races of the four corners of the world. Tobacco and chocolate were sent by the redmen of the new world. Coffee came from the black men of Africa. And tea was graciously served by the Chinese. And the Jews? How did they come into the picture? They were the catalytic, the distributing agent, the international go-between, who speeded the good things on their way. Anyone who regards as inferiors human beings who over long centuries developed such precious products—well, he's a fellow whose judgment is hardly worth taking into account.   ■

Lost on the great semantic sea

■ We have long been irritated by, and secretly envious of, the Communists on the score of their cleverness with words. They are masters of the art of giving a dirty dog a fancy name and passing him off as one of the hounds of heaven. Low-down, old-fashioned oppression is called the "new democracy." Control by a little bunch of infighters is labeled a "people's government." And the nicest people in the country, college professors and preachers, fall for it.

But one of my favorite columnists, Sylvia F. Porter, has pointed a finger at the fact that the boys of Moscow and Thirteenth Street do not enjoy a monopoly of the language that leads astray. We call our huge productive outfit the "free enterprise system," and what name could be sweeter? It's a fine name. Suggests all sorts of pleasant possibilities. We may not have free bread or meat or houses, but if we have free enterprise, what could be more agreeable? And now this Sylvia, about whose identity and intellectual acuteness there can be not one Shakespearean doubt, rises in meeting and snorts, "It just isn't free."

The lady's cue for launching this discussion of our system—if it is a system—was furnished by William Jackman, executive director of the Investors League. The league, she explains, is a nonprofit, nonpartisan organization of stockholders. Now stockholders, except for the biggest ones, are about as helpless as other folks. Probably Mr. Jackman's idea is to line up all the thousands of little people who own a few shares, the widows and orphans of whom we have heard so much, so that they can raise a feeble voice in the conclaves of the great corporations. It is an ambition that is, at least, humanitarian.

So this Mr. Jackman, who seeks a voice for all of the little chaps whom nobody consults, has thought up a scheme to put himself on the map. He has announced a contest. Instead of guessing who Miss Mystery is or how many beans there are in the jar, contestants are to compete in a "National Free Enterprise System Contest." Mr. Jackman, as general of the marshaled investors, has become convinced that "free enterprise" is a misnomer. So we are all asked to send in our pet cognomens for this whirling economic world of ours. Instead of giving a washing machine or a phonograph as a prize, the enterprising Jack-man should reward the victor with an automatic machine for turning out slogans. In her column, which I read in the New York *Post*, the Lady Sylvia sails merrily into all the names we thoughtlessly apply to our way of doing things: "Free Enterprise System? No, it just won't do. . . . Free Competition, then? . . . No. . . . How about Private Enterprise? No, sir! . . . The American Way? . . . I scream a protest." In the end she sums up: "Seems I've knocked down definitions without offering one of my own." But, she explains, this was just clearing away underbrush. The constructive work of definition is to go on from there.

Now, the funny thing about this spirited column is that the one name that is habitually applied to our productive system is that of a capitalist system. Soviet Russia is just as capitalistic as is the U.S.A. All the Soviet five-year plans make provision for capital investment. So does the City of New York. So do the cooperative associations. You just don't do things without capital—no matter what you call yourself or your system. When you call this way of ours a capitalist system, you are merely saying that we, like all other people in the world, use the things that we have produced in the process of producing other things. A fine piece of defining that is. You might as well call this the human system or the natural system or the inevitable system. In Russia, of course, the government owns all the capital, and a few fellows on the inside decide how it is to be invested and who will receive the benefits, but these are mere matters of administration.

The scintillating Sylvia writes but one sentence that I do not like. She says: "And in our modern civilization 'free enterprise' would be the most destructive economic way of life imaginable." As an ancient and time-toughened advocate of free enterprise, I rise to object. When Miss Porter wrote that sentence she was blinded by the twist the National Association of Manufacturers has given to the term. Real free enterprise is the best system for any nation and any time. For one reason, a system that is free is about the only sort that can remain enterprising. Any other variety soon suffers petrifaction of the brain and hardening of arteries. It makes little difference whether freedom is limited by an all-powerful government or a practically all-powerful clique of industrialists.

It is so obvious that we here and now do not have a free system that the matter is not worth arguing. The world needs more steel. But the big boys of the American Iron and Steel Institute have sufficient control to limit our productive capacity. For a long time between the wars it was taken for granted that only three concerns could produce all the automobiles this country needs. It took the Second World War to create the conditions that allowed Henry Kaiser to turn the triangle into a quadrangle—and now, of course, it's back to a triangle.

You read some time ago that various local trade unions had opened grocery stores to help their members fight the high cost of living. We did not have to wait long to hear the reply of the lords of food. Paul Willis, President of the Grocery Manufacturers of America, rushed into the breach. Such free enterprise was, he proclaimed, unfair and un-American. High prices and high profits for the big boys are, you see, tied in with our love of country. Somebody's right to exploit us is characteristic of this country. And—according to the GMA theory—in a free enterprise system some sorts of overrambunctious freedom must be limited. Many of us have taken the easy way of calling ours the "mixed system." That is about as vague as the word "hash" when applied to a type of food. But it has certain implications that are correct. Within our national boundaries there is opportunity for competition as between systems. The Post Office is one sort of thing; TVA is another; the New York Port Authority is still a different one. U.S. Steel is something else again; the cooperatives are quite different; and the corner grocery is different from all of them.

You may have guessed that I am for a free enterprise system but that I want it really free and really enterprising. That is something we have not had up to now. There is among us always the snide implication that if the people as a whole do something—through the United States Government or a state or a cooperative or a publicly owned corporation—by some twist of hocus-pocus that is not free enterprise. If words have the meanings the dictionary gives them, we could freely decide to run all our industries in the interest of all of us, and the whole outfit could truthfully be called free enterprise. The only question for reasonable people is whether we would get the best results that way.   ∎

Meteorological interpretation
of history

■ During a week in the garden I have been thinking of many things
—among others, about the weather. When you have your feet in the
soil and your hands busy with the plants on which human life de-
pends, your thoughts take on a slow and basic quality. You are not
content with the quick reactions that occupy so much attention and
serve as center of so much conversation in the superficial city.
Weather is one of the conditions that encircle man from the start
and to which he must direct his attention down to the final curtain.
It should not be considered in any light or frivolous way.

From the beginning our ancestors have been up against cold and
heat, floods and drought. Think of them sitting out the last of the
glacial periods in the earliest air-raid shelters. Consider those others
constructing their houses crazily on slender stilts to lift them above
the water. Picture all of the houses, walls, and courts built to keep
out the hot beat of the sun. Or imagine the stuffy igloos of the North
and the insubstantial and airy structures of the tropics. Animals of
our kind have spent a large part of their energy fighting the weather
and adapting themselves to it.

Consider the part weather plays in all art and the folklore of the
world. Without the storms and related dangers of the deep there
could have been no Odyssey. Shakespeare's plays, it is true, might
have been written, but there could have been no *Tempest* or *King
Lear*. Try to recall all the novels in which gripping cold, searing heat,
or resounding storms play the leading part. The poor characters
whom you have ingenuously accepted and learned to care for as if
they were neighbors and friends begin to suffer and wilt and wither
under whatever extreme the author chooses to inflict upon them—
until you curse the fellow for his relentless cruelty.

And, of course, the meteorological interpretation of history makes
the others look frivolous. Cold winters and hot summers have caused
famine and pestilence. Folk migrations followed, and brought wars in
their trail. Many a revolution resulted from no cause more remote
than the fact that the people were too hot or too cold or too hungry.

All these meditations floated through my mind as, beneath the beneficently brimming sun, I hilled up the corn or taught the pole beans how to climb. I was thinking of the millions of poor souls I had left behind in steaming New York. Of one thing I feel assured. Extreme heat will never drive them to revolution. To complete compliance and a subordination, perhaps. To revolution, never. If they are ever taken in by a Hitler or Mussolini it will be during a time when the heat has reduced them to imbecility. It seems to rob them of whatever brains or charms or ingenuity they ever had.

Here on our place in Delaware, on the contrary, life in midsummer is altogether delightful. Our house is wide and open to all the winds that blow. Our clothes are adapted to the temperature. That is, we all wear shorts. Our dining room is under a walnut tree. There, unless rain interferes, we eat all three meals. Song sparrows and wrens furnish table music and require no tips except the occasional crumbs. No one complains of the heat, and no one ever inquires, "Is it hot enough for you?"

Consider, in contrast, life in New York or any other American city. We are the wealthiest nation in the world and the most ingenious. But we live in the most stupid ways. The fellows who built New York—or the people who allowed them to build it—never took into account that for a great part of the year it suffers from a high degree of heat and humidity. Packing buildings in cheek by jowl along streets of unbroken cement or stone or bricks, they turned the town into an oven. By night of a hot day the people are all being baked.

The argument about trees on Fifth Avenue reveals the idiocy of our whole way of building a town. One of the great lords of ladies' wear whose palatial shop adorns the upper fifties objects to trees. He is an esthete. Green and growing things do not fit into his symphony of glass and concrete. And, worse yet, trees attract dogs. What could be more incongruous on the most expensive street in the world than a tree being saluted by a dog? We—rich people, smart people, advanced and intelligent people—have built a town that is unfit for dogs or trees.

I suppose it is commonly taken for granted that we must have a city constructed in about this way in order to house seven million people in a limited area. Every day that I spend "in town" I pass rows upon rows of little squat, decayed buildings that are for the

most part uninhabited. Under any rational arrangement they would
long ago have been torn down. A few handsome and well-ventilated
apartment houses would shelter all the persons who occupy the
neighborhood, and leave great spaces for trees, playgrounds and
gardens.

I can easily understand why Lewis Mumford sometimes gets blue
in the face and tends to sputter. We have planners and planners,
books and books, ideas piled on ideas. In New York we even have a
Planning Commission. I have seen grandiose maps of this magnificent
area as it appears in the planners' dreams. But practically nothing
happens. Everything remains just about as it has always been. We
take it out in talk, diagrams, designs. The uninspired realtors are in
control. They are far from having as much sense as the fellows who
put up the lake dwellings or devised the arctic igloos.

We have such an abundant supply of brains in this country and
they are so ill employed! Driven frantic by this thought, more than
one New Yorker during the past year or two has voiced what seemed
like a cruel thought. More than once I have heard men say, "If only
we could have had a bomb or two!" No one wants to contemplate
for his home town all the horrors that were suffered by London or
Hiroshima. But London was shocked into sense. Over there the
County Council consulted our own Lewis Mumford and gave him a
chance to apply his brains. But we have learned practically nothing.
We lack, apparently, the intelligence required to learn from the experience of others.   ■

The judgment of a nation

■ As I emerged from the exhibit of Le Corbusier's work, my mind
was a confused welter of notions. Perhaps this is as good a place as
any to undertake the job of putting them in order. They all had to
do with our ways of thinking about nations, ranking and rating them.

To my horror I discovered that I had succumbed to the current crude fashion of judging peoples, as we judge prize fighters. The man with the heftiest punch is, of course, the champion—and that is all there is to it. Judged this way, Joe Louis is a better man than John Dewey or Albert Einstein.

This sounds crude, but test yourself. Where does each one of our present nations rank on your private totem pole? Here is the way they stack up in the minds of most of us. At the very top are Russia and the United States. A little lower comes Great Britain. France and China we must think of next, but we do it with a skeptical grin, as if we were doing it out of good nature, knowing full well that these two powers are hardly comparable. Then we begin to think of the median powers: Brazil, Canada, Australia, Italy, and so on. Much farther down we place such negligible and easily-kicked-about nations as Belgium, Holland, and the Scandinavian states. And at the very bottom, of course, we discern Germany and Japan. Oh, yes, there is Poland. The Poles are hardly considered at all. A lot of them are dead and the rest of them are poor and miserable. They don't even get honorable mention.

Perhaps you have not been so much bowled over by our current crude standards as I have. Every week I look over dozens of newspapers and magazines. They are full of news, and the comment is by men without memories. The writers seem not to know anything about history. They seem, also, more or less devoid of knowledge of art, literature, economics, science, or industry. They judge all men and nations by the amount of power they wield at the present moment. So I have been infected by what may be called the newspaper mind —if you can call it a mind. My standard has been lowered to that of the current moment.

What I am working round to is the fact that seeing some of Le Corbusier's designs and reading some of his paragraphs upset the hierarchy of powers as it had been formed in my mind by men who have given complete acceptance to the present power standard. And when I began to think of men and nations according to different principles, I found my thought driven straight against almost everything that is now almost universally accepted.

It all began with thinking about France. In the average American's mind just now, that country ranks pretty low. The people over there often make a mess of their government. Before the war they were slow and corrupt and divided. Consequently, Hitler's tanks rolled right over them. But here is Le Corbusier. Before me in this exhibition were photographs of those shining, modern clean-lined buildings of his. There were designs of towns constructed for beauty, comfort, and efficiency all combined. What a man! And Hitler's tanks did not roll over his mind.

This artist, moreover, did not stand alone. In the very first poor little papers that came into this office from Paris after the day of liberation, printed every which way on pathetic half-sheets, I saw proofs of the indestructibility of the French spirit. Hardly had the sound of German boots echoed away when the theaters were advertising old and new French plays. Concerts were being given and art exhibitions held. Books and pamphlets were being advertised. There was a lot that the German tanks never got beneath their treads. Are these people a lot of no-goods? Are they all corrupt? Can they be left out of our account when we take inventory of the things of which we shall build the future?

The fair thing would be to judge nations as we judge men—or as we are supposed to judge them. Each should be ranked according to its accomplishments over a long period of time. For our contemporary nations a fair period to take into account would be five hundred years. We should ask: "How does this or that nation stack up alongside the others when we take into account all the things it has given to the world since the beginning of the Renaissance? This is a test that will give us fair and enlightening results. I cannot apply it here. I lack the necessary space. But you can try it. You will be surprised to note how many of your judgments are turned upside down.

The present giants, the Big Three, will stand high measured by any standard—though the two mightiest of them, the U.S.A. and the U.S.S.R., have only during the last two centuries reached the point at which their contributions to civilization could be taken into account. The first astonishing fact that emerges is that France, judged by this standard, would rank among the very topmost. Germany, too, would rank high. Italy, another nation that current fashion would shove into outer darkness, would have an honorable place. And think of all the little nations that would be seen to be important on the basis of their contributions to mankind. Consider Holland,

Switzerland and, last of all, Poland. These so-called *little* countries were producing great scientists, educators, composers, and writers before some of the present great powers were in a position to make any sort of bid for recognition.　　　　　■

A look at prehistoric America

■ His name was Wayne, and he was a gangling, towheaded junior-high-school boy. We were going with our guide along the edge of Pine Tree Canyon, from one excavation to another. The Indian dwellings, most of them six hundred or eight hundred years old, were exciting. The guide was jolly and full of information.

But somehow this whole experience did not come alive until this typical American boy caught up with us. He happened to overhear a few words from our guide, and promptly deserted his parents, who were taking in the sights on their own, and clung to us with his ears cocked to take in every word from then on. He would race along the sharp edge of the canyon or lean far out over it to get a better view of some point of interest. Through it all he never missed a trick. If the guide asked us to guess the use of some special feature of a structure, he was always ahead of the rest of us with a good guess. And often enough he would come up with a cogent question that gave the guide a chance to explain something he might have over-looked. At last, when we turned back toward our cabin after viewing the fortlike house the peaceful Pueblo Indians had built just before they retreated before their enemies, Wayne drew a deep breath and blurted out, "Gosh! I learned more today than I ever did in school."

This was a part of a day in Mesa Verde National Park. It is a spectacular wilderness in southwest Colorado owned and managed by the National Park Service. I had consulted my travel-wise friends before starting on a tour of our national parks. I had even dropped in at the headquarters of the Service in the Interior building in Washington. There I had taken council with Assistant Director

Hillory A. Tolson and that prince of salesmen, S. Herbert Evison. All these advisers made out a good case for Mesa Verde.

I was curious. What was there about this particular national park that made it a must? Why was it obligatory to spend time and money on a mess of old cliff dwellings and a museum full of ancient relics? In fact, why should the United States Government be spending millions of dollars to preserve and explain such an exhibition?

The Mesa Verde group of old Indian dwellings was first entered by a white man who left a record in 1874. In 1888 it was taken over by the government. In 1916 the Park Service was established, and this became a part of its domain. The Act of Congress establishing the Service provides that "the scenery and the natural historic objects and the wild life" in the parks are to be preserved "in such a manner and by such means as will leave them unimpaired for the enjoyment of future generations." This is all very clear and it gives a fine idea of the breadth of vision of the man who drew up the statute. There are two purposes: preservation and enjoyment.

Edith and I rolled into the eight-thousand-foot-high wilderness two days ago. From the point of view of fun, we have never had a better time. The canyons are breath-taking. The wild flowers are exquisite, varied, and gorgeously abundant. On horseback or on foot, the visitor can cover untamed wilderness to his heart's desire. But that is not what we wanted to know or to do. What about those excavated and unexcavated cliff dwellings? What about those prehistoric Indians?

The superintendent of the park, Oscar W. Carlson, and three of his archaeologists were endlessly patient in answering our questions. They took us from one excavation to another. They explained the peculiarities of Pueblo building and Pueblo life. And, especially, they made clear their own basic objectives with conscientious care.

The first object is, as Congress directed, to preserve both the natural resources and the archaeological treasures. The second is to exhibit and explain the remains of ancient civilization so as to give our citizens a more intelligent view of our own life and of a history of the various nations. Here was the Pueblo civilization beginning in this region about two thousand years ago. Step by step these Indians, whom we call savages, advanced through many phases of living. They had their troubles and their triumphs much like other peoples. Finally, about two hundred years before the tiny caravels of Columbus bobbed into our seas, these Indians suffered drought and were persistently attacked by warlike enemies. So they gave up and moved out.

This story, as revealed in the archaeological remains, is told with infinite dramatic detail to 200,000 visitors each season. Americans love their continent, our archaeologists told us, and they want to know what has happened here. If we come nearer to knowing and understanding our predecessors, we shall come closer to all the races and nations of the world. And possibly—just possibly—if we learn how the Pueblo folk lived and progressed, we may be more inclined to give our contemporary Indians a fair deal. One thing I can say for sure. Never have I seen a set of men more sure of their way of life and happier in their jobs than the archaeologists of Mesa Verde.

■

One world or none? . . . Well, none

■ I thought of calling this piece "Fin du Mondisme and the Man with a Hoe." I even toyed with a more alliterative variation, "The Man with the Hoe and Sidney Hook." The idea came to me on a Sunday when I was pepping up the soil with lime and manure. As a man with his head in one world and his hands and feet in another, I was bent on building a bridge from the frantic thinkers to the calmly ruminant toilers.

Years ago Sidney Hook sounded a warning about something important. Time out of mind all sorts of evangelists, politicians, and salesmen have been trying to stampede mankind. I could fill this page a dozen times over with the funny doings and sayings of people of different periods who thought the world was coming to an end. The point of the anthology would be that in the hours of what was thought to be the final crisis everyone did at an exaggerated rate just about what had always been his pet pattern. The cooks prepared extra food, the tailors tirelessly turned out clothes, and the preachers called to salvation till their lungs gave out.

Now we have the H-bomb. I read such a book as *One World or None* and am reminded of the Millerites. The followers of the prophet Miller—just about a century ago—were convinced that the world would come to its final hour some fine morning. They began to give away their property—a process that was very agreeable to their less sanctified and credulous neighbors. They ended by donning white robes, providing themselves with substantial lunches, and climbing the highest hills available.

The distinguished scientists who wrote the *One World* symposium are convinced that nothing matters but making peace. *Everyone else is loudly shouting with extra urgency whatever it was that he was shouting before.* The preachers proclaim that the bomb will catch us if we don't go to church. The Communists feel sure that the only safety lies in the universal acceptance of their faith. The sellers of toothpaste, soap, cathartics—anything—shout over the radio and television that there is something palliative about the use of their sundry wares. Everyone—from high motives, from low motives and, especially, to sell his copy to magazines—is yelling about his cure-all. When Sidney Hook named our desperate psychological condition *Fin du Mondisme,* he was using a particularly ugly foreign term for a desperately dangerous state of mind.

When the neighbors dropped in on Sunday and we leaned on our spades to gossip, we were at peace. The robins, cardinals, and song sparrows piped no note of *Fin du Mondisme.* There was no pessimism in the gay daffodils or the cloud of bloom that is the magnolia tree. Not that we are isolationists. We talked about people who are starving. One neighbor with a weak heart and another all crippled by arthritis are still bent on getting their seeds into the ground. The general opinion was that we must enlarge our plots and do our best. We were agreed on the proposition that food is a good thing and that if we have more of it, fewer people will starve.

But when it comes to "one world," we're agin' it to a man. The very idea is fearsome. It is natural enough in these superpower times. It is commonly proclaimed that since only a few great nations have power, theirs is the responsibility and authority. The implication is that the little nations may darned well take what is given to them and behave themselves. This sort of brutal thinking passes for realism.

When Wendell Willkie was talking about one world, Eugene Lyons rose to remark that there are at least two. I don't know why Gene was so modest. There are at least thirteen or nineteen or twenty-seven. The more of them we can preserve, the more chance there will be for liberty and blessed variation. It is customary to speak slightingly of the Middle Ages. In those far-off times there were so many little tyrannies that an individual had a break. A stout man on foot could escape from one sovereignty to another between dusk and dawn. But in the one world, if it takes on the ways that mankind seems most likely to adopt, there will be no escape under the sun. If it actually comes into being, the only hope of mankind will lie in the possibility of its breaking up—as did the Roman Empire —and furnishing the raw materials for a new fractionalization.

The frightening thing about the atom scientists is the way in which they throw their absolutes about. Technology is clumping on, and the little man had better pull his head in and do as he is told. We have had a few other such all-or-nothing theorists in the past. But life has gone on. After a century or so, their absolutes have seemed less terrifying. Like the sailor who had been condemned to hell by the irate boatswain, we didn't have to go.

Meditating upon these things I came upon Number I, Volume I, of a magazine called *European World*. Published in Rome by a group of Italians, it is printed in English as well as in Italian. Its purpose is "to fight, theoretically and practically, for the rapid transformation of our continent into a united, solid, active organism." I read the articles with more sympathy than hope.

The absolutists who are plumping for one world without considering what sort of world it is to be should give careful thought to Europe. Consider what civilization owes to the little—and now powerless—countries on that old continent. It is customary in this country to speak deprecatingly of Switzerland, Italy, Belgium, Holland, the Scandinavian countries. Each one of these countries has for centuries on end made unique and precious contributions to world wealth and culture. If at some time in the past any of them had been swept over with an iron broom and reduced to uniformity, all mankind would have been the loser.

From Rome the editors of *European World* now speak up for all that is fine and special in a cluster of countries that have given so much and now suffer in such a hell of poverty and weakness. There are in their first number some charming little essays on literature and music, symbols of a surviving interest in something beyond brute power. And there are political articles about Russia, about Turkey, about Trieste. In all of them one can sense the fear that rides the authors, fear of being engulfed either by the U.S.S.R. or by the Anglo-Americans. Their desperate hope is that through federation the European lands can get to their feet again and assert their independence. In the struggle toward the realization of this hope, thoughtful men everywhere will wish them well.

In standing up for the independence of so weak and backward a country as Iran, these men are defending the possibility of a variegated, interesting, and spiritually fruitful world. In our day we have seen two great organizers at work, two mighty erasers of national boundary lines. One was Hitler. The other was Stalin. So far as lay within their power, each advancing conqueror produced uniformity and sterility. Each was a believer in one world, his sort of world. Against such unified domination the editors of *European World* raise their voices. They have heard of the H-bomb. But they would still like to go on, think, write, sing, paint, eat, govern in their own ways. If this should prove impossible—well, let's call the whole thing off.

I am for *e pluribus unum*.   ∎

Not an exclusively American tragedy

∎ I recently asked an alive and alert young man what he thinks of Theodore Dreiser. He answered, "I don't think of him often and when I do I don't like him." It was more than enough. For fifteen or twenty years the ungainly figure of this man stalked among us as a sort of literary zombie. The young have been hardly conscious of him. This he did not deserve. There was scarcely another man of letters to whom America owes so much.

It is easy to understand what has happened. Dreiser lacked the brightness, the versatility, the wit, the style of Sinclair Lewis, John Dos Passos, John Steinbeck—to mention only three. His prose is unbelievably awkward and often mannered with old-fashioned and countrified turns of speech. And there was this business of turning Communist at the end of his life—just as some others toward the end, when the current runs low, turn to Catholicism. Dreiser scorned the Roman orthodoxy of his fathers at the beginning of life only to fall into the arms of the Moscow creed at the end. This completing of a circle from one rigidity to another could not be expected to rouse admiring enthusiasm among the young.

But the service the man did remains. It is a part of history. He did more than anyone else to jar America into the mood that has made possible the work of his more clever and popular successors. He is the bridge from William Dean Howells to James Farrell. The realism of Howells was smoothly polite and selective. Forty years ago Dreiser broke in abruptly, rudely, dramatically, with *Sister Carrie*. The shock was an important part of our national education.

It was not chiefly the Society for the Suppression of Vice that had to be conquered. When *Sister Carrie* was sent to the critics, the great majority met it with cries of outrage. Their moral vigor was in inverse ratio to their esthetic understanding. Down into the twenties the struggle continued—first about one book, then about another. And if now a novelist is free to write his best and expect a fair hearing, to this queer and awkward experimenter goes most of the credit.

In 1916 Henry L. Mencken hotly overstated his case. I wondered later, if he could still think of "no American novelist who seems so secure or so likely to endure." But no matter. Mencken had sounded a new note, and toward the end of his career—whatever opinions were held with regard to his critical judgment—he was universally acclaimed as a stout fighter in a good cause. In fifteen or twenty years our ways were sufficiently reformed to permit us to write and print and read as adults. It is one of the most important things that have happened to us. And to the stiff, unlovely, angular Dreiser we owe this change.

But old battles won for progress soon lose their glamour. How much is left? What of the books themselves? Is there any good reason why a boy or girl in the year 1962 should read *Jennie Gerhardt* or *The Titan?* There are no moral imperatives involved. Don't read anything that you find dull. But Dreiser has earned a right to a fair chance to everyone's mind. And I, for one, never find him dull.

There is, first of all, the fact that his characters, from Sister Carrie to Clyde Griffiths, come alive. It is a surprising fact. For the method of transferring the impressions of them seems woodenly mechanical. All good novels are, of course, autobiographical. But Dreiser always and naturally uses the honest, open, and cumulative method. His creatures live out their lives before us. The details would satisfy any social case worker. No matter how unattractive or unpleasant they may be, the author is always on their side. He never stands off and throws wisecracks at them as does Sinclair Lewis. The powerful effect of this method is best seen in *An American Tragedy.* As we read on, the people of the book, like those in the tales of Tolstoy, are as real as our own neighbors.

And there is the further fact that the characters live and move in a living and changing world. Dreiser, as far as I recall, made no pretensions of patriotism, but a deep sense of the quality of American society underlies every story. He never courts popularity by sliding snide remarks at his native land or at the humble folk of his little home town. The people, good or bad, smart or dull, are seen in their natural dimensions and given what dignity they are able to claim. If life is tough, Dreiser does not blame America for the fact. There is never the facile implication—as so often in Lewis—that in some other section or in some far country everything is swell, that there— far away—the artist is properly appreciated and no stupid conventions interfere with the course of true love. It is life itself—life anywhere—that wounds the seeking soul with lack of fulfillment. Nowhere does this carefully analytic writer use the jargon of psychoanalysis or of anthropology. But the insights of these sciences are a part of his natural endowment. So there is the sense not only that his characters breathe and grow but also that the whole society grows and changes as we read on. And the particular sector of society on view is a part of the human race, struggling and suffering under the imperatives of its existence.

No doubt Dreiser's fatalism had an unacknowledged part in creating his initial unpopularity. Eugene Witla is drawn by forces to which his eyes are wide open to a marriage that must end in tragedy. Clyde Griffiths, the most harmless of boys, is destined from childhood for the electric chair. It all runs counter to what was in 1900 the American faith. Every American, the theory was, could get rich and marry the prettiest girl in the world. And then along came this dour young chap and pictured us as having all the gay choices of a fly in a spider's web. It was a stunning clout over the head for the massed escapists.

The slanders both from the guild of critics and from the Society for the Suppression of Vice screamed of degrading foreign influence. But we have never produced an artist more genuinely native or more proudly independent. His enemies snarled of Zola. But there is not anywhere a trace of the French realist's ways. Dreiser himself acknowledges a debt to the Russian novelists. But they did little more than give him the comfort that came from the contemplation of their work. From the start—before he had read foreign literature—his view of life and his way of setting it down were fixed by an inner necessity. His sense of things was basically German, but it did not come from outside. It grew from within outward. It is, incidentally, no accident that Mencken, another man of German descent and temperament, was the attorney for the defense. But no one can say that in this case America owed anything of importance to foreign influence.

I don't want any young writer to imitate this man. One Dreiser is enough. But he had a quality that might be imitated to our gain. This stiff and serious author worked consistently, and turned out a long succession of works that all had the sharp stamp of his quality. The fly-by-night fellow who produces one good novel and then peters out in a descending succession of popular potboilers is the most tragic feature of our literary scene. To all such, Theodore Dreiser should stand forever as an accusing representative of artistic conscience.

■

The lake on top of a volcano

■ Because I wrote that California's Yosemite Valley is unlike any other place on earth, I may sound fickle when I proclaim that Oregon's Crater Lake is surpassingly beautiful and unique. There may be some body of water like it in some far place of Asia or Africa, but if there is I have never heard of it. The most exceptional thing about this lake is not that—six miles wide and two thousand feet deep—it lies on the top of a mountain, completely cut off from outside water except for rain and snow. Its main distinction is not even the fact that it lies in the crater of an extinct volcano and is completely surrounded by lava cliffs rising from five hundred to two thousand feet above the water level. Its real distinction is its breathtaking beauty.

As I sit in my room in the lodge of the Crater Lake National Park, I look down upon a surface of heavenly blue that all the ladies in solid phalanx assembled have tried in vain to describe. They have called it delphinium blue, Maxfield Parrish blue, purple blue, Mediterranean blue—and have finally acknowledged their defeat by describing it as Crater Lake blue. The water immediately below me has a color that is so intense it seems to be impregnated with some deep, deep dye. Farther off, toward the opposite shore, it turns to a lighter, gayer, more skyline hue. All viewers of this waterscape agree that they have never seen anything even distinctly resembling it. It gives the onlooker a sense of infinite elevation, perhaps because this vision is beyond reach. The gazing beholder cannot swim in this water, cannot even touch it.

The average visitor says almost automatically that the inexpressible color is produced by reflection of the sky. In a sense, and to a certain extent, this is true. The real fact is said to be that the rays of the sun are separated by refraction from the unusually pure water much as they would be by a prismatic glass. And the blue shade, being singled out and sent up from the surface of the lake, gives the effect of a deep-blue body of water.

The untechnical, rough-and-ready way of explaining how a fine lake could come into existence on the top of a mountain is to say that the mountain blew its top and then the rain and snow filled the resulting cavity with water. What actually happened is so complex and interesting that Howel Williams, professor of geology at the University of California, has published a detailed account of it. What especially fascinates me is his account of the great jagged rim that hems in the sheet of water. The rocks that compose it are of different sorts and have come to rest at various angles. Basing their calculations on the positions of these masses and on the glacial scratches on their surfaces, the scientists can determine the height and shape of the original peak.

My interest right now is centered in another man named Williams, Thomas J. Williams, the superintendent of this exceptionally interesting park. He came from a dirty little mining town in the East, and found the West big and clean and hospitable. In the National Park Service he has had a chance to preserve and expand the features of the country he has grown to love. "The job has a romantic side," he said to me. "We are trying to make people better by giving them a feeling for a mountain or a range of mountains. We have the opportunity to live in an ideal environment and to preserve and improve it. I really feel ashamed to take my pay."

The first purpose of the Park Service, Superintendent Williams explained, is to preserve the beauties of these regions that have been set aside by Congress. The second is to provide enjoyment and recreation for millions of people who have paid for these areas and who own them. The third is to increase their intelligence painlessly while they are having fun. "These three purposes," Mr. Williams drawled as we sat before the great log fire in the camp lodge, "are not separate. Through education and appreciation you secure wise usage that results in preservation. You can't get anything by playing the policeman. Put over the idea that the parks belong to the people, and they will help to defend them."

Crater Lake impressed me as an especially lovely place to spend a vacation. Wildflowers cover the meadows and play an especially prominent part in the community life. On this mountaintop, the evening air is too cool for the campfire talks that are a leading feature of the activities in other national parks. Instead, there are talks in the Sinnott Memorial, a fine stone structure halfway down the great rim. This place allows the speaker to point out the rocky features of his environment as he goes along. And then, every evening in the lobby of the lodge there is an informal talk on some feature of the region. The cheerful tone of the occasion is set by a short and amusing program given by young college people who do a good deal of the work about the camp. There is about the whole project a feeling of hearty enjoyment as of people come together for a good time in their own home.   ∎

A morning with Upton Sinclair

∎ When the accumulated files of Upton Sinclair's library were moved from his square, solid-looking house under the mountain in this town of Monrovia, California, to the University of Indiana, they weighed eight tons and filled an enormous truck. In the preface to his book *Life in Letters,* Upton mentions the fact that he has been a professional writer for sixty-five years and more. Since he is now over eighty years of age, he must have started when he was about fifteen. At any rate, the fireproof structures that he had built back of his house to preserve his treasures are now empty, and the Los Angeles smog grows steadily worse. Soon, I suspect, this enthusiastic Californian will desert his beloved palms, figs, magnolias, and oranges to content himself with the more modest growths of Arizona.

As we sat one morning in Upton's study I had a curious feeling that we were saying goodbye to a chapter of life. The glinting sun was kept out by heavy shades; we seemed shut in with the events of those sixty-five years. Having such a man with such a life, such memories, and such a memory, thus concerned, I could not be expected to forego the advantages of my opportunity, nor, to tell the truth, to deny old friend Upton an opportunity to reminisce.

First, I reminded him that pacifism is again becoming articulate, and I know of no one who has a better right to an opinion about it than he. The old boy straightened up and his voice rang out as if he were addressing a meeting. "I have never been a pacifist," he affirmed. "I am against war, but you can't end it by lying down and being walked over." Then he went on to explain that he had always been ready to fight Mussolini or Hitler or Stalin. "If we had been willing to fight them sooner," he added, "we might not have been forced to fight so long."

As to the Russians and the Stalin regime, he has had a long and complicated history. He was delighted with the March, 1917, Revolution, but for a long time did not know what to think about Stalin. He was opposed to foreign intervention, but against the dictatorship. At last, when the treaty with Hitler was signed, he surrendered the inquiring mind and wrote a pamphlet against Communist dictatorship. Old friends who continued to repeat the Communist blather fill him with disgust.

The Russians have translated and published over and over again some forty or fifty of his books. At the beginning he sometimes received small sums of money from Moscow, but that stopped long ago. The lack of financial reward, however, is not what troubles this honest American reformer. What worries him is the fact that Kremlin authorities publish *The Jungle* as if it represented the present conditions in the United States stockyards, and *King Coal* as though it were a true picture of the way things look in our mines. When publishers in other countries reprint these books, Upton insists that they include prefaces explaining that this is the way things were thirty or forty years ago. But in the case of the Russians, insistence does no good.

When I asked him which of his novels he likes the best, his face took on the plaintive expression you would induce on a mother's countenance if you asked her to choose a favorite among her children. The process of selection was obviously so painful that I was sorry I had asked the question. "Of course," he said at last, "*The Jungle* did the most good and made the most money. The story that I love the best is called *Our Lady*. But when it comes to selecting the best, it is either *Oil!* or *World's End*."

When I asked about other American writers, I set his mind to going back. His reaction is against the great men and women of the present. Faulkner he just can't stand. He may read a half of one of his novels, but he can never finish one of them. As I fished about, trying to find what was back of this judgment, I discovered that both the style and the matter of Faulkner are quite beyond Sinclair. He just doesn't get what the man is trying to do. When we mentioned Hemingway, we got another negative reaction. He doesn't really like the old adventurer's work, but after a little argument he did remember that he makes an exception of *The Old Man of the Sea.*

What Sinclair really cares for is the work of the men of his youth. He reads the new authors, but when it comes to what he really considers literature, give him Sinclair Lewis and Theodore Dreiser. "The best American novel," Upton said, "is either *Babbitt* or *Arrowsmith.* Both exhibit growth of character and both represent society as a vital and developing thing. I raved about both when they were published, and I still have the same opinion of them. Lewis was a great man. It is too bad that he ruined himself with drink." In a moment he remembered Dreiser's *An American Tragedy* and started the discussion all over again. "It's a great novel," he remarked; "it's wonderful to see how badly a great novel can be written. I don't know which of the three is best."

Then we walked out into the sun.   ■

Browbeating the highbrows

■ I still dream of getting out my columns in words of one syllable. Well, maybe not one syllable . . . but perhaps with an upper limit of three. You know what I mean. Plain words . . . the sort that you use every day . . . the kind that anyone understands without stopping to think or running to a dictionary.

I suffer from an unholy envy of the *Daily News.* It contains a lot that is bad and mighty little that is good. But, good or bad, it is human from beginning to end . . . and millions read it. And it is read by the poor, the very ones who would learn to serve their own interests better if they were to get their ideas out of the *New*

Leader. But most of them would no more than glance at our dignified weekly. It has no funnies, and more often than not it contains
fine, learned articles by fine, learned professors who just naturally
use fine and learned language. The folks who ruin their eyes by
reading the *News* in the subway would think they had encountered
a foreign tongue were they ever so much as to glance at these articles.
I can imagine their scorn and the short and lusty words in which
they would express it.

This whole subject was opened in my mind the other day when
someone dropped on my desk an article written by Arthur Koestler
and published in the London *Times.* A corporal in the British Army
had sent a letter to him asking about books—how to find the good
ones, how to know which ones to buy. He reported that he read a lot
of reviews in the press, but, he added sadly, "The reviewers are a bit
too clever for me."

Now, Arthur Koestler is one of the top writing men in this
world. He knows books and ideas as well as anyone. He has, in fact,
written one of the best of our novels, and his analysis of our current
stream of thought goes pretty close to the bottom. His answer to
this unlettered corporal is a fine example of straightforward thought
put down on paper.

There is a sharp passage about the daily run of reviews. The boys
and girls who do the writing must get on in the world. Their own
books will be reviewed in due course. They must not make too many
enemies. And the journal must get its share of book advertising. The
publishers must not be alienated. And, of course, the professional
book taster reads them by the dozen, by the hundreds. He is beside a
beltline, watching them go past. His taste goes flat and so do his
adjectives. In the end he manages to find that any volume in an
attractive jacket is delightful, fine, interesting, heartening, pleasurable.

But this is just by the way. Koestler soon gets around to the good
reviews, like those published in the *New Statesman.* He imagines
his corporal having a go at one of them: "After a few lines over an
allusion which you don't understand—a reference to Proust, or
Kafka, or Péguy—authors whom you have never read, but the writer
of the article seems to assume that everybody has read, or at least
ought to have read them; and so you begin to feel like a schoolboy

who hasn't learned his lesson, or, rather, like the uninvited guest at a party; left in the cold, humiliated, envious, resentful. And here we are at the crucial point: we are facing the wall, the tragic barrier which separates the progressive *intelligentsia* from the educated working-class. . . . It's no good trying to jump over the wall; our task is to abolish it. But that is a political, not a literary, task. It is, I believe, the main and ultimate task of Socialism.

"All of this talk about highbrows and lowbrows is a smokescreen. The brutal fact is that your critic's parents were unable to pay during an average of sixteen years so that he should read, browse, learn, soak in that spiritual nourishment for which you crave, at his leisure. You could go to school for only about nine years—and it was a different school and there was less leisure. This is what stands between you and him, between you and me. . . . I loathe the order which is its cause; but don't expect me for that reason to join in the popular game of highbrow beating. Wipe out the highbrow and you will soon march the goosestep. It is the Fascist division; our way is to attack the wall. As long as it stands, democracy is a sham."

When my friend Arthur gets down to the business of giving advice to the corporal he deals out some good stuff. He tells how much he enjoyed drinking French wines after he surmounted his fear of connoisseurs. A similar disregard for the critics he recommends to his young friend: "Read for pleasure, man, and don't bother about Péguy and *Finnegans Wake!* Go to the public library or the bookstalls, browse, open a book at random, read a page, and you will see whether you want to read that book or not. . . . If you don't feel that it has a direct bearing on your own personal interests, worries, problems—put it away."

I hope you got Koestler's point in defense of the highbrows. He has a fine passage in which he tells how they were pulled down and whipped into line in Germany and Russia. Every modern tyrant has angled for the support of the four-letter people by pitching into the intellectuals. There is no good in that. But there is this brutal wall, and our only safety lies in tearing it down.

Don't tell me that independent souls can hoist themselves up by their fingernails and climb over it. Just the other day someone was describing to me how Jack London did that. He managed to do it, but at bitter cost. It is a price few can pay. No. The only solution is to knock holes in the barrier, reduce its height, and finally level it with the ground.

We are always thinking of these distinctions in terms of wages, food, housing, medical care. But class differences in education, which are just as tragic, we hardly notice. You must have seen in the papers during the war the story of that colored regiment in Italy. Complaints had been made that the Negro soldiers were not up to the Army standard. A Negro officer was sent over to investigate. Among other things that he reported was the fact that most of these men were practically illiterate. Because they could not really read, it would have taken twice the usual length of time to give them adequate training. So they were sent into battle only partly prepared. Koestler talks about his corporal as having had only nine years of schooling. We have millions of citizens in this country who have never had anything like that. Our intellectual wall is the eyesore of the nation.

Sitting here at our desks, we cannot solve this problem. On second thought, I shall not even send a memorandum to our contributors asking them to use short words. To write their best they must feel free to dish out the whole dictionary. My dream of a *New Leader* in Basic English will remain a dream. All that I can suggest to our writers is something like this: Remember that there are fellows who are not professors or writers or experts; if you have a choice between a big word and a little one, remember the reader; he is, after all, the chap you are aiming at. ∎

COMMUNISTS AND CATHOLICS

The humor-haters

■ What this country needs is another Mark Twain. There are so many crooks, so many stuffed shirts, so many phonies, that we need a man who can start a snorting laugh big enough to blow them right off the stage. The incomparable Al Capp said over the radio the other night: "The great tradition of hard-hitting humor has died. No longer can the American humorist today hit out at the pomposities that abound in American life. There are too many taboos. They make it impossible for the humorist to laugh at anything except himself."

It would be interesting to make a list of things no one is supposed to laugh at. It would be longer than any laundry list. My mind started to work on this business one day some time ago when I happened on a long letter in the *Daily Worker* that Mr. Gus Hall, one of the eleven defendants whose sturdy figure was a part of the scenery in Judge Medina's courtroom, wrote in criticism of the new biography of Eugene V. Debs by Ray Ginger. Now, what Mr. Hall thinks about either Debs or Ginger is of slight importance. But quite unconsciously the careful letter writer reveals one of the more devastating aspects of Communism.

The horrible charge leveled against Debs is that he repeated "Negro dialect jokes." The great American Socialist even went so far as to print such jokes in the *Locomotive Firemen's Magazine* when he was its editor. He went even further in racist degradation. In 1903 he opposed the passage of special resolutions outlining the wrongs of Negroes and appealing to them to join the Socialist party. Debs was, according to the high-minded Hall, a pretty primitive and low-minded white chauvinist.

The interest of Eugene V. Debs in the problems of the Negroes need not detain us long. Every man who lived in those days knows the answer to that one. Debs was brother to all men and women. Color meant absolutely nothing to him. As a Socialist and trade unionist, he fought incessantly for union and equality. He knew that the white workers could not win without the help of black workers. So he struggled for the emancipation and elevation of the blacks because they are human beings and because their help is necessary in the struggle of workers of every color.

But it would have been impossible for a deep-down humanitarian Socialist like Debs to descend to the Communist political level. It never could have occurred to him to make special little dirty group appeals to any special crowd. That is the way Tammany Hall used to garner votes. But the Communists have reduced it to a science. How hotly they do love every little bunch from which they can lure a few supporters! People who conduct their politics on the red-light level can never be expected to understand the ways or the words of Debs. The theme of this essay, however, is not Debs and his detractors. I am talking about humor, the dearth of humor, the danger to humor. It would do Gus Hall or anyone else good to leaf through the files of the old *Locomotive Firemen's Magazine*. It came out once a month. In its early days it ran to sixty pages. Later it included more than ninety. And how it did blossom when it was in the hands of Debs! In particular, it was humanized. As you read, you can see Debs sitting there in his little office planning the issues. He must have said to himself: "By God, we'll print one trade-union paper that the working people will enjoy reading."

There are articles by Bill Nye, stories about Mark Twain, plenty of poems by Debs's dear friend James Whitcomb Riley. Ida Harper's Woman's Department aroused real reader response. There were poems—not too high class—in the style of "Casey Jones." And there were, to the distress of poor Mr. Hall, plenty of jokes. Debs didn't want his magazine to be as dull as the *Daily Worker*. The jokes are precisely like the ones you will find in *Puck* and *Judge* and other papers of the period. Some of them are about Irishmen, Germans, Englishmen, Yankees, Southerners, Chinese and—yes—Negroes. That is the crime of Debs. Negroes are not omitted. They are treated like everyone else.

Here we get back to Al Capp. In those days—back in the so much maligned nineteenth century—a man could make fun of anybody or anything. Now friend Al finds that while he is writing about Li'l Abner, or speaking over the radio or television, his characters must be forever looking over their shoulders to see who may be listening. So he blew up about this subject of the neighborhood censor. We have improved in some things, but not in this. The worst, however, has not come to pass. This country has not turned Communist. Humor has not been banished to Siberia or buried in a concentration camp. The Stalinists can keep their own precincts as dull as they please. But the rest of us can—with limitations—laugh. Perhaps the ninth or thirteenth or seventeenth freedom should be the freedom to laugh. I must write to Mrs. Roosevelt about this. ■

Art endures

■ The other day I was loafing about among the treasures of the Vienna Collection up at the Metropolitan Museum. The news that the United States Navy had guaranteed the safe delivery of these knickknacks of the Habsburgs had set me to thinking. Suppose that these paintings, these tapestries, these precious jewels had gone down to the bottom of the ocean. Millions of dollars in insurance which might have been paid by Lloyd's would have seemed a crude and stupidly inadequate substitute for this vanished beauty. So the State Department took charge. Admiral Conolly, commander of the United States Naval forces in London, arranged transport in the U.S.S. *Malabar*, with sufficient escort to guarantee complete security.

Here is a lesson in values. We often talk of human beings as if they had cockeyed notions of worth. Many people—even governments —seem to agree with John Milton that a work of art is more precious than life itself, for it is the essence, the very sum and symbol of the best of life. Since the war, during this time of all times when humanity seems reduced to its lowest term, we have had wide and official acknowledgment of the value of the arts. Americans have sent wheat, machinery, coal, and technical aid of all sorts over a great part of the world. When the Italians, the French, the Germans, and the British have thought to make a proper return, they have sent us pictures, statues, and tapestries.

There happened to be a comfortable couch opposite a painting by Albrecht Dürer. And it was there that I fell to musing. Once I disturbed myself to the extent of going near enough to read the date: 1508. These bits of canvas with designs smeared over them by long-dead artists, these fragile tapestries, these gaudy jewels wrought by supreme craftsmen for silly queens—many of them have gone down through the changes and chances of more than four centuries. What wars have swept over our continents! What revolutions! How many men of violence have reached the heights of power! How many have tumbled down in defeat and disgrace! It suddenly came to me that in this violent and uncertain world the most fragile things have the best chance of survival.

Here is this picture by Albrecht Dürer of the massacre of Christian saints. It was a mass operation carried on by a pre-Hitlerite Persian king. The canvas measures about a yard each way. You could easily carry it off in your arms. With one stroke of your hand you could destroy it. Yet here it is among these treasures carefully transported by the United States Navy. Empires have risen and fallen. Countless conquerors have disappeared. Yet this tiny and fragile-seeming product of man's love has endured.

The introduction to the catalogue of this collection was written by two curators of the Vienna Kunsthistorisches Museum. These men, top experts and writers, are servants of the tiny republic of Austria. It was there that the much diminished Habsburgs came to their end some thirty years ago. Now the sober and worried statesmen of Vienna find themselves the heritors of the high-class swag gathered in by their imperial predecessors. In their gratitude they send the cream of their heritage to be enjoyed by the American citizens who voted for the Marshall Plan and paid its bills.

I had, naturally, a couple of girls with me on this artistic expedition. They are a great help in the appreciation of the fine arts, especially of such jewels as the Habsburgs assembled for us. As we threaded our way through the vast halls of the Metropolitan Museum, I found myself unable to suppress a humbling thought that insisted on invading my stream of consciousness. I had recently been reading a biography of J. Pierpont Morgan. The accounts of his princely gifts to our museums were fresh in my mind. As we passed through that gorgeous display of Gobelin tapestries from his collections, my thoughts naturally reverted to him. I inevitably thought of him as our emperor-collector, in a real sense our American Habsburg. I told my companions how Mr. Morgan had bought these gorgeous fabrics, how he had loved them and parted from them for the public's welfare. Their eyes glowed as they looked at those magic presentations of mythical scenes. But in poor old Morgan they had not the slightest interest. American bankers and industrialists pass even as do European emperors—and leave hardly a wraith behind. In the end the great Morgan may be known exclusively as the man who for a brief moment owned these precious things.   ■

There are no white people

■ I recall once seeing a clown with his face painted white. And he looked terrible. It is fortunate that in the distribution of her skin pigments Dame Nature has kindly refrained from cursing any race or tribe with that sort of complexion. She has, on the contrary, shown appreciation of a wide variety of the livelier shades of color. We human critters range from the palest shades of pink and brown up to deep red or uncompromising black. Enjoying the advantages of Nature's miraculous versatility, there are hardly two of us who have exactly the same coloration. How, among the hosts enjoying such rich variety of shades, a broad classification of humans ever took it into their heads to call themselves white will forever remain a mystery.

These meditations on the obvious are called forth by a rereading of W. L. White's thin but thought-provoking book *Lost Boundaries*. I am thankful for it as a warm tale of experiences along the borderland between the Negroes and those whom we call "whites."

Dr. Albert Johnston, of Keane, New Hampshire, was a respected physician living in a fine house on one of the finest streets. He and his family were white—or, at least, they passed as white. Both Dr. Johnston and his wife knew that they had in their veins some "colored" blood. But, in order to get on in life and to secure a fair break for their children, they had just forgotten about it. Albert Johnston, Jr., was attending a high-class private school. Everything was on the up and up. Then, in 1941, when Albert was sixteen years of age, he heard his father say to his mother, "I'm going to tell that boy." A moment later Dr. Johnston entered the room where his son waited and calmly announced, "You're colored."

The story from here on is that of young Albert, the bright, promising boy of sixteen, after he finds that he is "colored." The reactions of his friends in his home town and at school, the deepening effects inside his own consciousness, his observations in a journey across the country to California—these give us a series of laboratory observations that are unparalleled.

I have never had the heart to write anything about Sinclair Lewis's *Kingsblood Royal*. In this slashing novel the creator of Babbitt tells of a young banker in one of his synthetic Minnesota towns who comes gradually and dramatically to the conclusion that he bears within himself a tiny admixture of African blood. He lives in a fashionable quarter of the town, has a slick wife and friends who are the ornaments of the Country Club Set. But in a manner not too convincingly managed by the adroit novelist, he feels constrained to reveal his connection with the Negroes and take what comes of belonging to the underprivileged minority.

I appreciate the daring of this conception. It took courage to think it through and send it out into the glare of the national arena. And there are some fine passages in the book—especially those picturing life among the Negroes. But when it comes to presenting the effects of the new psychological strain on the hero, Sinclair Lewis tries to recompense the reader for lack of insight by piling on crude and improbable drama. And I have a feeling that his sense of guilt as a white has compelled him to do injustice to his fellow white citizens. The Negroes in this tale are pictured with a warm and broad sympathy. But the words and actions of the whites—far-northerners, citizens of Minnesota—ring false to my northern ears.

Neil Kingsblood and his wife, Vestal, lived in the swell Sylvan

Park section of town. When Neil returned from the war as a hero, he was received with honor by the aristocrats of his set. But when he revealed the existence of his few drops of Negro blood, the whole town turned against him with raucous snarls. The story ends with a mob scene in which the upper-class leaders storm Neil's house with stones and guns. In the end, the innocent victims are herded into a police wagon while the mobsters go free.

The story never sounded true to me, but it was difficult to make out a case against it. How could one prove that white people would not act in that beastly way? Well, now we have proof. A curiously interesting thing has happened. First Sinclair Lewis gave us an imaginary account of what would happen if a respectable white person had his status as a Negro revealed to him and decided to cross the color line and take his place where he thought he belonged. Then this dramatic and revealing thing actually happened, and Mr. White in this book has set down the story with meticulous regard for detail. Never before did events so check up on an imaginative author. And I am forced to report that Sinclair Lewis comes off badly.

Dr. Johnston and his young son both had tough inner struggles in connection with their passing over. Many curious details are revealed in connection with the youthful Albert's trip across the continent. One's sense of the silliness of the whole segregation business is deepened as one reads along. But there is nothing to parallel the vulgar cruelty pictured in the fictional version of the experiences. In fact, in the good old New Hampshire town of Keane the patients of Dr. Johnston had long had a suspicion about his colored connections. But it made no difference to them. He was a good doctor and a good man. That was enough for them. I imagine that the folks of Minnesota average up about as well as those of New Hampshire. There really are no white people. There are just people. ∎

The Communist enemy within

■ As Alice remarked, this world becomes curiouser and curiouser. One morning I stepped up to a newsstand on East Fourteenth Street to buy a paper, and there beside me stood one of the chief Bolshevik functionaries of this country. He looked at me and I looked at him. He knew who I was and I knew who he was. But each one of us turned coldly away from the other.

That was a strange thing. I am not too good to speak to anyone. I have friends and acquaintances in every party, class, denomination, club, fraternity, or variety of human beings. And this Communist bigwig, too, is a right hearty sort of chap, born and bred in the West. If you saw him sauntering down the street, you would swear that he is a typical, normal, decent American.

Yet there we stood—the pair of us—our eyes glazed with unrecognition. Our minds were two sealed worlds. I suppose this man thinks he knows what goes on in my mind. In a way, I know what passes for thinking in his. But as the world surges toward large-scale war against Communism, the thought processes of him and of his fellows become more and more isolated. The distance between the followers of Stalin and our normal citizens becomes greater. What goes on inside these people's skulls gets to be constantly more and more of a mystery.

In Korea 200,000 efficiently organized and well-equipped Chinese Communist troops plunged against the forces of the United Nations. If this attack by outside forces had not taken place, the fighting in Korea would soon have come to an end. The open intervention, obviously arranged by Moscow, brought us close to the horrors of the worst war of all time.

This is a rough outline of the picture. All reports agreed about it. But in the face of this picture, the Communists thought and talked as if they were living in a separate universe. The editorial on the front page of the *Daily Worker* was headed: "Help Prevent Another World War—Recall MacArthur." The frantic essay that followed gave a completely upside-down account of the Korean conflict: John Foster Dulles and General MacArthur shoved us into it;

the Chinese delegation of "volunteers" made the journey to Korea in order to "find a peaceful solution to the Asian crisis."

The entire paper was of a piece. Every item of news, every opinion expressed, would fit neatly into *Pravda* or *Izvestia*. And then—as if to sum up and guarantee the completely topsy-turvy quality of the whole performance—a full-dress performance on the editorial page took up the subject of the "Foreign Agent Hoax." It is acknowledged that the Thirteenth Street oracles agree on every point with the propagandists of Moscow—even in their views of the Hitler-Stalin Pact. But—and this is really something—these opinions are held to be promoted in the interest of "The welfare, security and safety of the American people." The idea is simple. The *Daily Worker* presents, day after day, the ideas and policies of the U.S.S.R., but it does so because the men in Moscow know better what is good for us than we do ourselves. In holding this attitude the writers on the *Worker* are perfectly sincere.

Back in 1939 and 1940, I used to see a good deal of disloyal "German-Americans." These men, too, were opposed to America. If war came they were prepared to do all that they could in favor of a victory by Hitler. So great was their fervor for their "leader" that their words, their deeds, their whole manner and attitude had a look of fanaticism. But in comparison with the Communists these Bundists or Nazis, or whatever they were called, were stupid, simple-minded fellows. Most of them were just people who favored a victory by a foreign enemy to whom they were bound by birth and blood.

Here we are again at the beginning of what may be a period of danger and violence. Again we have among us a little coterie of disaffected men and women. But these people—the ones we call Communists—are no such simple disloyalists as were the Nazis of a decade ago. They are consciously, and in a sophisticated ideological sense, against our whole way of life, all that we stand for, all that we work toward and struggle for.

If the military situation grows more tense, we shall, in accordance with the law, put most of these people in jail. If that happens, let me warn you not to feel soft and sympathetic. No Communist would ever feel sorry for you or for anyone under any similar circumstances. They will be convicted on convincing evidence and they will deserve what happens to them. In the meantime, I wish every American could see the issue of the *Daily Worker* that I have before me as I write. It would mean the end of Communism in the United States. No one could read these open perversions of fact and logic without helping to laugh Communism completely out of court.   ■

The truth, the whole truth

■ For the past year I have spent at least one day a week in court, and, as a young lady remarked to me in the lively corridor on the thirteenth floor of the Federal Courthouse on Foley Square, "those courting days have been educational." They have given me an insight into life in these United States that would never have come to me in the ordinary course of affairs.

It was decided some years ago that if a man calls you a Communist you can start a suit for slander. He may designate you as a Democrat or a Republican, a Baptist or a Bahaist, a Mormon or a Mason. But if he ties you up with the Communists and cannot prove the connection—that may cost him money. The other week my neighbor column, *Heard of the Left*, reported that the magazine *Counterattack* had been so injudicious as to use the naughty word in connection with Mr. and Mrs. Frederic March. The handsome actor pair asked damages to the tune of $500,000, and would withdraw their suit only after retraction had been humbly made in public. It is a serious business.

You can join practically any party, club, school, clique, or religion and withdraw intact. But if you team up with the Communists, you cannot escape without running the danger of suffering devastating penalties. There is something strange about it. And incidentally, this circumstance places the United States Government at a crippling disadvantage when it brings Communists into court.

The tragedy of the ex-Communists was brought home to me as I listened to the testimony of Louis Budenz in the trial of the eleven Communist officials. I knew Mr. Budenz long before he began the Communist chapter in his life. He always seemed to me a straightforward, honest, and decent man. He still appears to be that sort of fellow now that he has left the followers of Stalin and is trying to explain them to his fellow Americans. But in the courtroom the eleven on trial and all their attorneys and supporters did their best to establish a psychological boycott of the witness. When he was asked to go into the audience to identify one of them, they would shrink from him as though he suffered from some contagious disease. Whenever they had occasion to refer to him it would be with some such epithet as "traitor," "stooge," or "turncoat." The effect was to turn the mind of the most unprejudiced listeners against the man who was trying to tell the truth.

But the disadvantage under which the reformed Communist carries on his labors goes deeper than the party's propaganda attack upon him. It stems from his total situation. How powerful and fatal it is becomes clear the moment we observe the cases of Mr. and Mrs. Whittaker Chambers. Many persons who attended the sessions of the Alger Hiss trial have a habit of saying, with a smug air of self-righteousness, "Well, it's a question of the relative veracity of two men, Hiss and Chambers, and of the two, Hiss sounds more as if he were telling the truth."

When you question these ready judges of the evidence, you find that their decision rests upon one or both of two reasons. They may say: "Chambers seemed fidgety and nervous on the stand. He acted like a man who has a bad conscience. And Mrs. Chambers was sometimes uncertain about the facts. She hesitated and sometimes went back and corrected herself." I know men who were familiar with Mr. Chambers before he was a Communist, while he was a Communist, and after he was a Communist. All of them agree that he has always been and is now an especially honorable and reliable person. Similar reports are made about Mrs. Chambers. But because of apparent nervousness or hesitancy, observers are slow to believe them.

Or you will hear it said by persons who have attended the trial from the start: "How can you be expected to believe people like the Chambers couple? They acknowledge that they have been Communists for years. Communists are, practically by definition, liars. They fabricate falsehoods even when they serve no useful purpose. Just for the fun of it, apparently, they apply for passports under false names or give wrong information when they apply for citizenship or for a dog license. They get out of the habit of telling the truth. A man like Whittaker Chambers who has lived for years in a mesh of lies can hardly distinguish between truth and falsehood. I wouldn't convict a man of stealing a nickel on his say-so."

As long as dogmatic "liberals" assume this attitude toward repentant Communists, we do irreparable wrong to a large group of fellow citizens and we place our country in an embarrassing predicament. A lot of fine, idealistic young people are swept into the Communist net. Their very idealism has made them easy game. And we are saying to them that repentance and rehabilitation are impossible, are forever closed to them, that they are disgracefully marked for life.

And to all the judges and juries and prosecuting attorneys we are saying that the testimony of men and women who have had actual experience with Communism is not to be received in court. These people, the ones like Budenz and Chambers, were the only ones who could give us complete accounts. They really knew. If we refused to believe them, we would have been sending our government into a life-and-death struggle with one hand tied behind its back. ∎

A place of refuge

∎ As was once remarked poetically of an even greater man, Heywood Broun "should'st be living at this hour." Communism as a religion, about which he wrote with both charm and insight, is once again in the headlines. Since his contacts with Communism had been close and, especially, since he ended as a Roman Catholic and, presumably, had been drawing toward Catholicism for months or years before his public conversion, it is fair to assign to him some authority in this field. If he, after his varied contacts, thought of Communism as a sort of religion, there must be some sort of validity to the idea.

Elizabeth Gurley Flynn may not end as a Catholic, but she started as one. I suppose this gives her standing equal with that of Broun to discuss these sacred matters. At any rate, she devotes a recent column in the *Daily Worker* to an act of public contrition over the procession of penitents leaving Moscow for Rome. Louis Budenz and Elizabeth Bentley are, it appears, only the most distinguished among a large number who have exchanged *Das Kapital* for the Bible. And at this fact the St. Elizabeth of East Thirteenth Street is much distressed.

To be sure, Miss Flynn's public lament at the losses being suffered by the foreign legion of Joseph Stalin does not openly state her feelings. She simulates, in fact, a good deal of joy at being rid of such poor creatures as Louis Budenz and Elizabeth Bentley. Monsignor Fulton J. Sheen, who is said to have been instrumental in plucking them as brands from the burning, is elegantly referred to in her column as "a veritable garbage collector."

What really troubles Miss Flynn is the effect of the herding of these lost sheep into the Catholic fold. In what must be designated as a bourgeois-sentimental deviation, she recalls an old aunt of hers, "a simple, devout woman, who identified clean living, truth, honesty, decency, good thoughts and neighborliness with her religion." This is a matter which the Sanhedrin of East Thirteenth Street really should look into. If a "reactionary" Roman Catholic can be honest and kind and neighborly, then surely the faithful are being deceived. But Miss Flynn's point is that such characters as her tearfully remembered relative will be debased by association with such low characters as Louis Budenz and Elizabeth Bentley.

One day a man stands high in the councils of the party. He edits their papers, he makes their speeches, he runs on their tickets. The next day, having deserted and denounced them, he becomes the lowest of the low. I never can keep track of Communist statistics. The last figure that I saw given as that representing the membership of the party was 60,000 or 70,000. The turnover is so great that there must be many hundreds of thousands of persons in the U.S.A. who have been Communists and have deserted the faith. One shudders to consider the moral effect of having among us so large a contingent of lepers.

Without making any extended examination of the rival theologies, I can note one simple reason why men and women may prefer the doctrine of Rome to that of Moscow. The Christian heaven has the great advantage of being postponed to the time after death. Whatever its attractions—and they are left rather vague in the New Testament—the true believer can never be disturbed in his contemplation of them. But the Communist heaven is on the map. From East Thirteenth Street via LaGuardia Airport it can be reached in a few hours. Many there are who have been there. And upon their return practically all of them have spread reports that throw the whole hierarchy into disrepute.

But Elizabeth Gurley Flynn has led me astray. I intended to make this column a serious discussion. I wanted to turn over some of the reasons why Communists turn to the Catholic Church rather than to some Protestant denomination. I think Elizabeth Bentley gave us the secret when she said to newspaper men that she had to go somewhere where she would be surrounded by the warmth of comradeship and continuous activity.

What critics of Communism outside the Catholic Church do not recognize is that the Communist "movement" has much to offer its devotees. They are relieved of the fuss and worry and uncertainty that engulf individuals cast loose in our turbulent and uncertain age. They are told what to think and what to do. Every minute of every day and night can be filled with what seems like purposeful activity. The little helpless individual feels himself caught up in a large and apparently successful movement that will give meaning to his otherwise meaningless life. Leaving all this, Miss Bentley felt that she had to go to some other organization that would give her something equivalent. The fact that she selected the Catholic Church might furnish food for thought for non-Catholics as well as for non-Communists. ■

PEOPLE AND THINGS

The man of faith

■ The *New Leader* office is a disillusioning sort of place. Every sort of political skulduggery is echoed there. There is an endless procession of democrats in exile. They used to come from Germany and Austria. Now they come from Poland, Czechoslovakia, the Balkan and Baltic countries and from Russia itself. From Spain, of course, they have been especially numerous since 1936. All of them are burning with tales of oppression and suffering that simply must be printed the very next week. Our place is a natural focus for all the horribleness of this present world.

But every now and then there comes rollicking in a man who is the exact opposite of all this. He comes in like a light, like a Christmas tree, like a glowing fire in a cold world. His name, appropriately, is Angelo Mascetta. Big, round, warm, glowing with enthusiasm, he represents a dual faith, the best of Christianity and the best of Socialism. My colleagues are all young, smart, sophisticated. They can tear the insides out of Kafka, Sartre, or Kierkegaard at the drop of a syllable. But this man, who is as simple as the earth or as a piece of bread, they unaffectedly love. He is a sample of the original stuff of the human spirit. Like a nugget of gold, he bears his own credentials —which they instinctively recognize.

I startled myself when I put Mr. Mascetta down as a Christian. He considers himself a notable atheist. For years he has loudly vociferated against priests. Sometimes I lure him into telling me why he never goes to church. It all started in his village in southern Italy. The priests were many and the people were poor. In his basic English Mr. Mascetta will sum the matter up: "There they were. All those priests, all those monks, all those nuns. All of those poor people. Did the priests help the people? Not on your life! Lies, they told them! They were to have things better in heaven. I couldn't stand it—even as a boy. All my life I have tried to find out the truth. And I saw I could not get it from them. Christ was born in a manger,

105

wasn't he? He grew up to be a workingman, didn't he? And he went round loving people and helping them, didn't he? He didn't put on a black robe and tell a mess of lies. Well, I made up my mind there was more Christianity outside the Church than inside. So I have never gone back there."

I sometimes try to explain that there are priests who are different. Angelo listens respectfully, but his ways and opinions are set. He will just go on trying to be good and kind and decent, as Jesus Christ taught us to be. As he talks I can't help wondering about that Church that he so strenuously denounces. If it is so bad, how could Angelo get so much good from it?

But usually it is about Socialism that we talk. For it is mainly to spend a little time among understanding comrades that this man comes to our sophisticated office. His Socialism is of a piece with his Christianity: simple, monolithic, indestructible. The only difference is that the priests of his political religion have never lost his allegiance or had his devotion turned to corrosive criticism. Eugene Debs, Victor Berger, James Maurer, and Norman Thomas are to him still saints whose virtues are never dimmed in his calendar.

Angelo's faith in his doctrine is complete, and, like many missionaries of the past, he is nonplused by the obtuseness of this wicked world. After every election he will come to me, his wrinkled brow picturing the seriousness of his effort to understand. "How can it be?" he will ask. "It is so clear. They don't need to go on worrying themselves sick about capitalism. Here is Socialism. It offers them everything. Why, why can't they see it? We have made all of these speeches. We have distributed all of these pamphlets. Are they dumb? Are they wicked? Do the capitalists have them bewitched?"

The idiocy of war troubles him in the same way. "If we could just have one generation without war," he will say, "maybe people would have time to think. Maybe they would see how much better Socialism would be. But we had the First World War, and the people said, 'We must fight just this one time more.' Then we had the Second World War, and they said, 'Well, this will really be the last!' Now we are getting ready for another 'last' war. When will this end? And we are all supposed to be Christians. I can't make it out. Can't we get rid of rulers who never did any good? Who just fool and divide the people? When will we do it? How long will it take?"

It is when I am with this man, when I sense his glowing faith in the future of Socialism, that I feel the most un-Christian animosity toward the Bolsheviks. We will be sitting there quietly in my apartment. Perhaps I will momentarily have made an impression by talking about the complexity of the world, the inevitability of social and economic slow motion. There are so many peoples, so many cultures, so many stages of development. And suddenly Angelo will begin to growl: "It is so terrible, what they have done to our Socialism. We always meant to make the world better. We wanted to end war. We thought we could get along without any robbers or robber system. We don't need to have poor, hungry fellows all around us. How much better the world would be without depressions! That's what Socialism has always meant. It was always democratic. The idea from the beginning was to make things better for the poor.

"And now see what they have done with our beautiful Socialism! It's like what Jesus Christ said. They have turned it into a den of thieves. And they call themselves Socialists. They are worse than capitalists. They won't let anyone talk or think or vote the way he wants to. And they have concentration camps like Hitler's—only worse, and more people in them. Maybe that's the reason lots of folks in this country won't listen to us. Maybe they think that what they have in Russia is Socialism." His face will grow deeply serious: "I think . . . I think . . . I think it is the awfulest, terriblest, most unholy thing that ever was done!"

I have tried hard, but I never have succeeded, in building a bridge from this present wicked world to Angelo's shining hope. He may talk about our two capitalist parties. They are, to him, but the left and right paws of rapacious capitalism. Then I will try to explain that here, with our two-party system, we get on better than other countries with five or nine or thirteen parties. The New Deal furnishes me a good part of my argument. Through the Democrats we got some reforms that the Socialists battled for through the years. Socialism, I will try to explain, is not just one thing. It is many things that, together, we hope make up a good life. And if we get these things one by one, and preserve our democratic ways, maybe we shall get on better than countries that achieve all at once what they call Socialism. Revolutions, too, have been disappointing affairs.

In Angelo's wide, honest face I can see mirrored his effort to follow my line of thought. He knows that a minimum wage is good, that old-age pensions are a help, that unemployment insurance takes a load off the workingman's mind. Yes, we are making progress. But then a look of desperation will come into the good man's eyes: "But I can't live forever! I will die. I want to see something better before I go up and knock on the big white gate. We have worked so hard! We have waited so long!"

The last time our faithful apostle of Socialism came in he told me that he was practically on the way to the hospital. I was shocked at the notion that a man so sturdy and so vital might be in danger from an operation. But he quickly banished my fears. "Don't worry," he said, "they can't kill old Angelo yet. I can't die now and leave this world the way it is. I must see something better than this before I go." And so, with his great voice booming, he went out of the door and down the stairs.

And one of the boys at a desk near mine, one who knows all the long words and all the social theories, said to me, "I just feel ashamed for our world because it has disappointed so good a man."   ■

Not first among the stuffed shirts

■ From the very start George Washington has got a dirty deal from biographers and gossipmongers. The egregious tale of the cherry tree is not the worst slander that Parson Weems planted on the great man's reputation. He pretended to quote an old gentleman who knew Washington in his boyhood: "He was never guilty of so brutish a thing as that of fighting himself nor would he, when able to prevent it, allow his companions to fight one another. If he could not disarm their savage passions by his arguments, he would instantly go to the master and inform him of their barbarous intentions." This clerical liar tried to make out that the six-foot George was not only a sissy but also a tattletale.

This miserable misrepresenter was later supported and enlarged upon by hundreds of writers who considered themselves respectable historians. The man whose toughness and courage made him our natural leader during those heartbreaking first years was transformed into the prime stuffed shirt of all time. We were told how he never missed a church service, never swore, never wasted time or money in gambling, never fooled around with girls. When the good ladies of Virginia, in 1925, published Washington's diaries we discovered that all these statements were the exact opposite of the truth. A few years later Rupert Hughes had fun writing a biography that proved that Washington was a great hunter, fisherman, horse racer, gambler, dancer, and admirer of pretty girls. The sizable bills that are recorded in the diaries as having been incurred in the purchase of ardent spirits need cause no one a headache now, for they caused the Father of his Country no headaches in his day. There is abundant testimony to the effect that he could hold his liquor better than most. And as to religion, he believed in morality, spoke often of Providence —and went to church when he felt like it. Once when the clergyman happened not to suit him, he stayed away altogether.

But aside from this imputation of Puritanism, there is another misrepresentation of George Washington that has a more serious aspect. Our first great general and President is thought of as the model and original of all conservatives. He was, for those days, a rich man. As leader of the nation for the first eight years of organized political existence, he seemed more often than not to side with the policies represented by Hamilton. So—though he tried his best to keep clear of political parties and was deeply troubled by the growth of the party spirit—it has been taken for granted that he was a natural and typical conservative. When present-day know-nothing, do-nothing reactionaries use those meaningless phrases of theirs, the "American system" and the "sacred principles of the Founding Fathers," it is Washington and the men about him whom they have in mind.

It never seems to occur to them that the conservatives of those days were the Tories, the fellows who fought against Washington. The men who had the nerve to start an entirely new sort of government in the wilderness were anything but conservatives. They were genuine revolutionists who risked their lives by taking up arms in a cause that looked shaky to all beholders. If the colonists had lost— and for five years it looked as though they would—Washington would have been the first one to be shot.

Persons who think of our first great leader as a conservative in our modern sense of the word show a lack of understanding of our Virginia leaders in the eighteenth century. Washington and Jefferson, for example, were different in some respects, but their basic concepts of people and government were not far apart. Those Virginia gentlemen, schooled in Locke and the French philosophers, belonged to the upper class but had a deep sense of the responsibilities of their class. They had both military and civil duties that it never occurred to them to evade or neglect. Both, for example, were ashamed of slavery and troubled by the problem of preparing the slaves for freedom and citizenship.

The ruthless, don't-care attitude of the typical present-day conservative did not become current until after the War Between the States. The notion, for example, that the government should merely act as umpire between capital and labor, that it is dangerous for the people to use the government as an instrument of progress, could not possibly have entered the heads of Washington or Jefferson and the men about them. Their attitude was the opposite of all this. When, at the beginning of the twentieth century, Theodore Roosevelt began to talk about conserving land, planting trees, and saving and using water power, he was picking up at long last ideas and policies that had been common property at the beginning of our history.

As a landowner, Washington was a planner. If our farmers and our state and federal governments had followed his ideas, we should have avoided enormous losses. He studied soil conservation, improvement in breeds of cattle, the introduction of better seeds and new sorts of grain and vegetables. And in his mind the interest in such improvements was not to be limited to private endeavor. In his very first message to Congress he stressed "the advancement of agriculture, commerce and manufactures." He asked "attention to the Post Office and post-roads and advocated the promotion of science and literature." He made a special plea—let all our America-Firsters take note—for the "introduction of new and useful inventions from abroad." You see? George Washington, the Father of his country, was a New Dealer.   ■

The world and Aunt Mattie

■ We buried Aunt Mattie the other day. She looked frail and somehow elegant lying there among the overgay flowers with the orchid in her work-worn hands. Friends and relatives who had not seen one another for thirty or forty years tried to make out in each other's aging features the lineaments they had known in youth. As I stood among them there, I kept saying to one after another, "She was born in 1857." The fact struck them into awed silence. It carried them back to a time for which their minds furnished no pictures. And while the clergyman was intoning a psalm about the age of the rocks and the mountains that go on from everlasting to everlasting, I was thinking of the mountains of history the human race has crossed between Aunt Mattie's birth and her death.

There was only one nook in Aunt Mattie's picture gallery that really fascinated the younger generation. They would listen voluntarily and avidly while the little old lady cleared her throat and told about how the soldiers filed into the trains to go off to the Civil War. The descriptions of the wounded veterans being carried through the streets on litters and, especially, the account of the halt of Lincoln's funeral train on the way from Washington to Philadelphia would hold them silent and awestruck.

The smarter ones among the youthful listeners realized that I was using these wartime memories as mere bait to secure interest in more educational items that were to follow. When the last thrill had been extracted from military memories, I would say, "Please, Aunt Mattie, tell us how you used to live on the farm."

Blushing shyly at being the center of the circle, the frail little woman would describe the alien sort of activities that absorbed the heart and mind and muscles of a little girl seventy or eighty years ago. As a child she learned how to card wool, to spin yarn and to weave it into cloth. The only artificial light was furnished by candles that were made in the kitchen in ancient candle molds. The grain and hay were harvested with cradles and scythes. The only power on the old farm, except that of the men and boys, was furnished by horses and oxen. From the time that she was a small child, she and the other members of the family would rise at four or five o'clock in the morning and labor without stopping, except for meals, until late at night.

The farm group was practically independent. The blacksmith performed the only service that was sought from the outside world. The only items acquired from the merchant were shoes and an occasional tool or piece of hardware. Oh, yes—salt and spices had to be brought in from outside. But as regards the basic requirements for living, Aunt Mattie's people in 1865 were as independent as their distant ancestors in the Middle Ages.

While the clergyman was speaking the fine and well-remembered words over the little old body lying there, my mind kept shuttling back and forth between 1857 and 1949. While the little girl was learning how to spin and weave, most of the inventions that have transformed the world had been made. The first railways were being built. Steamboats were crossing the sea. The telegraph was carrying its magic messages. Sewing machines were starting to hum. Mowing machines and reapers were making a new sort of music, replacing that of the scythes and cradles. Many new devices, in their first crude forms, were on the market. But they were not yet widely in use. Their transforming effect was not yet felt. Nearly all the people —in this and all other countries—still lived and thought as their ancestors had from the beginning.

But this one little wispy woman had lived to see our part of the world transformed. In her time, the population of this country had grown from about 30,000,000 to nearly 150,000,000. New states, new cities, new industries, new ways of doing practically everything had made each decade seem old and quaint in comparison with the next one. The telephone, the automobile, the airplane, the radio, the atom bomb had crowded crazily on one another's heels.

Aunt Mattie always commented on tales of these mechanical and chemical miracles in terms of self-congratulation. When our young folks would tell about their airplane trips, she would sit there practically breathless and murmur, "Wonderful . . . wonderful . . . wonderful!" And while the clergyman was speaking those sacred words about God remaining the same "from everlasting to everlasting," I thought how Aunt Mattie, too, had remained the same while the rest of the world had gone catapulting onward without ever inquiring about its direction. Mechanically, materially, America and Europe have advanced beyond the wildest dreams of Aunt Mattie's generation. But when I read Abraham Lincoln's speeches and compare them with those that are being broadcast around the world in these days, I wonder whether we have made any progress in our minds and morals. When Aunt Mattie was a girl, our ancestors took four months to cross the continent. Now we do it in four hours. But our thoughts hardly keep pace with our bodies. There is no jet propulsion about our thinking. ∎

The voice of individualism

∎ As one who has often called for good men to speak up for conservatism, I give thanks for Herbert Hoover. Of late he has come to represent some of the traditional attitudes of America much as Winston Churchill stands for the old order in Great Britain. Neither of these men can be smirched with the accusation of subservience to mere business interests. Both have given proof of devotion through long lives spent in public service. Both of them indubitably believe in their political and economic creeds with a faith that is close to religious devotion.

Herbert Hoover's statement on his birthday was not a reasoned discussion of the issues involved in the great debate on individualism versus Socialism. The old engineer limited himself to one set of proofs that government control is proceeding at a rapid pace. The

180,000,000 people in this country now spend a lot of their money by community action. Because we now spend more together than we formerly did, each one has, comparatively, less to spend on himself in accordance with his own whims. To our only living ex-President this seems bad.

But this man, magnificent as a symbol of an age that is passing, was not speaking as a professor of economics or history. As a man who for more than thirty years has played a leading part in our public life, he stood there in the stadium at Palo Alto and asked the American people to take thought. It is to be hoped that millions, including industrialists, congressmen, editors, ex-New Dealers, and New Frontiersmen, will give heed.

There are few men in the world whose experience gives them so great warrant to speak on these matters. The turns of war and peace, depression and recovery, have tossed him up and down and up again. He first appeared before mankind as history's greatest almoner. This vigorous individualist undertook the administration of a great charity fund provided by the taxpayers of the United States. In that emergency personal mercy was not enough. With the return of peace this businessman and engineer took on, as Secretary of Commerce, the task of setting the government to work in the interest of manufacturers and merchants. He did more than any other occupant of that office to make businessmen appreciative of government support.

Then came the four years in the Presidency and the tragedy of 1929–1932. It could not have happened to a more innocent man. Herbert Hoover believed that we must pay for the good of prosperity with the suffering of depression. Except for the inauguration of the Reconstruction Finance Corporation, he let Nature take its course. His theories may have been good or bad, but adherence to them had all the appearance of heartlessness. Politically, it was fatal. So Herbert Hoover, one of the most intelligent and public-spirited Presidents of our time, bowed out of Washington as a failure. Here was tragedy of the first order.

And now—by one of history's ironies—Herbert Hoover has completed a task that redounds mightily to the benefit of government controllers. The great weakness of the New Deal was that President Roosevelt was a bad administrator and had small respect for the mechanisms of government. Now comes the Hoover Commission. Between his seventieth and seventy-fifth birthdays, Herbert Hoover came out of his beloved library. At the call of a President representing an opposite party, he gathered a body of experts. He did a job of organization, of analysis, of reform and simplification that staggers the imagination. He must have been saying to himself: "I don't believe in government controls; but if we must have them, let us have a government that is set up to do business."

Perhaps the love for this man, which is so overwhelmingly demonstrated during his anniversary celebrations, may be due to the fact that he has gone through so much of our history with us. From 1917 onward he has been a participant in our life. It may, in some part, be due to the fact that Herbert Hoover represents our type of mind. He is typically American, both in his strength and in his weakness. He is a first-class engineer and businessman. As a political and economic theorist he hardly shines. But neither do we—or most of us. But probably the great change in feeling toward this old man is chiefly due to his profound and conspicuous sincerity. He may be right or wrong, but none can deny that he is a true, straight, and honest man genuinely devoted to the public welfare. ■

Rex Hobo

■ There have been too many "musts" lately, too many topics that had deadlines attached. So more than one matter that lay close to my heart was crowded out of this space in the *New Leader*. Among other things, I was forced to commit *lèse-majesté*. The King of the Hobos died on October 29, 1949, and I did not even drop a journalistic tear in memory of him. But Dan O'Brien was never in a hurry. Perhaps he will not mind too much.

During the last thirty or forty years there have been two distinguished wayfarers who have attached themselves to me in a rather desultory and haphazard fashion. One was Dr. Ben Reitman. Once every year or two he would drop into my office and bring me up to date about doings in the hobo world. Ben had a real sociologist's interest in his profession. It was with a distinct touch of pride that he would discuss different ranks among the knights of the road or describe in minute detail the fine techniques of their craft. But in the end Ben proved to be a traitor to his kind. Dan O'Brien would refer with gentle regret to the fact that he had turned respectable and lined up with the legions of law and order.

"He just wasn't quite good enough," Dan would sigh. "He couldn't take it. The lure of a fine house and a regular bed was too much for him."

How Dan O'Brien happened to be chosen King of the Hobos I never had precisely explained to me. Now and then there would be a convention of these wandering philosophers—in St. Louis, Chicago, San Francisco, or down on our own Bowery. The word would be passed "down the line." A hundred or two of them would get together. The questions of transportation and entertainment were easily solved. There would be tough battles for votes, but usually Dan won out. I suspect it was because he had the most effective ideological lingo.

He was born, of course, in Ireland. According to his chronology, it was ninety years ago. The basis of his intellectual life was laid by his father, who permanently set Dan's attitude by dying of overwork. Trinity College, Dublin, always occupied a prominent spot in his conversation, but whatever education he absorbed within its sacred halls must have been lapped up very rapidly, for he asked his friends to believe that he came to these shores when he was seventeen. Whether he had actually encircled "this small globe" twenty times, as he claimed, no man will ever know. And if his imagination somewhat exaggerated the learned and skilled professions at which he had proved his proficiency, God and St. Peter will certainly pass lightly over his lapses from factual accuracy.

On the day on which his obituary appeared in the New York Times, I went looking through an old letter file. And there—sure enough—I found some faded, pencil-scribbled pages signed "Rex Hobo." The dates were in the year 1930.

Once Dan wrote me about a poet named Graham who had been

jailed "by the capitalists." Why he had been incarcerated, I don't know. Probably it was not for writing bad poetry. But Dan had dedicated himself to the task of setting him free. He wrote to ask me to interest Heywood Broun. Heywood, characteristically, stood ready to do his best.

I am sorry to say that my files fail to tell the end of the story. Whether the persecuted poet was ever restored to the free light of heaven I cannot tell. The last sentence of Dan's last letter dealing with the matter reads: "The future is dark for those who challenge and dare the status quo in poetry and song. Yours for freedom for poets." This is sufficient to place my departed friend. His way of life was symbolic. It was a constant protest against the conventional way of things. This man wanted a less rigid world, a more fluid existence, a way of life that would offer the soul of man a greater variety.

It was usually on Union Square that he would call to me. I would be hurrying to an engagement and I would hear that high-floating Irish tenor: "Heh, Doc!" No matter what duty called me, the man was irresistible. I would drop to a bench beside him, and he would start all over again to tell me how silly I was to try to make the world better by hurrying from one class to another, one meeting to another, one luncheon or dinner to another. "If you would all just stop hurrying, if you would just all stop and think for a while, the world would be better, you wouldn't have to work to *make* it better."

Sometimes I would see a dark, sad look come over his face. Then I knew what had happened. He had caught sight of some bunch of strident Communists. This would be along in the 1930's, when unemployment was at its height and the Communists had taken Dan's audience away from him. "Look at them," he would say to me; "the capitalists are bad enough. But they don't want the whole world. They can't cover it. They leave little valleys, green spots here and there where a fellow can escape. But these guys! Where they get hold there isn't an inch left. There's no outlet for a man's body or soul. You can't breathe."

There was one subject upon which we could heartily agree. ∎

Kipling was wrong

■ One Sunday evening not long ago I received the surprise of my life. Madame Pandit, the sister of Jawaharlal Nehru, had sent out invitations to meet her distinguished relative. I made my way to the Waldorf-Astoria with pictures in my mind of making my way down a long reception line and shaking a tired hand.

But what I found when I stepped into the Perroquet Room was a party, just like a party at your house or mine—with Madame Pandit playing the charming hostess. Now, Madame Pandit is a very great person, learned, eloquent, really important. One year she made the most stirring address that I have heard at any meeting of the United Nations. But she is also a very pretty woman, which is a help. And she knows all the little tricks by which a hostess makes people feel at home.

There were a lot of Indians there, many of them handsome and impressive persons. There was no time to talk to most of them. Those I had a chance to meet impressed me with their tincture of Britishness. Politically India may have cut loose from Britain. Culturally, she never can. The American part of the assembly was notable for its pacifism. New York had poured out there, if not its beauty and its chivalry, about nine-tenths of its more earnest and energetic advocates of peace. India, the land of the nonviolent Gandhi, was being greeted by America's advocates of nonviolence.

Sooner or later everyone had a chance to join the group about Nehru and exchange a few words with him. Naturally, we were all thinking about him. Here he is among us. He will negotiate with the State Department, with our economists, with our businessmen. What kind of man is he? Is he a philosopher, a spiritual leader like Gandhi? Is he a practical politician? Will he succeed in making India a power that America can understand and get on with? Is he our sort of man or is he something queer and far off, perhaps too good for us—or in some sense not good enough. While I was talking with him, and while I was circulating about the room with my eye always more or less upon him, these questions were dodging in and out of my mind.

After a while Roger Baldwin, lounging informally upon a table, clapped his hands for attention and remarked that since we were all there together we might as well utilize the occasion to ask the Prime Minister a few questions. The questions, naturally, were about Indian progress, Pakistan, Communism in India, and the use of force. My chief impression was that this Indian leader is not troubled. He has complete faith that things will work out. Progress had not been so rapid as he had hoped. The long struggle with Pakistan had not been foreseen. But the princely states had been absorbed, production was rising, health standards were being improved. When asked about Communism the Prime Minister's answers were notably calm and reasonable. Communists are treated like everyone else. When they commit crimes they are punished.

Being in New York, the center of ideologies, Nehru was inevitably asked what sort of system they have in India—capitalist, Socialist, or some new sort of native brand. Nehru answered, as Hugh Gaitskell might have done about England, had he been there. You must be very careful how you use the word *Socialist*. It is a word that is liable to misunderstanding. But the government of India has had to furnish capital for some of the basic industries. No private persons or groups had capital in adequate quantities. The government believes in private industry and wants as much of it as possible. But the people must adopt the most practical methods to get things going. So they have a mixed economy.

I came away with two rather sharp impressions. In the first place, the leading pacifists of America are worried about Nehru. They feel desperately that he has betrayed their faith. He is now in power, the head of one of the most powerful states in the world. He has had to meet unexpected dangers and difficulties. He has a powerful army and he is ready to fight if he has to. The pacifists have a feeling that once again it is being proved that when leaders get power they tend to jettison the fine principles they advocated in their idealistic youth.

My own feeling is quite to the contrary. I said good night with a sense of satisfaction. Pandit Nehru is not a philosopher. If he is in any sense a spiritual leader, it is not in the same way or to the same extent as a Gandhi. But he is a statesman, clever, adaptable, practical. He understands that people must eat. He can talk our language. We can understand him and count on him. He is the prime proof that Kipling was as wrong as he could be. ■

St. George Bernard Shaw

■ In his old age Shaw made one skeptical of the joys of heaven and of the vaunted wisdom that is supposed to come with age. Far and away the greatest English-American writer of our age, he lingered on merely to remind us that even greatness must decay and that the progressive death of the faculties may leave mere cantankerousness in the place of brilliance. There was tragic sadness about the obvious disappointment of all those who piously pilgrimaged to Ayot St. Lawrence on the occasion of the great wit's anniversaries. But for the thoughtful among us the occasion furnished more important themes than those suggested by his churlish and somewhat childish efforts to maintain his reputation for epigram.

I belong to the generation for which Shaw was at once the prophet and the supreme man of letters. For those who were Socialists forty years ago, this man was the shining expositor of the truth. They—or most of them—could expound it only in modest, quiet, more or less underground ways: in small and musty halls, in badly printed leaflets, in hopeful but usually short-lived periodicals. Then into our theaters came the laughing, jibing Shaw. In *Widowers' Houses* and *Mrs. Warren's Profession* he expounded before the élite on Broadway the ideas that the patient and plodding propagandists were endeavoring to put across in all their desperately devoted ways. He was their knight in shining armor, their missionary to the upper-class heathen. The high tide of Shaw as the missionary of Socialism came between 1900 and the First World War. Since then, much of the great man's thinking, as expressed in *Man and Superman* and *Back to Methuselah*, tended to separate him from the Socialists whose chief interest lay in his propaganda value. The superman cult, to which he seemed to lend his authority, was not to their liking. And when Shaw made his brief pilgrimage to Moscow and tried hard to be shocking in his approval of the planning and power he found concentrated there, American and British Socialists were hard put to it to fabricate apologies for the erstwhile Fabian defender.

In one of his earlier prefaces Shaw ascribed his distinction to faultless vision. This account comes close to explaining both his strength and the weakness inseparably tied in with it. Shaw had the sort of clearsightedness that has been the mark of the greatest of the saints. All his work as dramatist, critic, preacher, and thinker has the stigmata of the man with the X-ray vision. He could look through the outer trappings to the skeleton of society.

Seeing thus to the very joints and tendons of things, he experienced a growing impatience with the great majority of the dull and the deceived. His gaze stripped bare the pretenses of the profit system in a way to delight the heart of the Marxist, but he was as far as any aristocrat from idealizing the working class. He never produced "proletarian" plays. In his view our social framework of pretenses produces stupidity both above and below. In such a society the only hero must be the man of fresh insights, the bearer of new ideas, the thinker as superman. And the obstruction to the free functioning of such a creative intellect is not the instinctive self-interest of the possessing classes, but the convention-bound stupidity of all classes.

Shaw's concept of his function, then, ran not at all parallel to that of the Marxian—or even the non-Marxian—Socialists. He had no faith in the much advertised historic mission of the working class. The mere overthrow of capitalism had for him no promise of improvement. Like St. Anthony or St. Francis or St. Thomas or any other saint, he had to break through the evil shell of traditional ways, somehow to melt down the congealed solution in which men were held, by some contagion to fire human creatures to rise to their possibilities.

Such a mission required attacks at many points. The most vulnerable traditional ideas about business, politics, religion, education, sex, art, medicine had to be held up to the shattering therapeutics of laughter. And so Bernard Shaw as dramatist had an inexhaustible supply of themes crying out for exposition. His plays are a series of operations on the body politic following X-ray tests and expert diagnoses.

But the objective was nothing so simple as a conventional revolution. No good was to be expected from a victory of the workers over their exploiters—since the classes were equally incapable of wise government. Somehow—as in Plato's *Republic*—a way must be found of harnessing brains to administration, of running society in a planned and rational way that would enable all men and all groups to rise to higher levels.

Both the strength and the weakness of George Bernard Shaw rise from this concept of his mission. His dissection of the ills of society and of the closely connected conflicts of individuals is brilliantly satisfying. The plays in which he presented them rise to great heights of comedy and tragedy. There are passages in his prefaces that equal the sharpest writing of the eighteenth century—when prose was really good.

But his objective, like that of the saints, was inhumanly high. He demanded that common, funny, narrow, limited human creatures apply the rules of reason to their individual and social affairs. His City of God was to be a heavenly commonwealth where every citizen was to be a Charles Darwin or an Albert Einstein—or, at the very least, a glorified Robert Moses. And—as in the case of Plato—the impatience of the farsighted apostle forced him finally into the way of the superman. Stalin—even Mussolini—appealed to him more than such gradualistic and realistic chaps as those who lead the British Labour party.

It is interesting now to look back upon Shaw's last considerable play, *The Apple Cart*. It was published in the year 1931, when Mussolini was at the height of his power and Hitler was not far from the German chancellorship. Those were the days when democracy was desperately on the defensive and when parliamentary institutions were the butt of ridicule among the paid propagandists of dictators on the Continent and among large groups of political lightweights both here and in Britain.

Yet this piece of special pleading by the great apostle of progress, George Bernard Shaw, is little more than a slashing attack on democratic government. Boanerges, the Labor member of the cabinet, is pictured as an inflated windbag one of whose first utterances was: "Democracy? Yah!" In the preface, which was actually an address delivered over the BBC, the author maintains that the people are no more capable of running their own government than they are of writing their own plays. The implication, obviously, is that inspired technicians should attend to both matters and that the uncouth and unwashed should keep their hands off. Actually, this is a Fascist play with only such overtones of the managerial revolution as most high-class proclamations of Fascism contain.

What the moral of this tale is I am not quite sure. In his youth and early manhood Shaw wrote brilliant plays and prefaces on the side of progress and understanding. At the age of seventy-five he gave us a testament of pessimism. Perhaps, to preserve their reputations, great writers should be shot at the age of seventy or thereabouts. A more humane procedure would be politely to disregard them after their decline has reached a certain point.   ∎

Ely Culbertson makes a bid

∎ Now that Ely Culbertson is dead, I have a feeling that my relation to him should have been closer and more rewarding. I must hasten to explain that my connection with the great authority on contract bridge had nothing to do with any card game. I am devoted to bridge, but I play a game which is more venturesome and amusing than scientific. I am sure that the great card shark never would have invited me to his apartment to discuss his one-over-one system of bidding. Once I was present when one of the card wizard's assistants came in to ask a question about his daily bridge column, but my business with him was of another sort.

I hope that some writer with sufficient interest and talent will some day put this man in a novel or play. His looks, his manners, his varied and mysterious connections—everything about him fitted him to serve as the hero of a mystery. The first time I was invited to his living quarters—as I remember it, they were on East Fifty-eighth Street—a secretive elevator man took me up some six or eight floors and let me into an apartment that was luxuriously furnished but entirely untenanted. Comfortable chairs and an abundance of books and magazines suggested pleasant ways of passing one's time. Bottles of Scotch, bourbon, rye, and soda were at the visitor's disposal. I poured myself a drink and made myself at home. In the course of time, I grew restless and began to wander from room to room. The books turned out to be concerned with engineering and international affairs rather than with card games.

There was not a sound. The carpets were so deep that my footsteps were muffled. After a time, in response to some sort of psychic tug, I turned around and there was a beautiful brunette in an evening gown. She addressed me by name and told me that she was one of Mr. Culbertson's secretaries. Soon we were deep in conversation— which she conducted effortlessly in the way of a society queen rather than a professional secretary. When Mr. Culbertson appeared, his entrance, too, was mysterious and soundless. Suddenly he was there. In carpet slippers, comfortable slacks and luxurious-looking blue velvet smoking jacket, he presented the perfect picture of a gentleman of leisure set to have a good time with his friends.

My invitation had hinted that the party was to be devoted to international affairs. The Second World War was coming to an end. Preliminary plans for the United Nations were on the griddle. As my fellow guests checked in, I realized that our host had called together a group of economists and historians. There were good men there from most of our New York institutions of learning—all of them obviously curious about what was up. Presently Mr. Culbertson called us into a circle in one of the larger rooms. With perfect ease and a good deal of charm, he gradually opened up the matter which he had on his mind.

The card player was making a bid for attention in the great game where the fate of the world was at stake. He was, we began to perceive, much more than a bridge expert. He had been born in eastern Europe of an American father and a Cossack mother. He had spent his childhood in Russia, had often visited the country, and was, consequently, never taken in by the Communists.

But he was not talking to his guests as an anti-Communist. Engineering had been his original profession. He had taken up bridge experting because he figured—and correctly—that that was the best way to make plenty of money in a hurry. He had succeeded at bridge by applying to it the principles of mathematics he had learned as an engineer. And now that people were furiously thinking about world organization, he proposed to approach that subject in the same way.

He had worked out a quota plan for a United Nations military force which would be able to maintain the peace of the world. I listened with interest to his presentation of the plan. Later, I studied printed expositions of it and attended meetings at which it was discussed. Several times, I sat on the platform as member of a discussion panel as Mr. Culbertson expounded his ideas. For a considerable time, the author's reputation brought the scheme into a good deal of prominence.

From the start, I was of the opinion that this project, brilliantly though it had been developed and presented, would never be adopted. It was too mechanical for this disordered world. Most of the academic experts agreed with me. But we all respected the patience and cleverness with which its author continued to present it.

In time, the UN was established without a military force. Mr. Culbertson's contribution to the discussion was forgotten. I continued to read his bridge column, but had no occasion to visit him or keep myself informed as to what he was doing and thinking. Now that he is gone, it seems to me that I made a mistake. I allowed an interesting and important man to slip away from me without getting from him what he could have given.   ■

Richard Wright

■ A couple of weeks ago I was writing about novels as roads to understanding. All round us are groups of people who are different. Differences inspire fear. Fear is dangerous. The realistic novel gets beyond peculiarities of speech, dress, and manners. It takes us inside men and women who may be our neighbors but are kept alien to us by their words and ways. We realize that inside they are not so different as they seem. We begin to see things from their point of view. Because it prods us to sympathy and understanding, a conscientiously written work of fiction may be worth a dozen books on social theory.

I was saying things like this in connection with a discussion of *Two Solitudes*, Hugh MacLennan's fine novel about the Canadian French. Since that time people in this country have been stirred and shocked by *Black Boy*, the autobiography of Richard Wright. The

Negroes are our greatest unassimilated and misunderstood group. Through this book—as well as through a number of others published during the past year—we have a window opened straight into their hearts. It is important that white folks take a look through that window and take careful note of what they see. Our friend W. E. Burghardt Du Bois raises a question as to whether this is straight biography or fiction in biographical form. To biographers of Richard Wright the question is important, but not to us. Wright is a talented and successful author. From the vantage point of his present success and popularity he looks back and—no matter what were the exact details of his existence—he sees his boyhood as a tough and bitter time. His pictures of the people—whites and blacks—must epitomize the impressions he carried with him into his manhood.

In reading *Native Son*, I had my suspicions aroused by the sketch of the Communist leader. The man was too saintly, too wise, too devoted. Nobody could be as good as all that. But I can understand how Richard Wright came to draw that picture. He came North bleeding from a hundred wounds suffered by his ego. What happened to him later on is to be disclosed in a later volume. This one takes him only to the moment when he departed from Memphis for Chicago. I can easily understand how the Chicago Communists took possession of him and gave him the recognition for which he had yearned. All the world knew from his *Atlantic* articles how that brief honeymoon ended. Richard Wright is direct, honest, violent. He could not long be fooled by anyone.

I notice that Negro writers are more cautious than whites in expressing approval of this book. On the face of it, this might strike you as strange. Here was an ambitious and dynamic young writer. When he wrote the book he was in his early thirties. Despite all his handicaps, it is seldom that an American author achieves such distinction in so few years. You would think that other Negroes would have rallied round him, boosted him, hurried him along to a position from which he could get the ear of the entire reading public. Instead of this, they accepted his book with reservations.

This attitude is easy to understand. I confess that I blinked when I read the following sentence (Page 33): "After I had outlived the shocks of childhood, after the habit of reflection had been born in me, I used to mull over the strange absence of real kindness in Negroes, how unstable was our tenderness, how lacking in genuine passion we were, how void of great hope, how bare our tradition." Absence of real kindness among Negroes? I have known hundreds of them. I would have said that on the average they are more warmly affectionate to relatives and friends than the average whites. But who am I to argue with a colored man about such a topic?

I can see that a great many Negroes will be suspicious of this book, afraid of the effect it will have upon white readers. For it presents a picture of the deep South that is horrible. Other writers, both white and colored, have tried to play up Negro virtues. That is natural and right. These people, more than 13,000,000 of them, have been generally played down. Their talents, ambitions, hopes have been disregarded. Our whole treatment of them is based on a widely accepted notion of their inferiority. To counteract this state of affairs, it is natural that advocates of equal opportunity should swing the other way. White enthusiasts, especially, tend to overglorify every evidence of talent or virtue.

Then came this ruthless Richard Wright. He was a black Erskine Caldwell. To him whole sections of Mississippi and Arkansas are nothing more than an endless Tobacco Road. He defends himself against it, his aunt and his uncle, with razor blades. In all his experience in church or school he never makes a friend. The religion of his relatives is mean, low, sordid. The white is just as inimical as the black, and more dangerous because of the power that gives backing even to the humblest of them.

But I am proud of Richard Wright. America did, after all, produce him, and he was man enough to write out of his own soul without regard to what other, blacks or whites, may think of him. He was an authentic artist and he demanded the freedom that is necessary to artists. He could not write as a Negro, carefully calculating what would be the effect of his words on public opinion. That way lay mediocrity. Conformity he simply would not stand.

I recall seeing a tall, handsome, dignified Negro walking along a street down in Richmond, Virginia. Suddenly a white man approached from the opposite direction. Instantly the Negro was transformed into an obsequious, grinning monkey. He bowed and cringed and uttered degrading sounds. The white man strutted on his way. The Negro straightened up and became once more the handsome and self-respecting being, but now, it seemed to me, with infinite sadness added to the lines of his face. His whole being was in protest against the part he had been forced to play.

Wright speaks of "the sensitive controlling mechanism" that shuts off the minds and emotions and actions of Negroes. From babyhood he objected to it, rebelled against it. "It never occurred to me," he says, "that I was in any way an inferior being."

The origin of his impulse to rebellion was never indicated. There is the continuous implication that it was instinctive. But whatever the spring of experience from which it started, the impulse was over-powering, irrepressible. Only death could still his voice.   ∎

Ego against environment: Thurber

∎ I suppose I have read a dozen articles about *The Thurber Carnival.* I have had no fault to find with any of them. All the authors expressed the greatest of admiration for the drawings and text. Some of them went so far as to suggest the birth of a Thurber cult. There was an apparent effort on the part of each of them to top the others and to take some credit to himself in connection with his super-admiration. Each critic seemed to be saying to the others: "Look, I am closer to this man than you are and I understand him better—so I deserve some credit for his achievements."

And I—in the very act of pounding my typewriter—am lining myself up alongside the others. We have all grinned and laughed and squealed and howled our joy over the pictures and the prose. We have grabbed relatives and friends by the lapels or the forelocks and compelled them to listen. We have read the book through and then gone back and picked out this section or that until we have gone over the entire collection again and again. But when you come to write about it, what can you say that makes sense? I recall that

John Burroughs tried to describe the song of a meadowlark. Old John could write, but that time he fell flat on his dignified face. The thing couldn't be done. And—in the same way and for similar reasons—the essence of Thurber cannot be translated into our pedestrian prose.

But the topic has a fascination. You may say that the fact that he and I grew in the same old town, that I knew the same instructors and professors, gives me no special license to approach the holy altar with rude and unsanctified hands. You may say that I am the sort of unfeeling guy who would write a grocery list on the wing of a butterfly. But I have a notion that this sensitive and erratic man coming at this time and writing in this way does have a special meaning for us.

To put it bluntly and inaccurately, James Thurber is a persistent and pertinent protest against mechanization. He hates what science and the belt line threaten to do to human nature. He is equally at odds with Ford and with Freud. Ford makes a man stand in one place and do one thing. Freud attempts to analyze mysteries of his inner being and hopes to produce a state of normalcy devoid of hallucinations. Thurber prefers inefficiency and dreams to high production levels and sanity.

Now, don't expect me to back up my theory with carefully marshaled citations. Let some candidate for the doctorate do that. Just read *Carnival* over again and find—or fail to find—my proof. Think of the treatment of characters. Take the father, for example. A lot of authors have written about their fathers. The others all give economic details, tell how their progenitors made their livings. They fit them into our social scheme. Nothing less will make the old man seem respectable. But Thurber presents his immediate ancestor sleeping, dreaming, waking, doing completely irrational and ridiculous things. You sense the man's inner, irresponsible, flighty and insubstantial ego. Instead of being a respected citizen of Columbus, Ohio, he might have come straight out of Shakespeare or Barrie.

There is here a whole series of tales in which the most conventional little men discover within themselves the most amazing resources. Walter Mitty was such a one. His wife has a very practical idea about buying rubbers and being sure to put them on. But he lives adventurously in his dream world. Mr. Samuel O. Bruhl, the most typical and inoffensive of white-collar workers, goes, in imagination, the whole way to romantic gangsterism. And then there was the bookkeeper who rebelled against the efficiency expert and did the most unbookkeeperly things after business hours. It all goes to show that a respectable citizen may have a fairyland encircled by his conventional derby.

And the procession of servants at the Thurber establishment all suggest paths that lure straight into Nonsenseland. Or perhaps nonsense isn't mere nonsense. Possibly they are to be regarded as links with the eternal verities. Barney Haller, who might be just an ordinary hired man to you or to me, "had a lightning playing about his shoulders, thunder following him like a dog. . . ." Dora Gedd, "the mousy girl of 32," shot a man in her room and shouted at him things out of Shakespeare. Juanemma Kramer could be instantly hypnotized by practically anything or anybody. Vashti was involved in the most improbable love affair. Mrs. Doody had the religious conversion of the household on her conscience and took after father with a bread knife. Mrs. Robinson, fat and very black, was always hearing voices and seeing visions.

If the servants were on the edge of fairyland, the cats, dogs, and other domestic animals were constantly scurrying back and forth across the border. Dogs are the real heroes of the Thurber universe. Rex, the American bull terrier, is its noblest inhabitant. His simple motivations make human creatures seem messy and unsatisfactory. Muggs, the dog who bit people, is given a complete character sketch with due regard to both conscious and subconscious motivation. Even the mice are taken in and given a point of view. St. Francis had nothing at all on James Thurber.

The lame wood duck brought the magic of dark forests and limitless space to the most stubbornly utilitarian surroundings. There you have your humans, ordinary and unromantic Connecticut villagers, buying apples and cider at a roadside stand. Commonplace automobiles whiz by on the dreary concrete highway. It was just "a small, trim duck," but it was wild. A couple of weeks ago it had dropped in out of its world. A speeding car symbolizes the impact of our mechanized might on the free and happy denizens of forest and field. The duck is knocked unconscious. Two hunters whose business it is to kill ducks are strangely affected. The whole group of humans unite to protect the wounded bird against the attack of a lame and crazy old setter who feels automatically impelled to do his stuff. The bird recovers and makes for the woods: a sure and atavistic urge was guiding him; he was going home. "Our painfully artificial existence is, after all, surrounded by the original wilderness—which may be home to many a creature outside the duck family."

I have a feeling that I have been skirting outside everything important. I could have written an essay to prove that Thurber side-steps sex. I could, also, have written one to prove that fear of sex is at the heart of all that this man has written or drawn. I will close with a remark about his attitude toward the automobile. To him this internal-combustion engine is as mysteriously menacing as whatever it is that makes human beings tick. The machine that is to the rest of us a simple vehicle is to him a threat reaching out from the assembly line. With it he carries on none of the simple foolery that we get from S. J. Perelman. The Get-Ready Man, who kept shouting, "The world is coming to an end!" was thought of as being but a mere adjunct of his big Red Devil car. And I suspect that our beloved Thurber took the shouted warning more than half seriously.

■

George Norris

■ Born in 1861, George Norris was part of the post-Civil War generation. The Midwest, where he started life, was the very heart of Republican conservatism. Here reactionary, big-business politicians dominated politics right up to Wilson's administration. They won the war and freed the slaves—so for nearly fifty years they could put across almost any sort of skulduggery wrapped up in the national flag. Joe Cannon and Mark Hanna were good representatives of their sordid and cynical realism. Norris was young and impressionable precisely when such plunder politicians were at the height of their power and prestige. He was, inevitably, a Republican. With his brains and vote-getting gift, he could easily have been a member of this pirate crew. He could have become rich and successful. But he happened to be different. He went his own way. He achieved great success, but his triumphs were those of the American people.

When the senator was twenty-four years old he moved to Nebraska. From then on, he was in the Populist belt, and that was just the time when Populism was seething to its climax. Sockless Jerry Simpson was a hero, and William Jennings Bryan was right around the corner. Fake cures for all political ills, like patent nostrums for physical ills, were surging on the western air. The fact that 16-to-1 could become the slogan of a national crusade was a measure of the political crudity of the day. On the one side was fat Republican conservatism and on the other, lean and raucous Populist radicalism. It is a measure of young Norris's intelligence that he fell for neither one nor the other.

Midwestern idealism has been given too little place in discussions of the road we have traveled. You get it at its best in Senator Norris and the elder La Follette. But there was a big dose of it, too, in the Bryan of the earlier years. Contemporary commentators often noted how the Populist campaigns approached the fervor of religious revivals. There is in those wide areas—or at least there was—a simple sort of Sunday-school belief in the basic virtues. It was mixed with the traditional notion that the country is more honest than the town and that poor and ordinary folks are better than the rich and refined. The East, of course, being far away, partly metropolitan and, theoretically, rich, was considered less virtuous than the West. And Europe, being even farther away and, presumably, more sophisticated, was thought of as a pretty rotten den of iniquity. Strange as it may seem, this attitude accounted for the most honest and decent part of American isolationism. Its roots are in the impulse to preserve something good that goes back to simple, rural days.

It is easy to make fun of this impulse and of all the notions that cluster about it. But the basis of it is a fine thing. It sprang from Protestant morality, a code the young people of a generation ago took seriously out there. It was these great Midwest regions that sent most missionaries to foreign lands. Their isolationism did not interfere with their developing a relief movement for backward nations long before there was any United Nations. And if a young fellow went into politics, he was rather likely to feel that he had a missionary function. It was his duty to carry the Bible virtues into the dark places of political chicanery. There was fanaticism in it, of course. Oftener than not the whole thing became ridiculous in its upshot. But no one can doubt the basic genuineness of this sort of moral perfectionism no matter what form it finally happened to take. The elder La Follette sounded strange to unfriendly ears when he ranted on about the wickedness of Wall Street. But he did put through the Seaman's Act and establish the Interstate Commerce Commission, to mention only two of the reforms that he sponsored.

Out of the same impulse to put plain decency into politics came George W. Norris. I have looked through his speeches in vain trying to find any consistent ideological creed. What he wanted was concrete things that were better. He worked to give the average citizen a richer life, to make government a more effective instrument in the citizen's hands. He had a saving grace of common sense about him. And he was more honest than most of his contemporaries in liberal politics. His liberalism never wove a web of weasel words. The real, rousing western radicals of those days were weak in reasoning power. They did not even try to show how inflation or any other sort of panacea would make anyone happier. They adopted a slogan and wound themselves up to put it over as does any peddler of any nostrum on any street corner. They were not dishonest as Mark Hanna was—nor as Boss Platt—but they were crooked in another way. They sought office under false pretenses. When Senator Norris said, "My hands have never taken a bribe nor my lips consciously uttered an untruth," he was near enough to the grave so that no doubt could be cast on his simple sincerity.

Except for two or three of the very greatest, no other American has left such dynamic reminders of his life and work. When he died every paper in the land published some sort of eulogy of the man, and it must have been tough going for some of the reactionary scribblers. They fought against every proposal of his, and after he died they spouted his praises with tongue in cheek. Practically all of the eulogies mention the Norris Dam as the senator's great monument. I prefer to be reminded of him by the graciously designed town of Norris. There are pleasant, curving drives, wide stretches of greensward, homes half hidden among the trees, and a wide-stretching park from which one can enjoy the lake held back by the noble dam. I felt while viewing these fine creations—everywhere I went—even far up in the coves of the mountains—a spirit of optimistic cooperation in something splendid. There is a community of interest in work, in cooperative accomplishment. All of the citizens are better off because each one of them is doing his job. There is here a picture of the future America. It is what Senator Norris must have dreamed.

This practical, regional, geographical, industrial achievement represents one important phase of the senator's life. From the beginning he fought to give the people the benefit of the inexpensive power that can be produced through great government-owned dams. To the very end he was planning means to put through the Missouri River Authority, which will make the TVA look like nothing but a pilot plant. This is "free enterprise" at its best, national and regional enterprise, freely supported and freely enjoyed by all the people.

George Norris's Lame Duck Amendment and his transformation of the constitution of Nebraska stand for another drive in the senator's lifework. He saw the machinery of government getting in the way of the people's desires and interests. The old forms were too stiff, too little responsive. So he helped to put through the Twentieth Amendment to the Constitution. This change makes it impossible for defeated congressmen to put through legislation the people do not want. When the Upper Chamber of the Nebraska Legislature got in the way of things that were good, he said that there was no longer need of a House of Lords. So the constitution was rewritten and this state has become the only one of the fifty to experiment with a one-chamber legislature. The senator's profound belief was that if we make the machinery of government simple and intelligible, the people will see their way clear to achieve their ends.

Senator Norris was profoundly pacifist. Along with Senator La Follette, he opposed our entrance into the First World War. But he was marked off sharply from narrow-minded, parochial, nationalist, know-nothing isolationists by his devotion to the second worldwide struggle against dictatorship.

It was fitting that the last honors were done the senator on Labor Day. By training and experience he had little contact with the labor movement. But he was passionately devoted to fairness. He wanted every citizen to have an even break. So, naturally, inevitably, he lined up with the labor forces to secure essential reforms.

In this field the Norris-LaGuardia Anti-Injunction Act is his best known achievement. But though he was always on labor's side, he always reserved the right to criticize. And it was inevitable, too, that this sort of nonpartisan statesman should be for the New Deal and for a constantly newer New Deal. He believed in concrete and practical improvements, but he could never get enough of them. He was that sort of realist. He sought, by definite changes, a constantly improving reality. At the very end he was thinking of the changes not yet made. In this man, this life, this series of achievements we had a true representation of the American ideal. ■

A certain wise liberal

■ What is a liberal? Well, William Allen White was one. If we can get a picture of this man, it may serve in place of a definition. The editor of the *Emporia Gazette*, who handed in his last copy in 1944, looked soft and pudgy. When I first observed him strolling to lunch along lower Fifth Avenue, it seemed impossible to identify the fighting editor with this slow, gentle, and friendly westerner. But I soon discovered that as soon as civil liberties were mentioned, he would stand up and fight like a man. That is one part of the definition of liberalism. It is a combination of gentleness and a sure sense of when the time to fight has arrived.

The heart of this man's thinking was neighborliness. There are two sides to every question. Keep your shirt on—listen to the other guy—things like that. His stress on reasonableness grew out of life in Kansas. His father had hastened his migration from Massachusetts through Ohio westward in order to reach the dark and bloody ground of Kansas and take his part in the Free-Soil fight. Bill was born in 1868, when the wounds from that feud were still bleeding. He grew up among men who had shot the other fellows instead of listening to them. In the new struggle between capital and labor he wanted reliance on ideas rather than on guns. He idealized Lincoln rather than John Brown. At some moment in his boyhood he must have decided that thinking was better than shooting.

And the distinctive mark of the man is that he did think and did change—right down to the end of his life. He started with the theoretical furniture provided by his time and place. To start with, he was a standpat Republican. His earliest editorials were in support of McKinley, the very symbol and picture of conservatism. In 1910 he practically apologized for the editorial that made him famous. "The editorial was pat," he wrote; "now it is not." The times had changed a little. Bill White had changed a lot.

What was this famous essay that set out to answer the question "What is the matter with Kansas?" It was nothing in God's world but a smartly put-together lot of catch phrases designed to make poor people look silly and richer people look good. That was during the Bryan campaign in 1896. The Populists were on the rampage with hope of victory putting new fire into their eyes. The twenty-eight-year-old writer threw all his talent into his effort to make them look silly. Mark Hanna circulated more than a million copies of this satirical script as part of the most scurrilously corrupt campaign we have ever had in this country.

One part of the thing was good. There was an element of blatherskitism about the Populists and Free Silver Democrats. The boy editor sneered: "We have an old mossback Jacksonian who snorts and howls because there is a bathtub in the statehouse; we are running that old jay for governor. . . . Kansas has been raising hell and letting the corn go to weeds." What she really needs are more men "who can bellow about the crime of '73." The state has "started to raise hell, and she seems to have had an overproduction. But that doesn't matter. Kansas never did believe in diversified crops." All right. There was a lot of foolishness about the Populists. But young White's masterpiece also firmly set up a picture of well-dressed and prosperous capitalists talking the sure good sense that would lead to universal wealth and ease. Mark Hanna and William McKinley, who remained unmentioned, were established as foundations of wisdom. Bryan was quoted: "There are two ideas of government. There are those who believe that if you just legislate to make the masses prosperous, their prosperity will find its way up through every class." On this analysis young Bill, future liberal, pours his biting scorn: "That's the stuff! Give the prosperous man the dickens! Legislate the thriftless man into ease, whack the stuffings out of creditors. Whoop it up for the ragged trousers. Put the greasy fizzle who can't pay his debts on the altar."

That is the writing that made Bill White famous overnight. No wonder he apologized for it fourteen years later.

Writing in his town of 13,000 inhabitants and for his paper of 7,000 readers, Bill White had, first and last, a lot to say about Socialists and Socialism. He liked the ideas of Socialism first-rate and thought they would just naturally be coming along—would, in fact, come much faster if the fanatical Socialists didn't get in their way. In 1920 he wrote: "This is a funny country—not exactly pharisaical, but object-blind. What it does not want to see, whether immoralities, or human nature functioning in the good old-fashioned way, or social evils—it simply won't see. It's that way with classes, and the Socialists might as well quit."

In 1913 he thought like this: "If you were a Socialist, wouldn't you chuckle and chuckle? About half the Socialist platform of 1904 is now on the statute books of one-third of the states, and much of it is in the platforms of at least two of the great parties. The Socialists might as well go out of business." Here you see the soft and mystic side of liberalism. Like the drunk, this very practical man actually thought that Utopia would just naturally come swinging around in its own good time.

But when the Socialist assemblymen were thrown out of the New York Legislature in 1920, this social somnambulist suddenly came to life. Listen to this: "To deny the right of representation is vastly more un-American than the disloyalty of the Socialists. It is to our shame that this thing is done by the Republican Party." Every time a Negro was lynched or denied a job or otherwise wronged, this man stood up in holy anger and swung with both fists.

In 1922 they had a railway strike out there in the West. Editor White was all for conscience and conference and compromise. That was in the days of the Kansas Industrial Court. Businessmen of Emporia put cards in their windows proclaiming their support of the strikers. The Industrial Court ordered them taken down. Editor White went red. Here was a fighting issue. Free speech was at stake.

Instantly a placard went up in the famous editor's window—and he dared the court to arrest him. The dare was taken. He was arrested. But the fight grew hotter. On July 27th came the free-speech declaration that brought the Pulitzer Prize: "You can have no wise laws nor free enforcement of wise laws unless there is free expression of the wisdom of the people—and, alas, their folly with it. But if there is freedom, folly will die of its own poison, and the wisdom will survive."

Just about that time Bill White wrote of himself: "What a fine old reactionary was the callow editor of the *Gazette* in his twenties!" Perhaps the moral of this business was a piece of good news for us all. Some Republicans can improve. ■

Thomas Mann

■ Professional literary comment on Thomas Mann's quartet of monumental volumes splits naturally into two blocs. The boys and girls who do the writing divide themselves according to the amount of literary awe that went into their making. Those who took the required courses and have heard about Goethe are distant but respectful. Those who came up by the journalistic route and made a virtue out of judging by the taste that a book leaves on their tongues take infantile pleasure in throwing a couple of clods at the fine Goethean shirtfront. The two schools are united by the fact that neither one offers much proof of having read the novels or having any distant notion of what they are all about.

Which leads me to the fact that I have been taking a vacation. Thomas Mann requires leisure, and I have been having it. At the end of my garden there is an orchard. A good fat book just fits into the crotch of one of the apple trees. As I would finish a row of corn or beans, there *Joseph the Provider* would tempt me into the shade. While I admired the ears growing round and long on my own cornstalks, I read about Pharaoh's dream of fat and lean ears and years.

That spreading tree, through the branches of which I could glimpse the far sky and the occasional transport plane, was a strong incentive to far-ranging meditation. Thomas Mann and *Joseph* would start me off, and the flights included wide stretches of history and geography. Then it began to dawn on my somnolently soaring mind that these four books uniting Israel and Egypt are really a commentary on civilization—on all civilization.

It took nerve to write such books in those days of the 1940's. At least I suppose it did. What we call realism had long been accepted as the natural literary form for practical and common-sense folks like us. We expected a straightforward and preferably a funny tale of what happened to Joe or Annie or old Grandpa Goople. When a man began to write about distant and ancient regions, customs, gods, ideas, religions—we got nervous. It was a world in which we were not at home. Evidently a lot of things mentioned had double meanings. They were symbols. Symbols suggest ideas, and ideas made us uneasy. The best defense against our unease was to pretend that the whole business is phony and doesn't matter much.

The symbolic form has the great advantage of universality. Far things become near and ancient things are contemporaneous. The author evidently had a lot of fun doing this writing, and I can imagine his quiet smile as he penned some of these passages. More than one of them had a modern sting in its tail.

Nearest the surface is Joseph as the Egyptian Roosevelt. This Hebrew upstart at the sophisticated court of Pharaoh was the first economic planner. Having no graphs or Gallup poll, he depended upon dreams. But there is a continuous hinting that dreams and their interpretations are the thoughts that form behind half-closed eyelids. Joseph and Pharaoh are two men thinking about government, prices, finance, and foreign relations. The benevolent dictator shall investigate and find out where the grain "is to be distributed gratis and where sold, shall arrange that the little people shall eat . . . and shall harass the great in favor of the crown, that Pharaoh shall become excited over gold and silver." And after laying down this neat little program Joseph goes on to pay his respects to the economic royalists—or perhaps Dr. Mann was thinking of the Junkers of his day in Germany. For there were in those days, as in ours, "remnants of the old" that still defiantly persisted. They, said the smart economic

planner, shall pay "such kind of prices that their eyes shall run over
with tears and they shall be plucked to the last pinfeather" so that in
the end these who "sit defiantly on their estates" shall be turned into
tenants.

To each according to his need; from each according to his bank
balance. From beginning to end the common people supported
this program, and you can well imagine what the "remnants of the
old" thought about Joseph and what they said about him in their
clubs.

The implications about dictatorship and democracy are far too
many and too subtle to indicate here. Joseph is pictured as the
supreme politician, and a good politician must be basically democratic. This politician manipulates both the theoretical dictator on
the throne and the common people, who are theoretically slaves. As
you feel the tug of all the classes and sects of Egypt, you have the
feeling that little has changed.

But all this is on the surface. It is what George Babbitt might
select for comment. From beginning to end the book is a search for
the truth that lies in back of names. The ancient peoples went from
their animistic deities to the earth to the moon to the sun. Joseph
and Pharaoh are both seeking something deeper than the earth and
higher than the sun. There is an eternal conflict between the person
and the pattern. "The traditional comes from the depths" and blinds
us, "whereas the I is from God and is of the spirit, which is free.

"The search of the free spirit for truth and his twistings and turn-
ings to adapt himself to society—this is what furnishes the bones
of this story underneath the luxury of oriental trappings."

To get into the spirit of the thing, you must read every word, and
you must read slowly, with time out now and then for excursions to
other stretches of history and colors of climate. Perhaps this is the
source of critical shortcomings. A man with a deadline to meet is in
no proper mood to seek meanings that lie beyond meanings.　■

FREEDOM AND INDEPENDENCE

Father's German Revolution

■ On May 16th Americans and Germans met in the old St. Paul's Church of Frankfurt, Germany, to celebrate the hundredth anniversary of the Revolution of 1848. Orators from both countries pointed out the similarities between our New World ideals and those treasured by the Germans who gathered in Frankfurt exactly a century ago to draw up a democratic constitution for the Fatherland. As the speakers elaborated this chapter of history there amidst the rubble of that ruined land, a distinguished poet, Fritz von Unruh, fell in a faint and had to be carried from the hall. This gave an appropriately tragic touch to one of the greatest of history's tragedies.

I suppose I am one of the very few persons who have something like a memory of that German Revolution of 1848. I recall it in the sense that I have in my mind living pictures of the scenes that were passed on to me warm and vivid from the recollections of my father. The present collapse of the proud old empire brings back the tales to which I used to listen as we circled the winter fire with Father sitting there in his worn old armchair and turning his mind back to the scenes of his youth. In the manner of their telling, these narratives had a simple and folklorish quality, but I can see in them now a wisdom that goes far toward explaining Hitler and all the horrors that have scarified the Europe of our day.

My picture of the events of '48 has nothing to do with the high drama of Berlin, Leipzig, Vienna, or Frankfurt. Father's part—and it had a quiet heroism—was played in Remptendorf, a tiny feudal village deep in the Sächsische Vogtland. The 1,300 inhabitants were, during the first half of the nineteenth century, practically as docile as had been their ancestors during the Middle Ages. In fact, it was only a few years before this that my grandfather, as burgomaster of the place, had had the nerve to put an end to unpaid feudal labor that had been rendered to the prince of the realm time out of memory.

Father's little episode in the great Revolution that stretched from Vienna to Berlin began to roll in the narrow street before the stoutly built house that had sheltered my ancestors for five generations. I heard the story many times, and while I will not guarantee the historicity of the narrative, I will swear that my reproduction of it is practically perfect. For this story, like other folk tales, had been rehearsed so often that it had taken on a final and perfect polish.

Father, then, on that historic night in 1848 had retired to the depths of his ancestral featherbeds beside the fireplace when he was roused by the clamor of shouts and all the commotions of a crowd milling about in the street. People were calling him by name: "Heinrich! Heinrich!" When, finally, he had prepared himself for so public an appearance, Father was given more accurate information about what was up and what was required of him. "Come," the neighbors shouted, "you must lead us! There is a revolution. In the cities things are going great guns. You be our leader and we will go and smash the windows of the Herr Pfarrer." The village preacher was, I should explain, the nearest thing to a representative of royalty that the provincial village could boast. Striking at this symbol was the quickest way of hitting at ancient authority. So there was King Mob looking for a leader.

Now, Father was both a republican and an atheist. You might think that this was just the moment for which he had been waiting. But the revolutionists of '48 had their minds set on different things. When Father would reach this point in his tale his face would assume a religious solemnity. Here was the village Patrick Henry facing his people. What should he do or say? Whither should he lead? "Good friends and old neighbors," he would recall his words to us, "you tell me that there is a revolution in the cities. If that is true, this is an important moment in our history. We want to have a republic, and if our revolution succeeds, we shall have a free government like that in America. But do you know what it means—to have a republic? It means that you will have no king or prince to guide you. You must guide yourselves. You must write a constitution. You must understand and defend it. You must elect representatives who will pass laws, and the laws that they pass you must be ready to support and obey. That will not be accomplished by smashing anyone's windows. I advise you to go quietly to your homes and consider the meaning of our revolution."

There are those who maintain that the outburst of 1848 would have accomplished more if more windows had been smashed. At the very least a really red revolutionist would feel sure that the docility with which the good burghers submitted to Father's plea augured ill for the success of the popular movement. The people were too tame to dare much or to make dramatic changes. For it is related that the crowd quietly dispersed. And later Father and the village storekeeper were chosen as delegates to the Constitutional Convention.

The story of the failure of the German Revolution of 1848—like that of the failure of the Russian overturn of 1917—is one of the great tragedies of history. This failure led straight to Kaiser Wilhelm II and the First World War and thence to Hitler and the Second. So the reasons for the lack of success are important. The docility of those feudal peasants on that dark and narrow village street gives one the clues historians seek.

Further explanations appear in Father's account of the convention that tried to write the new constitution. He and Kaufmann Nuss made elaborate preparations for their effort to assist in the establishment of a free government. Father used to tell us proudly that he read the Constitution of the United States and the speeches of Thomas Jefferson. The people in that village where that farmer read Jefferson a century ago are now ruled by Russian army officers. The spirit of Jefferson is, I suspect, no nearer than in Father's day. ∎

The failure of democratic Germany

∎ So the German Revolution of 1848 was—theoretically—successful without a fight. In my father's little principality—with the preposterous name of Reuss, Greitz, Schleitz, und Lobenstein, Jüngere Linie —things were all set for the constitutional convention. The people's government was to be put on a going basis. The hopeful founding fathers were to meet in the castle of the reigning prince. This feature of the arrangements always seemed rather strange to my brother and me as we listened to the oft-told tale. In our school history we had read what Sam Adams and Patrick Henry said about George III. Over there in Father's little corner of Germany, the King George part was being played by the prince, and the constitutional convention was to be held in his palace. It had a queer look. There was something obviously unrevolutionary about it. Nevertheless, Father and Kaufmann Nuss set off with high hopes to do their part toward setting the new state on its feet.

The prince of the realm, it must be confessed, did things up in style. He received his peasant constitution makers with a swell banquet. The occasion was notable for the pair of delegates from Remptendorf because it was the first time that either of them saw or tasted ice cream. The good Kaufmann, it was recorded, partook gingerly of the dainty and strange confection and succeeded, despite its frigidity, in swallowing some of it. To his regret, that was not the end of the tale. The merchant-turned-statesman felt ominous rumblings in his interior and was soon forced, in fact, to leave the table amidst the curious and embarrassed glances of his fellow solons and relieve himself in whatever sequestered spot he could find in that aristocratic environment.

But I am getting ahead of my story. When the delegates entered the banquet hall, stepping timidly on the deep pile of the carpet, they were awed into silence. Father recalled that as they passed through the door he murmured to his faithful companion, "Look, Kaufmann, this is the way our rich rulers have it. Perhaps if you and I lived this way, we would be as bullheaded about staying put as they are." The prince's strategy, you see, was having its effect.

Every delegate was presented to the provincial dictator. Father's face would grow extra solemn as he approached this part of his narrative. While the hereditary monarch held his hand and heard his name, he said, rather sadly, as though recalling happier days: "Bohn, Bohn. Yes. I remember that name. Your father was always a faithful subject." That was the word that had touched Father to the quick in his youth and brought that look of mystic solemnity to his eyes in old age. Looking around the little circle of his children, he would say, dropping each word separately: "I didn't want to be discourteous. After all, we were there representing the dignity of the people. But I just had to say something to let that old man know what we were thinking. So, standing there on that soft carpet and looking down the length of that long table to which we had been invited, I said to him, 'We aim, sire, to be good citizens.'" Then there would be a dramatic pause. We would wait—knowing well what was coming. When at last the pregnant combination of words and occasion had had time to sink in, Father would proceed: "Yes, children, little do you know how fortunate you are here in republican America. But never forget—there is a world of difference between a subject and a citizen."

After the ruler had exhausted the propaganda value of feasting and soft living, the convention finally settled down to the business of constitution making. My brother and I, who already considered ourselves experts in American history and government, would ask with suppressed eagerness: "What did you do, Father? How did you know how to write a constitution?" Then Father would raise one of his worn and farm-browned hands for emphasis: "It didn't come easy to an inexperienced worker like me. I didn't say much, but I studied day and night. I read especially"—and here my brother and I would feel little shocks of electricity run up and down our spines—"the Constitution of the United States."

That is how the framework of government was hammered together in that corner of Germany away back in 1848. Their task completed, the amateur statesmen retired to humbler and better-understood tasks at home. The rest was all anticlimax. Father would grow shy and reticent over this chapter of his Odyssey. He would require prompting, which my brother and I, from the heights of our American experience, were not slow to supply. "What was the matter?" we would ask. "Why didn't your constitution work the way ours did?" "Oh," Father would murmur, "it was all their fault. They wouldn't leave things alone. One article of that constitution after another they annulled. What could we do about it?"

At this we might nudge each other, but we had enough respect for Father to refrain from sophisticated criticism in his presence. It was only when we were alone on our way to bed that we would remark in superior tones: "Imagine the dopiness of those Germans! They wrote a constitution and left it to the aristocrats to enforce. No president, no congress, no court, no people's army. No wonder it failed. All they got from America was the words. They never found out what makes things go."

And having spilled our upstart wisdom out of Father's hearing, we were ready for the deep sleep of boyhood—little dreaming that Father's failure so long ago would rise to plague us and all mankind in two great wars. For the failure that the Allied representatives assembled at Frankfurt to celebrate in 1948 began before Father's house in Remptendorf on that night in 1848.   ■

Gullahs have good memories

■ One Christmas Day some years ago I learned that we were near Pauley's Island, one of the old rice and indigo islands that have taken on a folklorish charm for the readers of Julia Peterkin's novels. *Scarlet Sister Mary* has made the Gullah Negroes a fabulous people. Inevitably I experienced the yen to go in search of them. A kindly officer of engineers made arrangements that smoothed our way—and off we went.

The island proved to be only the length of a bridge from the mainland. But of strange features and arresting atmosphere it has no lack. The hospitable host of the inn took us out among the dunes and then deep into the pine forest. He did not promise us real Gullah Negroes, but, at the very least, such Negroes as we had never seen before.

Black man Number One was an ageless fellow who had long ago given up counting his years. He was engaged in conquering the jungle, pulling it out of the ground and consigning it to the fire. This rude labor he was not unwilling to relinquish to receive us with singular grace and good manners. But when I asked him about the Gullah Negroes he seemed taken aback that I should be interested in such no-'count folks. "They is," he said slowly, in his soft and musical accents, "a kind of rough people that can't rightly talk American. They got some kind of African language that they kin understand but no one else kin. If I was you I wouldn't bother much lookin' round for 'em."

A winding and primitive track through the pines led us to a bridge and across it to the mainland, and soon we were in talk with a man who was expecting soon to conclude his one hundredth year. That meant that he was fifteen or sixteen years old when the War Between the States began and about twenty when he was released from slavery. By the way, he seemed puzzled when I referred to the War Between the States or the Civil War. After quite a bit of explanation his brow cleared and he exclaimed, "Oh, you-all mean Abraham Lincum's war." So we had our bearings and the talk could proceed.

Yes, he remembered well. During that war Lincum's soldiers had come near. It must have been Sherman's troops on their way from Savannah to Columbia. What he remembered was that the slaves had been herded back into the woods. The slaves and the silver were both hidden at the approach of the Yankee marauders. I wanted to know what the slaves did when they heard that they were free. "Why, Massah," he said, "we jest went on workin'. There was nothin' else for us to do. We stayed on the old plantation, and then maybe ten or fifteen years afterward some of the young folks got the idea of goin' somewhere else to work." You note that he called me "Massah." The women of our party he addressed as "Missus." For seventy-eight years he had been a free man, but he still used the language of slavery.

Naturally, we wanted to get some picture of slavery times. But it took a lot of poking about in the old man's mind to bring any of them to the surface. He had a deep aversion to displaying them. There was, evidently, something unworthy, something disgraceful about them. "Some black folks," he remarked, "was well enough off. It all depended on the kind of white folks. Some of the massahs was mean, and then it meant the club and the whip. But I ain't a-goin' to say one more word about that." And he clamped his lips tight shut.

Some twisting and turning along another winding track lined by Negro shacks brought us to the country store and to our last black Methuselah. He laid claim to only eighty-nine years, and his value as a witness about times past was vitiated by his evident desire to display his learning. But to him I owe an experience that I shall not soon forget. He led me into the store, which was run by his son. There I found half-a-dozen Negro men sitting about the fire. These were younger men, and when I was introduced to them they did not address me as "Massah." My time with these men was short, for mine host was after me. It was time to go. The storekeeper addressed me with solemn formality: "You are a white man that thinks enough of Negroes to stop by and talk with them. We are powerfully worried about what is going to happen to us in this land." I had but a few moments, and I cannot recall what I said to him. But as our guide fairly pulled me out of that place I had a feeling that those colored men were trying to hold me with their eyes. They wanted help that I had failed to give. ∎

Free as a bird—or a turtle

∎ Some time ago I wrote a column about the unconquerable depths of the sea. Following the thought waves of the saintly Thoreau, I found pleasure in the notion that some areas of creation never will be subdued by what we call civilization. Over a recent weekend I found myself practically forced to pursue this line of meditation a step further.

I spent some days as the guest of a charming gentleman who was born to be a dictator. He has lately purchased an estate among the mountains of Pennsylvania. No sooner did it come into his possession, than its birds and beasts became, in his imagination, his dependent subjects.

The wrens, rather than being left to their own devices, had charming little ranch houses constructed for them. Along with the thrushes, robins, song sparrows, and catbirds, they had their domestic arrangements looked into. Even their choices of mates were criticized. Their selection of home sites was made the subject of derogatory comment. But, except for the wrens, our winged and musical guests exhibited little appreciation for the attention showered upon them.

One family of brown thrashers, however, gave a notable exhibition of independence. Their cleverly hidden nest was discovered in a great bush of boxwood at the kitchen door. It was amazing to find such wild and timid birds so close to the haunts of man. The beautifully constructed nest had been so carefully hidden that it never would have been discovered had not the lord of the manor seen one of the pair slipping into the secret hiding place. The whole family was called to view this wonder, this pair of wood birds established here within inches of a human dwelling. And then we went to breakfast.

After the cheerful feast of fruit and bacon and eggs, the natural wonder had to be viewed all over again. Our host had even prepared us for appreciation by delivering a lecture at the table about the changing habits of wild creatures. As they become acquainted with friendly men, we were told, they gradually become domesticated. Soon we may expect them to live as quietly and stupidly among men as do the pigeons.

It was a pleasant-sounding theory. But the brown thrashers had never heard of it. When, finally, we left the breakfast table and went to pay our respects to those wild things who were responding so rapidly to man's civilizing and dominating—not to say imperialistic—influence, they were nowhere to be found.

All day a diligent search was made. The trees, the shrubbery, the neighboring gardens were all carefully examined. Those birds had simply disappeared. Their domicile had been sullied, debased, desecrated. Its secrets had been pierced by the evil eye of enemy man. It was no longer fit for the rearing of a proper brood of free and high-flying wood thrushes. The birds had fled as from a pestilence.

I made similar observations upon the performance of a turtle. I saw him first laying distance behind him at a terrific pace as he made his way over a wide stretch of lawn. Head up, giving every evidence of alertness, this old hard-shelled fellow obviously knew where he was going. My host, who was able, of course, to explain all the mysteries of the animal kingdom, pointed out that turtles are excessively fond of mulberries. A tree weighted down with this delectable fruit was approaching its period of ripeness in a neighbor's yard. Doubtless this old reptile, recalling the dainty feasts enjoyed during previous summers, was on his way to repeat such pleasures. He reminded me of the classical turtle with which Steinbeck opens his *The Grapes of Wrath.* Our turtle had, no doubt, a similar purpose.

My host no sooner saw this enterprising explorer than he had all of the creature's future life mapped out for him. Just such a fine turtle was what he wanted as a permanent ornament for his estate. A pool would be dug to serve as his bathtub. Every delicacy would be served for him without his having to scrounge for it.

This grandfather of the turtle world was installed in his new kingdom with enough of the promised luxuries to serve as a guarantee of what was to come. The final act you can easily guess. After a couple of hours, when we went to make sure that His Turtleship was completely comfortable and happy, we found that he, too, had disappeared. He preferred the ups and downs of free enterprise to all the ease and luxury of a limited world.

The moral of these simple tales need not be pressed. The wild creatures have more sense than millions of humans. They have, at least, a fair estimate of the value of freedom. ▪

Inlander by the sea

▪ Down in Delaware we have our own Atlantic City. It has a biblical name, Rehoboth—though there is nothing biblical about it except for the fact that the time is divided into day and night with the sun to mark the one and the moon the other. Last weekend I was down there by the sounding sea and thinking all of the thoughts that roll in with the waves. The world of the water and the sand and the rimming pine forests was more than usually a world by itself. It happened that the friends with whom we lived and boated and hiked did not take a daily paper. For three days we were shut away from Congress and from conferences of foreign ministers. Strange as it may seem, in the presence of the wide-stretching sea and sky the last hot headlines faded out of memory. The sight and sound of the deep had wrought a change in us. We had no more interest in current events than had Thoreau strolling along the shore of Cape Cod a century ago.

Any native of the inland plain yearns for the ocean or for the mountains—perhaps, as in my case—for both. My youth was spent where there was no water wider or more dangerous than the brook that purled across the meadow. The other day when we motored into Rehoboth a wild storm was lashing across the sky. But I could not wait. Despite all scoffing and warning, I had to hurry down to the beach. The others, bred within sound of the surf, could wait. But for me, who had not even seen or heard the ocean-sea until well past my twentieth year, the storm had no terrors. In fact the surface of the waters lashed to fury is so different from the safe and calm world of my boyhood that it has always held a special charm.

I was glad that I went beyond the dunes and down onto the beach on that wild afternoon. The scudding foam was tossed so high that sea and sky could hardly be distinguished. On land the mingled surf and sand was being carried far up over the roadways and houses. It was the sort of watery world out of which it would have seemed normal to see strange monsters writhing forth.

I inevitably compared the wild, wide, and practically unexplored ocean with the completely tamed and systematized expanses of my boyhood world. I am told that there are on land a few spots that have not yet been pried into—in South America, in Africa, in the secret recesses of Asia. But very few of us will ever spy out those far places. The ocean is the only unplotted waste that we shall ever know.

Books on oceanography I have always lapped up as children devour the funnies, or romantic maidens the best-sellers. But every time I go through a new one, I am struck by the thought that much of the bottom of the sea is actually unknown. There must be countless beings there below that have not been weighed and measured, described or classified; among them, doubtless, creatures as strange as any that have hitherto been brought to our wondering gaze.

We shall, in time, widen our knowledge. Perhaps in the end men will understand all, or almost all, of the strange forms of life. But I believe and hope that they will never completely conquer the watery wastes. They can sail over them. They can fish up the inmates of them. They can even, in submarines and diving bells, penetrate deep into them. But I have a fixed belief that they can never completely conquer them, master them, make them tame and common and ordinary and harmless. Those who go out to sea will forever be challenged by mighty and mysterious forces.

There by that troubled tide—as always by the sea, whether in calm or storm—I find myself thinking of the Greeks. Their words keep coming back: "the sounding sea," "the hollow sea," "the dark sea." The Iliad and the *Anabasis* seem as near as yesterday's newspaper. It is probably not just because the Athenians wrote so supremely well of marine experiences. It must be, rather, because by the water one has far horizons. Sea and sky stretch away and away. So one's mind, being symbolically stimulated, tends to look both forward and back. And when we look back, the men we see first are, most likely, Plato, Aristotle, or Achilles.

These meditations naturally led in the direction of Toynbee and the successive rise and fall of nations. Our tragic situation, viewed in the perspective of the endless succession of civilizations, seems less fatal than it usually does to our nearsighted eyes. A certain stoicism— if not hope—may be attained in their perspective of millennia. But this does not by any means tend to reduce man's view of his own importance or his faith in his own will. In the long look across the ridges of the past, what is most conspicuous is that the nations that shine out are the ones that knew what they believed and were willing to stand up for their beliefs. ∎

With magnolias

∎ About ten years ago both Frank Lloyd Wright and I were in Washington at the same time. The argumentative architect made a speech that showed he had been doing some bad thinking about a good subject. He talked about the green and gracious city that serves as our capital. He reported that he disliked the domed and pillared buildings that house our government. He proposed that the nation's political heart be moved to a spot somewhat near its physical center—

say, along the Mississippi, where the great architectural innovator and his followers might shake off the combined influences of Rome, Palladino, and the eighteenth century and build on the wide plains the functional palaces of the future.

So far as building design is concerned, I should be delighted to have the Frank Lloydians given free rein to show what they can do. But as to the location of the capital, my vote is in favor of leaving it precisely where it is.

The Mississippi is a noble stream, but it doesn't really separate anything from anything. The people and institutions on one side of it are, by and large, the same as those on the other. You can travel three thousand miles from Portland, Maine, to Portland, Oregon, without encountering any significant shift in opinion or pattern of life. But run your car a mere hundred miles from New Jersey or Pennsylvania to Virginia—and you pass from one world to another.

I am sure that many readers will agree that folks from Dixie have much to assimilate from more enlightened politicians and visitors who frequent Washington. The struggle at last summer's Democratic convention and the fall campaign of the Dixiecrats have put the attitudes and ideas of the old Rebel country on the spot. The South is far more leavened with liberalism than ever before, but the conservatism of the old Confederacy is replacing original sin as the whipping boy of the universe. Right now a large section of northern opinion is further from understanding the South, compromising with the South, appreciating the charms and virtues of the South than ever before.

I need not explain that with regard to civil rights and racial equality, I am a northerner down to the bone. My brothers helped to fight the Civil War. In my youth I just naturally took for granted that that war had been won, that the Negroes had been liberated, that racial equality had been achieved. I was wrong about some of the facts but right about the ideals. With regard to civil-rights programs, the North is on the winning side. With regard to such matters the folks down yonder have a lot to catch up on.

But this is not what I set out to proclaim. I am writing this column in order to say to all my friends in New York, New England, the Midwest and Far West that there is another side to this matter of regional dissidence to which we ought to pay attention. It may be that we have as much to learn from the South as the South has to learn from us.

The notion came to me the other morning as I was eating breakfast in my hotel dining room. It was gay and sunny. There was a cheerful flutter of activity and of talk. I suppose there were among the guests about even numbers from the North and from the South. I looked and listened—and I fancied that I could go through the room and divide the sheep from the goats.

The distinguishing marks were quietness of manner, ease and readiness in communication, ways of acting that betokened confidence in old and well-tried patterns of living. These were the stigmata of the southerners. The representatives of the North and West were less uniform. Many of them might with profit have been sent to school a few hundred miles nearer to the Equator. Their voices needed toning down. The movements could have been less jerky and angular. Their personalities lacked softness.

I suppose I shall be told that I am wasting my time on superficialities. Correspondents will complain that what southerners have to learn from us is basic and what we have to learn from them merely ornamental. I doubt that anyone can make good on this distinction. Tone of voice and manner of speech symbolize things that lie deep in character and culture. Failure to appreciate the value of that which we lack is in itself a deficiency.   ■

The weir people

■ With the end of vacation looming ominously ahead, we started out aimlessly through the spruce wood that borders the beach. It was Duffy, our affectionate and enterprising hound, who determined our course. Briskly she set out with nose to the ground and tail wagging like a banner. The way in which she turned to the right along the path following the shore suggested that she had definite business in that direction. Happy, amused, content to have our decisions made for us, Edith and I followed along.

This route would take us, after a short walk, to the weir of Seal Cove, and we had half a mind to look once more into this trap for unwary fish. A half-hour of following Duffy's eager lead up and down and about that springing carpet of spruce needles brought us near enough to our destination so that we could see that something was happening. The men were out on the weir drawing their nets. There would be boatloads of fish to see and fishermen to talk to.

A weir is a comparatively primitive device to snare the dumb and unwary denizens of the deep. The art of building it our friends inherited from the native redmen, and we have made but slight improvements on their original techniques. It consists, essentially, of a triangle of spiles and net that lures the poor fish into a great enclosed square from which there is, so far as his intelligence reports, no escape. Two men own and run this weir. They not only built the structure themselves; they produced the raw materials from the surrounding forests and constructed the great spile driver, floating on a scow, with which the spiles were driven into the ocean bottom.

I have written more than once about the seaboard people of Maine. I hope that it is not merely a notion of mine—this idea that they are an especially stout and admirable lot of people. But now as representatives of the entire upstanding and independent tribe, I should like to name the weirman of Seal Cove and his charming wife. A handsomer couple I have never seen anywhere. Tall, clear-eyed, fair-spoken people, they show what qualities humanity can achieve free from any sort of compulsion and far from crippling crowds.

When we arrived, the men were out on the weir pulling up the nets and dipping the fish into their boats. As we waited for the men to come ashore, we chatted with the weirman's attractive wife. She has lived among the fishermen some three or four years. In the wintertime they make or mend their nets. Some of them build lobster pots. There is plenty of work.

Time to think? "Yes, there would be time to think if they had anything to think about or to think with," said the weirman's wife. She had organized a hobby club last winter, and the youngsters thought it was wonderful. She would do it again. These waterside kids, she thought, deserved some sort of break.

By this time the men had pulled a dory up onto the pebbly beach with a load of mackerel. While they shoveled the fish into boxes and baskets they kept up a running comment on their business. For most of their catch they were paid from $1.15 to $1.50 a bushel. That means from about a cent to a cent-and-a-half a pound. The bigger fish bring 12 to 15 cents a pound. It isn't, obviously, enough. The same fish bring high prices in the Boston and New York markets. It is the old story.

My mind ran back to a time many years ago when I tried to interest an outfit of Maine fishermen in cooperatives. I had found a schoolteacher who was willing to undertake the necessary correspondence. The Cooperative Association was ready to go ahead with the project. Finally, I recalled, an organizer had been sent up into the Penobscot Bay region, not far from this very cove where these men were shoveling out their fish. So I said to them: "Look! Haven't you men ever thought of starting a cooperative, having your own refrigerating plant and packing and selling your own fish?" "Oh, yes," the weirman said, "there were some people here not long ago tried talking up that idea, but it didn't take. The men would be all right as long as they were in a meeting. It all looked fine. But when each fellow would be out in his boat, he would forget all about it." "But what about Nova Scotia?" I put in. "The Catholic priests helped along, and now the men have their own storage plants and run their own business."

Then my weirman gave an answer to which I should like to give wide circulation. "That's all right for Catholics," he said, "they'll stick together. But Protestants would never do that."

By this time Edith had got so interested that she could not keep out of the conversation. She asked why some Protestant preachers couldn't take the lead.

The weirman laughed aloud. "If any preacher tried that," he said, "he would soon find that he was a leader with no one behind him. Just let me tell you what these men are like. A half-dozen lobstermen come up here from Southwest Harbor and other places to get bait for their traps. They need a couple of bushels apiece. Well, every darned one of them burns the gasoline to come up here in his own launch to get his own coupla bushels. They don't have sense enough to club together and divide the transportation cost by six."

I still like them.   ■

Mark of the craft

■ I have been amused—sometimes touched—by the enthusiasm with which my New York friends have received my vacation sketches of Maine fisherfolk. I will meet some well-known and successful man— a fellow who enjoys all the advantages of living in the heart of the metropolis—and he will say: "Wonderful people, those fishermen you wrote about. I'd like to live the way they do." But he probably does not at all mean what he says. He is probably merely voicing a general discontent with life in this beehive of steel, glass, bricks, and cement. To outsiders, the denizens of New York seem to have everything in the world, but they really feel fenced in and deprived. My tales of the lobstermen and weirmen opened windows on a life that seems more free and individual.

Mr. Waclaw Solski, who has lived on many of the coasts of Europe, writes to me: "I very much liked your stories about the fishermen of Maine. What struck me while reading them was that these people, individualistic as they certainly are, have very much in common with the fishermen of France and England. During the war I spent a few weeks at St. Ives, which is a small village in Cornwall. Everybody knows everybody and they are all very proud, but they did not mind talking about their most personal matters with a foreigner. I remember that because of the strong winds I got in-flammation of the eye while living there. There was a doctor in the village, but the fishermen did not like doctors and advised me against seeing him. They gave me some tea leaves to put on my eyelids, and they served the purpose very effectively.

"It would be interesting to compare, not only fishermen, but people in other professions in different countries. It is striking how similar they are. They look the same. They talk the same. Fishermen in Bordeaux, France, and Ostend, Belgium, tell the same jokes which are related by the followers of their trade in America. Perhaps you will some day write a piece on this subject."

The only European fishermen I have ever had any dealings with were the patient watchers of the lines along the banks of the Seine. Though I have often waited patiently for signs of life at the ends of their poles, I never saw one of them capture so much as the tiniest specimen of any underwater species. But these ancient representatives of their craft were never disturbed by their lack of success. What they actually sought, sunshine and contentment, they seemed to be absorbing in large doses.

Quite in accord with Mr. Solski's theory, I have seen along the Mississippi—and many a smaller stream in this country—patient men nodding over their rods with precisely the same satisfying philosophy as that which oozes from anglers of the Seine. Since receiving his letter I have learned that the evidence supporting his theory comes from world-wide sources. Fishermen everywhere—even in China and India—have a way of thinking for themselves and looking out for themselves. I am told that even in Germany those who draw their sustenance from the sea are averse to taking orders. Perhaps here lies a key to that education for democracy about which we have talked so much and done so little.

The other day, in the midst of a great shower of rain, I found myself in need of a taxi. Just at the right moment the door of one opened at the curb directly before me. As I moved quickly to assert possession, the piquant face of Martha Graham—better known as Miss Hush—emerged from the interior. After she and I, despite the downpour, had exchanged a few cheerful words I said to the driver, "Did you know it was Miss Hush you were carrying around in your car?"

His rather disgusted face was turned halfway round to me: "Miss Hish, Miss Hash, Miss Hush. Whaddu I know? Whaddu I care? Celebrities or no celebrities! They all look alike to me. In this trade they come a dime a dozen. But whether you get a decent tip—that's something else again. How do I know? Maybe you're a celebrity, too. Most of 'em look dumb enough."

Nearly fifty years ago I heard a Paris taximan make an exactly parallel speech. He too was fed up with famous folk, was glad to transport common people if they would only express their appreciation in palpable terms. Drivers of taxis, pullers of jinrickishas, providers of metropolitan transportation the world over are brothers under the skin. They are alike in their hatred of the police and in their opposition to the drivers of trucks and private cars. They are all tired of the city and, like barbers, have their eyes on just the right spot beyond the glare of traffic lights.

In this little essay I had intended also to consider waiters, mail carriers, policemen, and beggars, all the far-flung special squadrons of the workers and loafers of the world. How different they are from the way in which a certain distinguished pundit named Karl Marx has pictured them! ∎

Envoys of the air

∎ Every time I make a trip to the Voice of America studios, I sense that I am getting a glimpse into the future. Here a new technique of international relations is being worked out. Hitherto international affairs have been almost exclusively government affairs. A striped-pants ambassador with his staff represents us in each foreign capital. For each foreign government such a dignitary and staff carry on in Washington. The range of affairs with which these persons deal is strictly limited. The average citizen never sees an ambassador and no ambassador ever sees him.

Foreign relations as conducted by the script writers, broadcasters and, in general, policy explainers of the Voice of America are of an entirely different sort and on an entirely different level. To get a picture of what is happening it is necessary to bear in mind that the same thing is going on in London and Paris. Every now and then we receive letters from far-off places that make comparisons between our programs and those of England and France. So I know that people throughout great parts of the world can choose among the broadcasts of these three representatives of Western democracy.

The Russians, of course, are in this thing in a big way. And other countries, too, are trying their hands at it. Broadcasting by governments is a rapidly developing method of carrying on propaganda war. But it is, to an even greater extent, a growing instrument for the development of world unity.

The difference between the old way of reaching foreign countries and the new way is revolutionary. Under the old diplomatic system, government communicated with government. Under the new, a government communicates with the individual citizens of another government. The method of communication is warm, informal, individual, human. The men and women who do the writing and broadcasting for the Voice are as different as possible from traditional diplomats. Though they must cultivate some of the arts of diplomacy, most of them remind you of good newspaper men or good salesmen with a touch of the showman thrown in. They have a human-interest story to tell, and it is their business to put it over.

The broadcasts to which I have listened most often are those from the German desk. They are bright, sharp, up-to-the-minute, sometimes witty, warmly and intimately delivered. I can tell from letters that I have read from France, India, South America, and China that the programs beamed to other countries have the same good human qualities.

A charming young lady whose business it is to classify mail gave me what might be called a mail clerk's view of the nations of the world. The Italians, she reported, send their letters in orange-colored envelopes. The Spaniards use purple typewriter ribbons and half-sheets of paper. The Brazilians love envelopes decorated with stripes of white, yellow, and green, the national colors. The French seldom use typewriters, but their handwritten letters are carefully done—often with purple ink. From Great Britain comes much high-grade stationery, and the notes, restrained and genteel in tone, are usually written by hand.

The Germans require special treatment. They are the great letter writers of the world. Out of about six thousand letters that arrived in an ordinary month, more than three thousand usually come from Germany. These are written on all sorts of stationery, and generally without regard to design or color. Practically all of them are long, closely spaced, and typewritten. Many are warmly personal. One that I happened to pick up told the story of a man's life, beginning with an unhappy childhood and ending with the account of the death of the man's wife. One of the young ladies in the mail department told me that never has she come across a German letter in which the author acknowledged any personal responsibility for Hitler or for the war. But I seem to sense in many of these letters a desperate yearning to be understood and to be recognized. This might account for the unconscionable length of these lucubrations and their almost unpleasantly personal quality.

Communications from Anglo-Saxons are generally like those that any American might write. From Europe and Asia, too, arrive many short and practical letters about migration to America, about the probability of finding jobs, or about other aspects of life on this side of the water.

What finally remains with me after going through a pile of this variegated mail is that men and women almost everywhere are lonely, scared, uncertain, insecure. They hear this voice coming out of the air. It comes from New York—rich and, they think, happy New York. In the answers that return to us I seem to detect a desperate human cry.　　　　　　　　　　　　　　　　　　　　　　　■

Independent people

■ We were sitting on the racked and weather-beaten wharf after having taken a dozen lobsters from Will Dunning's float. The tide was out and the water calm, on this sunny Sunday morning. Even the gulls seemed less raucously assertive than usual as they scouted for their breakfast. Behind us the Fisher Village was sprawled in contours dictated by the granite ledges of the shore. Little groups of fishermen lolling against the well-weathered cottages seemed like figures in a stage set or in an impressionistic painting. The whole scene, under the comforting rays of the sun, seemed timeless.

When Will spoke, he might have been an actor, a perfect actor in this perfect scene. His theme was set for him by the environment. Behind us the fishermen loafed in Sabbath quiet. Before us, the craft of their trade rode at anchor in the still water. Nets were spread out to dry on either hand, while here and there a lobsterman was fussing over his gear. It was church time, and we had been joking about the fact that we were sitting in the open under the sun rather than in the church under the spell of the pastor's sermon. So there was some suggestion of religious solemnity about Will's voice as he began a vocalized revery:

"Yes, it's a good life. We generally work six or eight hours a day setting traps or moving 'em around. And then, o' course, you have to fix up your gear now and then. And when we get a good load we have to run it up to Portland in our boats—an' that makes a change.

"But there's one nice thing. Once in a while there's a stormy day when you can't go out. But the traps are out there with the bait in 'em. And while I'm loafing around here spinning yarns, I know that out there the lobsters are finding their way in. I ain't doin' nothin', but yet the traps are makin' a little money for me.

"I ain't sayin' that we haven't seen hard times. During the depression, while the children was growin' up, there was times when we had trouble scratchin' up enough to eat. But lately here, with better prices, we generally have three or four hundred dollars more than we need in the bank. That wouldn't seem like an awful lot to you fellows in New York, but this year we put new flooring in my house and most every year we make some improvement. And we don't have a thing to worry about. Nobody can discharge us, and if worse comes to worst, we can eat what we catch. Yes, it's a good life."

The next day we went out fishing with Alvah and Winfred Wallace, father and son. As we put out into the bay at four o'clock in the morning, I began to think of the contrast between the life of the Maine fishermen and that of the farmers of my boyhood. An average farm may be worth just about the sum represented by Alvah's fishing outfit. But the fisherman's boats and nets deteriorate rapidly. Every few years he must buy a new motor at a cost of $1,000 or $1,500. If he goes out deep-sea fishing, he may lose his entire investment in a single storm. Alvah, in fact, told me about one year when he put his traps out in deep water and actually lost everything in one big blow. He told of it as calmly as though it were the regular thing. It is all a part of the game.

We had a good day out there on Casco Bay. We were set to catch silver hake with a dragnet. This contraption is ten fathoms wide and five fathoms deep at the mouth—with floats at the top to keep it up and a chain at the mouth to keep it down. From the mouth it narrows rapidly and runs back about thirty fathoms like an enormous stocking.

In the still-dark morning, we began to chug slowly in wide circles from Flag Island to Mark Island and back again. Stars were beginning to pale, and the flashes from four or five lighthouses out to seaward grew gradually less vivid as they went on and off with their carefully spaced signals. The net was drawn about once every thirty minutes. In between we had time for talk—sometimes in the cozy cabin where we had hot coffee from a bottomless pot and sometimes out on the deck watching the changing colors as the sun rose.

Out of the talk of Alvy and Winny Wallace rose a picture of their life and of the entire separate sea-and-shore civilization they represented. Alvy was the father, stanch and strong at the age of sixty-five. Winny, the son, had been his father's partner through all sorts of weather and fortunes since his boyhood. Their last name was seen on half the headstones in the little neighborhood churchyard behind the village. These same people—and their ancestors—have fished these same waters from homes on these rocky shores for more than a century. Some few young men have gone off to sea. A few have disappeared in the great cities to the south. But through all the years—marked by such changes in the outside world—this Fisher Village has remained constant. Its people, about a hundred of them with hardly more than five or six family names among them, have always fished for a living. The faithful sea has supplied their wants. Even though it might cruelly deprive them of life or property, they have remained true to it. It has never occurred to them that there may be better ways of making a living or other—possibly better—places to live.

The two men, father and son, served as the crew of an outfit that ordinarily would have taken five men to operate. Their cooperation was so perfect that it was a pleasure to watch them haul in the long net and deposit the tons of slithering silver fish in the hold. It was a rather complicated process. A single haul might amount to a ton or more. The great stocking would be lifted on board section by section by means of block and tackle attached to the mast and connected with a winch that was powered by the vessel's gasoline engine. Ropes would creak and tackle squeal and strain as each new catch came over the gunwale.

By midmorning the wind had freshened to a gale, the mast swayed from side to side, and with the whole process made more difficult by the changing weather, we saw what to less calm and seasoned craftsmen would have been a minor tragedy. A strand of one of the ropes broke with a resounding snap. The great stocking of fish streamed out behind, and there we were with the wind blowing harder every minute. Without exchanging a word, the two men made a rough and rapid splice. Winny climbed the swaying mast to run the rope through the block—only to find that it would not go. Half an hour had already been lost. Then the young man had to climb down, get another rope, attach it to the other gear, and climb the wildly weaving mast a second time. Then, finally, after an hour's patient labor, the whole outfit was adjusted, the winch started to turn, and another load of splashing silver fish came slithering aboard.

What struck me was that during all this trying and dangerous work, much of it performed at the top of that crazily moving mast, neither one of these men uttered a cussword or even one syllable that expressed impatience or ill-temper. Seamen are famous for profanity, but not these fisherfolk. I have often noted the calmness of their manners, the slowness of their words, their whole patient and gentle approach to life. But here I observed them in a moment of crisis. Nothing snapped in them, nothing gave. Whatever had to be done was done quietly and quickly—without the slightest sign of surprise or impatience.

Ever since those hours I have been turning over the thought of these men in my mind. Obviously, we have here what the psychologists would call men who are well adjusted. From childhood they have felt sure of themselves and of their environment. The sea never goes back on them and, as Will Dunning said, nobody can discharge them. Each one owns and runs his own business. Each one lives in a house that he has built or inherited and that he can alter to suit his needs or tastes. These dwellings are not even aligned in coordinated and arbitrary rows along streets. They are dotted among the rocks according to the taste of the builders. These men and women are less suppressed, less tied into an externally imposed pattern, than any other group which I know. And their way of living is so old, so well and easily accepted, that there is no conflict between inner drives and outward pattern. Life is accepted just as are the tides and storms of the sustaining sea. And the total arrangement seems to produce results that our educators aim at with but indifferent results. ■

Cultural autonomy in Pennsylvania

■ Here are three items that happened to lodge in my consciousness last week. First, I read an account of how the farmers of Russia were socialized during the early 1930's. A lot of Communist party members from the towns were sent out into the country to pep up the harvest, see that all the grain was threshed and that the government got most of it. Many of these boys had never seen a farm before and didn't know which was the business end of a fork or a rake. A reaper or a mower was something entirely outside their philosophy. But they had been provided with revolvers, and knew perfectly well how to operate that sort of instrument.

How grain can be harvested with guns was demonstrated to the satisfaction of the party Commissars and much to the discomfort of the farmers. Such tillers of the soil as failed to step lively and do as they were told were quickly and efficiently taken care of. Some of them were shot and hundreds of others were loaded into freight trains and headed toward Siberia. So the grain was reaped, threshed, and loaded into cars to be sent off to the government storehouses—and the farmers were left with far too little to feed themselves and their families until the next harvest.

The second item is a bit snipped from an address delivered by Jerome Davis at the Eastern Sociological Society meeting at Columbia University. I came across it in Sunday's *Times*. Mr. Davis, according to the report, "declared that minority groups within the Soviet Union have cultural autonomy. It is part of the national planning to develop each group economically and to encourage the preservation of its customs."

On the same day I caught up on my reading in the Philadelphia papers, and there I came across a luscious item of news that has roused one comment after another in the press of the great state of Pennsylvania. It has to do with the Pennsylvania Dutch, a "cultural group" that has been contributing to the livelihood and liveliness of this country since the days of William Penn. For about 250 years these lusty folk have tilled their soil and gone to church, and for a good part of that time they have doggedly voted Republican. I don't believe they know what a "cultural group" is, and as far as I remember our Constitution says nothing about "cultural autonomy." But since I read what happened in Lancaster County, I have been wondering what would happen in that prosperous region if a bunch of Commissars were sent down from Washington or Harrisburg to facilitate the harvesting of grain with revolvers.

Among these so-called Dutch, the Amish are one of the most persistent and determined of sects. They are a sort of German Quaker. You know them instantly, for they "go plain." That is, they wear the kind of clothes that were in style when their sect was started. The garb is as sacred as the Ten Commandments. No razor ever touches a male visage, and no lipstick defiles that of a female's. No church is adorned with a useless steeple, and the church service is conducted with traditional simplicity. The rules of life are strict and are far better enforced than such regulations usually are. The faithful neither smoke tobacco nor indulge in alcoholic liquor—though this law does not prevent them from growing endless acres of tobacco that contribute to the downfall of the more easygoing gentiles. But don't get the idea that these folks are completely abstemious. Their cooking is something to write whole books about—and many books have been written about it. This is a subject to which I must return.

All of this will convey to you the notion that the Amish are a bit set in their ways. They know the road to heaven, and nothing can divert them from it. Among their rules is one forbidding the use of power-driven machinery. Their fathers used horses, and so horses have what is practically a religious sanction, like sacred cows in India. The whole cycle of fluster and bluster that led to the writing of this column began in Lancaster County with one young bearded farmer who figured out that he could get more done if he attached a tractor to his plow rather than a pair of animals. His plowing went famously, but he plowed himself right out of the church. As soon as the elders of the denomination, who are called bishops, could get around to him, he was expelled. That was more than he could stand. A bigger harvest, easier work, greater wealth were all very well, but not enough to lose heaven for. So the young man sold his tractor, did penance, and was returned to the bosom of the congregation.

But this was far from being the end of the tale. A certain Clyde A. Zehner, who, if one is to judge from his name, found his origin not far from these very pious Germans, was once serving as chairman of the Pennsylvania Agricultural Adjustment Administration. He was—that is, at that time—the nearest thing that America can supply by way of a Commissar of Agriculture. Mr. Zehner crashed through with a statement that if the Amish would substitute tractors for their old Dobbins, they would produce enough extra grain to save exactly 32,000 starving Europeans from death.

Now, behold how such things worked out in this country where nobody makes a special boast about the "autonomy of cultural groups." The bishops of the church respectfully replied to AAA that they would not, could not, attach the new-fangled tractors to their plows. About that little matter they were fixed, set, unchangeable. But they did want the greatest possible production and they were all in favor of food for the hungry. So they made a proposition to the government. If the officials really wanted more wheat, why not release from the prison camps some hundreds of their boys who were incarcerated as conscientious objectors. These lads were senselessly held far from home and their customary labors for three or four years. It was a fair proposition.

Don't get the idea that these Pennsylvania Dutch are isolationists. They are pacifists. They don't want war. One of their most numerous sects, the Dunkards, heard that the people of Poland were up against it, that their work cattle had been killed. So, instead of sending a letter to their congressman or adopting a resolution, they got together a carload of horses and sent one of their members to see to it that they were distributed to the farmers of Poland. I call that a sensible and constructive move. Well, the other day this Dunkard who made the delivery got back to his native heath, and his religion did not interfere with some straight talk. He reported that the Russian soldiers rob the Polish farmers and that the farmers often respond by bashing a soldier in the head and throwing his body into the river. So the peace-loving Dunkards are far from content with what is going on over there.

You may have guessed by now that I rather like these people. They go their ways and live their life, and there is no one to regulate them or level them off or herd them onto communal farms. And it is all so natural to us that no one like Jerome Davis feels called upon to rise at a meeting and boast that we have something called "cultural autonomy."   ∎

Heaven is not far from Hollywood

∎ I knew from the start that this would happen. California was bound to catch up with me. My Delaware garden is all right. The onions and kale and other things that persisted under the snow look fine and green. The strawberries are in hopeful bloom. Our long-term planning is represented by ten trenches of asparagus from which we expect nothing until 1947. But I must admit that—except for the flowers, which are gay beyond reason—spring is in this region mainly a season of promise.

And while I am still in the midst of humble beginnings, my old friend Louis Mertins, "Beeswax," for short, of Redlands, California, sends me a hymn of California fruitfulness that puts to shame the Forty-Niners' tales of gold. On a day when I had been spreading lime and manure on soil that had not yet been turned, I received from him an airmail letter that began: "In my Far Hills garden I have today (March 20) corn and beans well above the ground, strawberries red and ripening, and new potatoes as big as marbles. There is only one month in the year (February) when I cannot go out and pick fruit, ripe and tasty, from vine or tree—and this year even in February I plucked a huge cluster of Emperor grapes, luscious and sugary.

"Nor do I include citrus fruits in this boast. That not a day of the year comes that we cannot pick oranges, grapefruit, lemons, from the trees—that goes without saying. But I mean non-citrus fruits. In March the strawberries come on and last in profusion till well into July, lingering along fitfully through fall and winter. In April the loquats ripen. They are a Japanese fruit, and even before Pearl Harbor were little considered. But they make fine jelly, so we let them stand. In May the first robin peaches (as pink and lovely as a California maid skilled in the cosmetic arts) ripen, followed in June and July by half-a-dozen apricot trees, different varieties. Then the sugar plums, as big as your fist and as sweet as honey—and improved prunes and satsumas and more peaches. By July 15, the boysenberries are ripening and the black raspberries and the blackberries. Meantime, the strawberries are plugging along with shortcake and just plain strawberries and cream alternating on the table. August sees our first grapes (Thompson seedless) coming ripe—with a battle royal between the birds and ye old dirt farmer. Then come the muscats, the tokays, the concords, the malagas and the other sundry varieties—going on until January. And in August, Elberta peaches— like—like nothing you ever tasted.

"My home stands at the approach to Smiley Heights, six acres which lie on the flat above an arroyo that drops off sheer 30 feet. This arroyo is filled with trees and vines. Possums, skunks, jackrabbits, gray squirrels, cottontails and more birds than we really need in fruit and berry time, hold carnival there. And this arroyo that edges our land meets Omar's requirements. It 'just divides the desert from the sown.' Beyond is the limitless sandy waste just as it has stood since the Eo-cenery.

"My vegetable garden occupies a terrace on the bank of the arroyo. Most of the year we live on what comes out of it. I might explain that I am not too good a potato-digger. There are always volunteer vines which come up from vegetables which have been left in the fall. These I transplant. Twice this year Jack Frost nipped my potato tops, but they are coming great, and soon we'll have our own new crop. Last year I had several hills which produced seed from the flowers. Burbank once tried planting these rare seeds with interesting results. I have planted them and will let you know what I produce. It would seem, Bill, that these seeds take the potato back over the long road of artificial selection to the potato that the noble Red Man had to eat. We shall see.

"Our proudest crop is sweetcorn. I am often tempted by the blandishments of friends and the offers of free seeds to plant various new strains. Last year it was an Iowa hybrid. This year my daughter sent me some blue Mexican sweetcorn which I must give a whirl. But I always go back to golden bantam. I plant it on March 1 to ripen about May 10, and each succeeding two weeks thereafter we have corn coming ripe, sweet as sugar, until November 1.

"Now don't get me wrong, Bill. I wouldn't for the world make you feel bad. For you gardeners of the East I have both sympathy and respect—sympathy for your misfortune and respect for your courage and optimism. Some years ago my wife and I visited Robert Frost at Ripton, Vermont, where every summer between the last frost in July and the first frost in August he raised a garden during the interims of his work at Breadloaf School of English.

"We were there in August, on the day when they had their first corn. It is a hurried business, this raising a garden in Vermont. Out in California we plant in leisurely fashion in January, February, March, and reap our harvest at our ease in July, August, September, October. The plants are never in a hurry. They have all four seasons for their growth. In Vermont, if they don't hurry they're nipped before they're nibbled. 'Frost on the air,' said Robert that night as he lifted a knowing nose toward the north. And that was in August.

"That, I suppose, is why Frost writes poetry for the market and calls it farming. The frost that shows in his hair seems not yet to have nipped the product of his pen as it often has that of his garden. And if I could write poetry like Robert's, I'd be willing to forego the garden stuff."

My old friend Beeswax really is a kindly chap. He would not willingly hurt the humblest insect clinging to the Eastern seaboard. And there is something engaging about his enthusiasm for his bursting and bumptious land. Perhaps that is the heaven to which all good gardeners will go when they die. Just where Beeswax will go, I can't imagine. If they threaten to remove him outside bounds of his golden state, he will probably go on a sitdown strike.

But I shall wait for someone else to write a proper answer to him. I should prefer a reply from Vermont. It is a state of which I am ridiculously fond. Some frost-bitten gardener from under the shadow of Mount Mansfield ought to be able to give this Californian his comeuppance. ■

FATHERS AND SONS

The little red schoolhouse

■ It really was red and it certainly was little, but in my imagination it stands as one of the greatest educational institutions in the world. Along with my picture of it there always comes to mind a saying of Emerson's to the effect that every gain is accompanied by some commensurate loss. All my life I have been defending whatever sort of teaching was called modern or new or progressive or experimental at the time. But as I look back on the total life together in that one-room red-brick building, I feel sorry for the boys and girls who nowadays get so much less in their expensive and elaborate institutions.

Our tiny district school among the farms out there in Ohio had one great advantage. It was in the heart of a community of people who knew who they were and what they were and what they wanted. There was only one good-for-nothing fellow in the whole neighborhood—and he was a bachelor, so nobody had to worry much about him. There were no churches and no preachers. As far as I recall, nobody went to church. There were no drunkards and no criminals and, in particular, no juvenile delinquents. We young people had no experience with any judge or policemen or sheriff. The people knew one another. There were no outsiders, none of those terrible minority groups. The families all owned the farms they worked. All of them worked hard and behaved themselves and helped one another. Nearly all the inhabitants had come from New England. The names of our neighbors were Smith and Clark and Kittredge and Thorpe.

The fact that we were all about alike and that we all knew one another greatly lightened the teacher's task.

When I first put my hand into that of my big sister and walked the mile to our miniature temple of learning, our teacher was a girl named Georgia Thorpe. She was a neighbor's daughter who had spent a couple of years in a high school in some not distant village. She had no idea of what is called pedagogy. The hard words of

177

psychology would have alarmed and puzzled her. But she was well acquainted with every child in the district. She could picture what went on in his home. She loved them all and liked being their teacher. That was something.

Our equipment was primitive. In winter a big old potbellied stove consumed great quantities of wood and kept us unevenly warm. The biggest boys considered it a great honor to be allowed to come to school early and start the fire so that the place would be warm and cozy by the time the pretty teacher arrived to open the day. Two blackboards, a globe, an awe-inspiring dictionary and a water pail with a tin dipper completed the outfit, for which the school directors periodically voted expenditures. In the modern sense of the word, we had no playground, but outside our little building we had a whole gorgeous world. On one side, our school grounds bordered a forest that might just as well have belonged to us. No one ever objected to our playing and exploring within its boundaries. On the other side we could jump the fences into practically endless pasture lands. We needed no traffic cops to protect us from the cattle and horses that populated these fields.

I can see theoretic objections to having all twenty-five of our pupils in the same room and taught by the same teacher. Class periods were short and there were frequent interruptions. The urgencies of the very young might interfere with the intellectual interests of the older pupils. Everything was going on simultaneously. The class that was reciting would, naturally, distract the attention of the pupils trying to perform their tasks at their desks. There are obvious advantages in having every grade by itself with its suitable equipment and its teacher trained to meet its special needs.

But there is an argument to be put up for the old way, for having big and little learning their lessons together. We were a big family. The youngest would be tots of six. The oldest were strapping young men and women of eighteen or twenty. The big just naturally took for granted that it was a part of their business to help the little. In stormy weather they might carry them to school—at any rate help them over the danger spots. In the games and athletic sports they would instruct and encourage. And often enough the older pupils would turn teacher in order to show off their learning. The whole way of living was a natural and accustomed one. It encouraged affection and thoughtfulness. It promoted mutual understanding. And, on the whole, it made for pleasant and natural growth.

Another great advantage was that our tiny educational system was autonomous. There was no principal or superintendent over our beloved teacher. She was it. The school program was infinitely flexible. We could do just what we wanted to do—adapting our program to the season or to our whims. On a fine day in the fall when the pawpaws were ripe in the gully we would play for what seemed endless hours in that alluring wood. One of the lessons that we learned there was that the world is not such a bad place. There was, of course, no hydrogen bomb in those days.   ∎

The good old days are gone forever

∎ For weeks past I have been warned and lectured and threatened. All my fellow workers on the staff of the *New Leader* have been conscientiously preparing me for the glory that is to come. As the gray and gooey-looking cocoon suddenly astonishes the world by bursting forth as a dancing butterfly, so we are to take on the gaudy look of a slick paper magazine. And I must be slicked up along with everything else.

I don't even know the meanings of half the words they use in telling me how I am to behave. The general idea is that I am to be strictly limited—somewhat as I was in my boyhood when the words went around that grand company was to be expected and the family was to move into the parlor. Young people were told to do this or that—and not to do certain other things.

We inherited our original form from the old New York *Call.* That was a daily paper—so we started as a weekly with all the habits and freedoms of a full-size daily. That meant that practically every story could be a front-page story and we could have headlines galore.

The dullest piece of exposition from the Balkans or from the inside of some department down in Washington could be dressed up with a rowdy head and played as spot news.

I am told that in prehistoric cave-dwelling days—before I came to the paper—freedom and adventure ranged even more widely. Away back there, foreign correspondents used to be invented—always with high-class names. And, since their expense accounts were negligible, they could be spotted over the earth with carefree negligence. The stories were written at or near 7 East Fifteenth Street or at the printing plant down on Lafayette. But without tribute to Mackay Radio or Western Union, they were accredited to our versatile and agile reporters in Constantinople or Peking.

Even in my early years the impulses of daily journalism were still strong. Perhaps this was partly because the *New Leader* was constantly reinforced by energetic men from among the star reporters of New York's greatest dailies. In those days we printed on Thursdays. By ten or eleven o'clock on Thursday morning, these members of the Newspaper Guild would drop in at our printing plant to go to work. What piles of copy were turned out and rushed to the linotypers! What gigantic objurgations were flung at Hitler and Stalin! When a pepped-up writer hit upon an especially juicy phrase, he would intone it aloud.

Theoretic differences had to be settled on the spot—mostly by lung power. The inner nature of Leninism, Stalinism, Hitlerism, the ultimate destinies of capitalism, the possibilities of democratic defense—what tumultuous battles raged about these matters! And because these eager beavers sometimes held up the presses until the very last minute in order to scoop everyone and to be scooped by no one, the united staff sometimes turned against the patient printers. Sometimes there occurred battles of truly epic quality.

In the end, the miracle always happened. A paper was turned out. As I glance back at the old numbers in the files, they look crude to me. But as the first copies came from the press each week they invariably seemed to be supreme achievements. Then off we would go to celebrate in the nearest barroom. All theoretical differences had been smoothed out. Even the most recalcitrant printer was recognized as a human being. And what jolly and understanding topers we used to find leaning against the bars near the corner of Lafayette and Canal streets! I wonder if any loafers half as attractive are still to be found in that neighborhood.

Those days are, as the cartoonist has it, gone forever. For years past we have been mending our ways. As time has rolled on, we have become more and more conscientious, less like a newspaper, more like a magazine. Now the final step is to be taken. You will read these words on slick paper in what I hope will be a really beautiful weekly magazine.

But I hope the slickness will be confined to the paper and the print. In the past we have been honest and straightforward rather than smooth. We have never been deluded by Stalin or Hitler or any of the American fools who have trailed along with them. We believe in America. We believe in democracy, we believe in humanity. We hope in this new form to attract myriads of new readers. But our hearts are still the same. Our readers will find us fighting the same old forward-moving battle.　　　　　　　　　　　　　　　　■

The little gray schoolhouse

■ Every now and then as I stroll along the placid reaches of lower Fifth Avenue I am stopped by a very dapper and very New Yorky elderly gentleman. I can guess from his looks that he is a banker. Everything about his clothes and his bearing proclaims his profession. But this supermetropolitan person immediately begins to tell me what wonderful times he had when he was my pupil in a district school out in Ohio. My conscience always begins to bother me. That is why I am writing this column. My homily on the charms of the little red schoolhouse called forth such praise that doubts began to creep into my mind. Letters expressing agreement and applause came from famous educators, Harvard men, Princeton men, even University of Wisconsin men. Georgia Thorpe would blush if she could know what high approval has been heaped upon her wood-stove-heated educational institution.

So I feel impelled to do something to set the record straight. There were disadvantages about those simple-celled and autonomous schools. This I discovered later when I turned teacher. At the age of sixteen I was educationally ready for college but financially somewhat retarded. To achieve the necessary degree of solvency, I signed a contract to teach school for a nine-month period in Middleburgh Township. The little, unattractive temple of learning that now became for nine months the center of my activities did not doze beside a forest or near a brook as did the school of my childhood. On the contrary, it was perched on the edge of the railroad yards of the New York Central system. Appropriately enough, it was not painted a cheerful red but a dull and depressing gray. And the children who were sent thither to negotiate their first steps in formal learning represented two contrasting segments of population. A few came from families of the original Anglo-Saxon farmers of the region. The majority were the offspring of immigrants from three or four European countries.

My dapper banker who greets me so effusively near the Washington Arch has been through Harvard and is otherwise so far removed from that old school, and has so far transformed it in his creative memory, that I have not the heart to remind him of the realities. In that school we had forty-nine pupils and twenty-nine classes each day. It is easy to imagine how skimpy and inadequate was the teaching. But that was not the worst of it. There was a total lack of that social solidarity that I described in connection with the country school of my childhood. We had, it is true, a little flock of children who were easy to teach. But we had, too, a group of disaffected and violent older boys. I was sixteen; some of these young giants whom I was supposed to teach were about twenty, great hulking fellows who came to school just to make life miserable for the teacher.

I mentioned as one of the advantages of the little red schoolhouse the fact that its educational system was autonomous. The teacher had no one over her (or him). In my experience as a country teacher, I discovered that this independence has its disadvantages.

When rebellion showed its ugly head I was dependent upon my own resources.

The revolution broke out, as most revolutions do, in springtime. I had been out on the playground playing ball with some of my be-tween-age pupils and was about to call the school to order. Just then through a window I saw approaching, armed with various crude weapons, the entire contingent of disaffected young men. Darkly glowering, they approached, opened the door, and rushed in, evidently bent upon putting an end to education once for all.

Do not expect me to give an epic account of the battle that ensued. In this struggle I had two advantages. The danger was so sudden and near that I had no time for thought. And the woodbox, which proved to be the arsenal of war, was on my side. The poor little children hid under the desks or sought protection wherever they could find it. Sticks flew. Heads were cracked. The considerable vocabularies of my opponents were exploited to the full. Many words were used that have never been sanctified by any lexicographer. All that I know is that in the course of time the hassle was over. The enemies of education were on the outside and, with the younger children, I was on the inside. Among the latter, of course, was my future bank manager who now tells me whenever we meet what a successful pedagogue I used to be.

On the last day of school we had a wonderful party. Its climax was reached when I saw the county sheriff striding across the yard. He had come to secure information about my disaffected contingent —who had never returned to school after their defeat. I suppose they had regarded their education as completed. But the sheriff had the intention of adding a postgraduate course. He had, in fact, come to gather information about these energetic and enterprising chaps. They had all been arrested after breaking into some freight cars not far from the school. So one group of pupils from this one-room schoolhouse graduated into the state penitentiary. I thought this item should be set down in order to keep the record straight. ∎

The old man of Belvidere

■ I had never heard of the town of Belvidere. It lies in one of the dimples of the northern Illinois prairie on the edge of Wisconsin. We found it because we were tired of the Turnpike. Someone in our car said, "Let's get out of here and go somewhere where we can see people and towns and cattle." After an hour or two spent rolling past herds of Holsteins quietly and unsuspiciously chewing their cuds, we came to Belvidere.

It might just as well have been in any other moderately prosperous northern state. The chief artery of travel and trade was appropriately called Main Street. It was dignified and thrown into deep shade by a row of huge elms on one side and equally impressive ancient maples on the other.

The next day was Sunday. The sun was shining, the birds were singing—and never was the wide world more inviting. I had everything to make life perfect except a Sunday paper. So I had a motive for strolling down the middle of a town as fresh, as capable of surprises, as if it had just been created.

I saw first that the magnificent trees we had noted the evening before had sent out such mighty roots that the ancient sidewalks were heaved and humped all out of shape. Then it began to dawn upon me that the places I was passing were of an old and upper-class sort. The houses had the size and solemnity of Victorian architecture. They had great porches, gables, and porte-cocheres. The trees had grown to such proportions that place after place was deep in aristocratic shade. Evidently at some time in the past there had been prosperity and freedom to indulge upper-class tastes for architecture and decoration. Now the town was slowly running down.

In the meantime, my quest for a Sunday paper gave little promise of success. The stores were all tightly closed. There was not even a wandering citizen to whom I could put a question—at least not until I had passed most of the town's shiny automobile establishments and a couple of locked-up drugstores. Naturally, I was growing hungry and I thought that if I could find a restaurant my whole problem might be solved. With a cup of coffee I could stand my disappointment.

About the time this fruitful thought occurred to me, I came upon a thin and hunched old man sitting on a much carved and whittled wooden bench before a tightly closed grocery store. When I asked him where I could find a restaurant, he responded: "Well, friend, there used to be a purty good eaten' place down the street a piece, but nothin' lasts long in this town. It folded up quite some time ago." I was tired from my long walk, and because the old boy seemed eager for companionship, I accepted an unspoken invitation to share the ancient bench.

The old man's name was Jake Staubell, and he was not at all averse to revelatory conversation. He, too, was waiting for a chance to buy a Sunday paper. The *News*, he explained, would be delivered at this very spot. "These cussed youngsters we have now," my friend mumbled, "they can't be depended on to do anything. The papers was supposed to be here sharp at seven in the morning—and here it is eight-thirty. No wonder the world is going to pot."

This was enough to put old Jake's memory into action. He proudly proclaimed that he was eighty-six years old. "And by God," he went on, "I have earned my living since I was eleven. Look at this town!" he shouted, and looked up and down the empty street as if to challenge anyone to take issue with him. "Eighty-six years I have lived here. We used to have business. We had factories. We made sewing machines. We turned out furniture. We made cloth. The working people worked. They didn't belong to any of these fool unions. They stayed at home and spent their money in their own home town. The best vaudeville players came to our theater, and people laughed at real jokes. The employers tended to business. They knew how to make whatever they were supposed to make, and the workers had respect for them.

"And then what happened? The old men who owned and managed their businesses gradually died off. The young sprouts who took their places thought this town wasn't good enough for them. The auto was invented. Horses didn't go fast enough. They began to run all over the state—to Milwaukee—even Chicago. Their hindquarters was socked down in the cushions of their cars instead of at their desks.

"Nobody looked after his own business. The sewing-machine factories failed. The furniture factories discharged their people. So the workingmen had to find jobs in other towns—and of course they had to have cars to travel back and forth. And soon their wives got into the habit of buying their stuff in bigger places where there was bigger stores. That's why things is shut up here. First thing you know, we didn't have anything left but a couple of churches—and they don't furnish much income."

A mighty thump announced the arrival of the news and the end of our enlightened converse.   ■

The village church

■ In these days no one is inclined to give anything like due credit to the little Protestant churches that were scattered over the country during the nineteenth century. I am not thinking of the great official establishments with their seats in the few large cities. The Methodist Church had conferences, the Episcopalians had dioceses. But a boy in a country town saw little and heard little of these. What he did hear about was the little church on the public square and the saintly preacher living in his humble "parsonage." This church, guided and nurtured by this gentle shepherd, was not just an ecclesiastic institution that preached to people on Sunday and subsisted on the "offerings" they contributed. It entered deeply into the daily life and thoughts of most of the people—except, of course, the Catholics.

It is difficult to know whether to start with the people or the pastor. The whole institution was so deeply democratic that it is hard to decide which comes first. I lived in my lovely town of four hundred neighbors from 1886 onward. Fifty years before that, the circuit riders had been making their circuits, baptizing, burying the dead, and preaching to the living. There were no salaries and hardly any churches. No one expected organization, honors, or ease. It was a tough life with everything to give and little to get. But that's the way the new country was built—and it proved to be a first-class method.

The preachers had never attended any famous theological seminaries, but for their work they had just about the best sort of training you can imagine. They went straight back to John Wesley—and through him to Martin Luther and the Holy Bible. Their doctrines might sound a bit old-fashioned and overorthodox now, but those men believed in them completely and lived up to them with a devotion that was convincing. I knew some of these men intimately—so intimately that I would have discovered any traces of dross in their make-up. No matter how little they received or how disappointing life might be, their saintly calm was never disturbed.

Among all of those whom I knew, there was only one who furnished such a variation as might have furnished forth a story by Mark Twain or James Thurber. There came to our hamlet a man named Eastman. He differed from his fellows in several ways. In the first place, he was not content with the black and rather shiny garments that served as uniforms for his profession. His rather plump middle was covered by an emphatically gay waistcoat. And he was not content with the modest accretions to the church that were brought about by the regular increases in the population. No, by cracky! He wanted action. Whether we liked it or not, we should have revival services and crowds. And we did have them, but the treatment was not very successful.

All preachers, in those days, had horses. Without such an animal as assistant, you were stuck. And this man Eastman had an extra fine and shiny one. One bright sunny day my brother and I were on a hike far out among the farms—and suddenly we heard behind us a great swish and clatter. From the roadside where we sought safety we quickly viewed in a cloud of dust the pious preacher in jockey's uniform and on a racing sulky going down the road with his son on horseback beside him. The terrible truth flashed over us: The holy disciple was a racing man doubling as pastor. As soon as the news became common property, the oh's and ah's blew the fellow right out of the pulpit. Think of it! The wickedness of it! To drive a race horse! A few of the sporting men who frequented the mysterious and shadowy saloons endeavored to defend him, but failed to get much of a hearing.

But this was the one exception. All the other pastors I knew were really saintly men. Even if now and then one came along who could not preach very persuasively, the old ladies would say, "He lives such a good life, no one would complain." But even if these men were not distinguished by learning, if they did not pretend to turn men to virtue and church membership by their eloquence, their lives were a constant and effective sermon. Especially was this true in relation to the young people of the village. It could be taken for granted that "the preacher" knew every growing boy and girl in or near the village. He followed with special interest each young hopeful who showed any promise of scholastic talent. In those Midwest states we had a little college in nearly every county, and it was part of the duty of the pastor to see to it it was filled with ambitious and promising youngsters. As soon as a youth showed the least sign of brains, the preacher would get busy discovering to what college the boy would prefer to go and how the necessary funds could be raised. Many a man who played a part in the development of that great agricultural section owes his education to the interest of a devoted five-hundred-dollar parson.

The influence of the country church and its educational value depended far more upon its democratic activities than upon its preaching or its doctrinal teaching. All the members took part in something. The young people who had any intelligence or energy took part in many sorts of organization. Some joined the choir and helped to select and rehearse the music. Others formed a young people's society and set programs for its meetings. Those who were interested in study or made more pretentions to learning would become teachers of Sunday-school classes and arrange for the study of the Bible. It is characteristic of the time and place that all these things were arranged and carried through by the members of the church, young and old, and not by the clergy. The growing youth had more experience in organization—in life in general—in connection with the church and Sunday school than in any official educational institution. ∎

Father wins the race

■ Father, who came to this country in 1852, never tried to conceal his puzzlement over the fact that this "free" country tolerated Negro slavery. He always tried to make it clear to his younger children that during the abolition struggle his attitude had been strictly American and 100 per cent for liberty. When President Lincoln issued his first call for volunteers, Father, who had been born in 1816 and was, therefore, forty-five years of age, seriously considered signing up. But his oldest boys, my half-brothers, were at that time eighteen and sixteen. So father took the practical step of calling them into conference.

The short address he delivered on that historic occasion has doubtless been given the benefit of some literary polish with the passage of time. According to the account that was passed on to my brother and me, Father addressed his offspring in words something like these: "My sons, you know well that we fled from Germany because of the failure of the so-called German revolution. The Prussian government robbed us of the liberties we thought were guaranteed by our constitution. We came to this country, not to become citizens of a slave state, but to enjoy freedom. In order actually to create the free conditions which we expected to find, either one or more of us must now enlist and do our part upon the field of battle. I am a bit old to take to the field, but if you find soldiering too distasteful, I will go." This offer, of course, was promptly turned down. Both of the boys entered the army and served through the four long years.

But just at the moment my interest lies in another aspect of the antislavery conflict. I have it in mind to tell the little tale of how Father, though remaining at home, did accidentally and almost inadvertently play a tiny part in the emancipation movement. Cleveland, Ohio, was some ten or fifteen miles from our home, and it happened to be an important station on the Underground Railroad. Once a fleeing black man got aboard a boat for Canada, he was forever free from bondage. One morning just before the beginning of the war, Father was cheerfully rumbling along the rough and rutty road on the way to the great city. In his wagon box he carried a heavy load of the farm produce on which he depended for his livelihood, and before the rude equipage paced the finest pair of horses Father ever owned. For a pair of workhorses these two bore the special distinction of having their names passed on from generation to generation. Father always referred to them as Bill and Gen—as the hero-animals are referred to in fairy tales. I have always had a suspicion that it was the part played in the following events by these fabled creatures that gave this affair its high place in Father's saga. Well, the sun was shining, and Father, according to his wont, was humming a German roundelay. Despite the dark spot caused by slavery, life was moving along in a very satisfactory way.

But then, like a sudden cloud, the dark spot moved before Father's eyes on that sunny highway in antislavery Ohio. For there, scurrying along, breathless and obviously alarmed, was a Negro family consisting of father, mother, and several children. Father recalled that Chagrin Falls, a village lying beyond his house, was also a station of the Underground. It took but a moment to reconstruct the dramatic situation. Escape depended upon instant action. A quick glance showed that the officers of the law were in hot pursuit of the poor fugitives.

Father motioned the fleeing family into his wagon. A word was enough for Bill and Gen. The race was on. On general principles one would guess that a pair of farm horses attached to a heavy wagon would have little chance of a victory over a buggy horse pulling a light vehicle made for rapid travel. But one making a bet on this basis would have been leaving out of account the qualities of Bill and Gen. Obviously, they were farm horses who had long had ambition to exhibit their speed. This was their chance. At last they had an opportunity. They could go the limit. And my father, too, was a jockey at heart. He, also, had an accidental justification for letting himself out.

The pursuers were not far behind. Who they were we were never told. One of them may have been a Southern officer of the law. Over the ruts and stones jounced the clumsy wagon. Father held the horses in just enough to maintain his control and not to cut down their speed. Every now and then the pursuers would come close enough to express themselves in heated exclamations. Then Father would draw away and leave them once more well in the rear. Through the streets of Cleveland this exhibition naturally attracted astonishment and attention. In those days there were, fortunately, no lights to bring traffic to a stop. All that the startled police could do was to try to save the pedestrians from destruction. Around the corners and up and down hills rushed both vehicles. At last, and still in advance of their pursuers, the steaming farm horses slammed round the turn onto the dock of the Canadian Steamboat Line. And the boat, as good fortune would have it, was tied up and ready to receive passengers. By the time the slave catchers were ready to retrieve their property, the frightened slaves were theoretically on Canadian territory and out of the reach of any slaveholding law.

Father never learned English very well, and so was never able to report just what the Southerners said to him or about him when they faced the proof of their failure. There was some loud talk about a fight, but when the pair of them took a good look at Father and at the group of Northerners attracted by the fracas, they changed their minds about the matter. In the form in which it reached us, this tale gave chief honor and credit to those two horses Bill and Gen! What a pair! What heroes! ∎

The artists are right

∎ I began the year among the artists, and they turned out to be a swell lot of people to start off with. During the hazy, happy hours while one year melded into another, no one mentioned Russia or war or the Communists. We talked, instead, about pictures. One man had a cargo of them loaded in a station wagon; he was on his way to give a show in Miami. Another had spent the day arranging his canvases for an exhibition on Fifty-seventh Street. Things were going well. With only slight assistance from the circulating punch, the talk fairly sparkled.

The next day, January 2nd, I spent the afternoon among the

van Goghs at the Metropolitan Museum. Just to be in the same room with such paintings, just to be among people who were called together by such works of art, made the world seem fine and good and—yes—even moderately secure. No matter what happens, even if war comes and atom bombs destroy much of the world we love, the things that van Gogh tried to express, the impulses that have motivated all those who have piously tried to follow him, the dreams of all those who have worked in the various art forms—these things are too deep and strong to be destroyed by any calamity that may befall us. The devotees of beauty and justice may seem weak, but their activities arise from a source so deep that in the end they cannot be destroyed.

As I strolled about the wing of the Metropolitan that contains the van Gogh exhibit, I happened to meet one of my old students, and he reminded me of something I had forgotten. In 1915 Vincent van Gogh, the nephew of the great artist, visited this country, and my student and I had been among those who shared the privilege of meeting him. This nephew was—no doubt still is—a Socialist. By this I do not mean to say that he was a doctrinaire politician. He was, on the contrary, a man deeply sensitive to human suffering and in earnest about promoting human welfare. And away back there years ago he used to speak of his uncle as more interested in people than in pictures or painting.

After my hours with the dark paintings from the early Dutch period and the blazing bright ones from the South of France, I came away fairly shattered. I had had no idea that there could be such a massive expression of the human soul. I had had such a blazing revelation that I could find no words for it, could not connect it with any other fields of experience. In any case, it is stupid and dangerous to attempt to interpret an artist in terms of the inartistic world.

But I could not get out of my mind the things that "young" Vincent had told us. And I recalled that van Gogh himself had struggled hard to be a preacher of the simple and human Christ, but had been rejected by the church because he could not learn Latin or Greek. I thought of his devastating experience among the miners and then I recalled his painting of the peasants' hands, those terrible gnarled, deformed, work-worn hands. Their picturization cries out more loudly for change than all the books, speeches, pamphlets, platforms, and proclamations of all the politicians and theorists. As long as those hands call out to us, no one can be at peace.

If the dark depictions of the murky North are in a sense socio-logical preachments, then the bright visions of the sunny South are a deeper revelation of something vastly more important. They are a powerful attempt to give voice to a concept of biological relativity. The stars and suns that shone for van Gogh were brighter than those that shine for astronomers with an eye to candlepower. They shone for more sensitive eyes. For this palpitant person from the dark North, sunflowers and other golden blossoms fairly flamed from the soil, revealing the inner vitality of the earth. Every plant, every tree was an emanation from the center in which we all originate. To this man's deep-seeing gaze nothing is dead. We are all sparks from the same source of life.

To a man who feels toward the world as van Gogh felt, all violence, all oppression, all enforced uniformity, all crippling poverty are malign insults. The very nature of the world demands freedom for individual development. In the end, human creatures, being parts of such a world, must resist tyranny. If tyrants now and then win a victory, their conquest can be but for a time. According to the artist's conviction, life will conquer death. All oppressors, all who attempt to impose a dull uniformity by force, will, in the end, be defeated. ∎

Who—or what—done it?

■ The first President I ever saw was James A. Garfield. He lived not far from us out among the fields of northern Ohio. I recall that on a frosty autumn morning I was with my father at the fence that ran across the front of our farm. A neighbor had stopped to chat, and they were discussing something that was not of much interest to me.

My attention was attracted, however, when I heard the neighbor remark, "There goes Garfield." I looked up and saw two men approaching in an ordinary "top-buggy." One of them was obviously the bearded dignitary whose appearance had been made familiar during the campaign just ended. He lingered long enough to show the proper respect for two voters by the roadside, but the picture of him has remained a permanent part of my gallery.

Since then I have seen fourteen presidents come and go. There have been eighteen political campaigns of which I have some recollections. My earliest memories are, to be sure, somewhat on the primitive side. Our section of the country was Republican and my father was Democratic. Instead of preelection polls, we citizens on the make indulged in preelection fights. They were equally indicative of the ultimate outcome and they were vastly more fun—especially for the Democrats. For though in our school we were always a minority, we always won. It may have been because the Irish were on our side. The Irish are fine fellows—especially when they are on your side. In those days a physical struggle seemed a much fairer way of establishing control than any mere counting of noses. It allowed some play for courage and strategy.

So far as I was aware, there was at that time no talk about educating for citizenship, but politics was more in the air than it is now. There was continuous hot discussion both at home and in school. No child with normal curiosity could remain indifferent. Very early we took to scanning the newspapers in order to cull arguments that could be used as weapons against fellow pupils or teachers in the opposite camp. The whole thing was a lively and contentious business.

The papers that I read in those days came from Cleveland. The *Plain Dealer* represented the Democrats, and the *Leader*, now forgotten in the graveyard of forgotten journals, furnished ammunition for the Republicans. One thing about these journalistic gladiators fascinated me from the start: Their language was free and unrestrained. The cartoonists were permitted to use every repulsive symbol in the animal kingdom, including the skunk, the snake, and the rat. In fact, often enough I had the feeling that these four-legged or crawling creatures had reason enough to complain about the literary associations that were set up and forced upon them. Up to the moment when the votes were cast, the candidate of the opposite party might be painted in terms so disgusting and repellent that it seemed practically impossible for an honorable and upstanding American citizen to vote for him.

On the Wednesday morning after election, however, a strange and sweet calm settled over the land, and especially over the editorial pages of the warring journals. The people, in whom all wisdom is said to reside, had spoken. Those on the winning side had always had faith in their patriotism and good judgment. Those who had lost might hint that the innocent voters had been deceived and that by the end of four years they might reverse their decision. But in the main, defeat was taken in good part. The victorious candidates had, after all, some hitherto undiscovered virtues. On second thought it seemed to the editor that the country would, perhaps, not go completely to the dogs under his leadership. It was the duty of all of us to rally round and make the new administration a typical American success and a credit to our country.

I recognize the value of these proofs of basic unity. It is well that no defeated candidate has had to flee to Mexico or Canada. And there is great virtue in the fact that Democrats and Republicans do not snipe at each other between elections. It would interfere with industrial production. But it seemed to me in my early days—and it still does—that men who wield influence as writers should be able to recall on the Monday before election that they will be alive and writing on the morning after election.   ■

Face to face with the ceiling

■ A couple of days after Christmas we were headed for a party. On the way we stopped in for a call on my physician. There was to be nothing professional about this visit. After a drink or two, we expected the jovial doctor to join in the evening's pursuit of pleasure.

But when the physician got one glimpse of me he put one or two quick questions, and then came the verdict: "No party for you—you go to bed for a month." From this sort of verdict there is no appeal. To bed I went, and for a month I have been contemplating the ceiling.

From many points of view the experience has been a salutary one. The world—including the *New Leader*—has got on beautifully without me. And I, having my field of vision limited to a ceiling utterly devoid of interest, without even a crack or a spot to inspire the imagination, have been forced to think of myself and of all the world. As long as you can keep yourself pepped up over things that seem important, you can postpone to a more convenient season the examination of all your pushing and doing and making. But when you lie there horizontally, under orders not to move, not to sit up, not to plant your foot upon the floor, there is no way to fend off thought.

When all your neat psychological devices have their gears stripped by enforced inaction, your usual process is reversed. While you are busy with work or play you manage to keep yourself convinced that the world's troubles are all due to someone else. In the international realm it used to be Germany that originated the evil. Nowadays it is Russia. Within the domestic scene it is the Sixty Families, the economic royalists, or some other crowd that messes things up. It is never one's self, one's own crowd, that runs the train off the track. But when you lie there looking straight up, the first fellow you take apart is yourself.

You start in by thinking about your life, whether it has been of any use, whether you could have done better by following a different profession. From yourself you pass on to your country. You like it, of course. But what is wrong with the people? Why haven't they done better with their government, their schools, their industries? Then you start a mental survey: our books, movies, radio, churches, sports. Why is it that so much of our life is cheap and foolish? To a fellow prone on his back the quick and easy answers fail to satisfy. We could make life a lot more wonderful for a lot more people if we could just get together on a few general ideas.

At long last, working from within out, you come to the wide, wide world. You don't picture it in headline style. You lie there and make a picture of all the people everywhere. You see the folks in Africa, in Asia, in South America, in Europe, on all the islands. As in an endless movie they troop before you, dressed in their different clothes, living in their various sorts of houses, doing their work in their endless variety of ways—and most of them having a pretty poor time of it.

Then you begin to figure out why so many of them—after all these centuries of religion and science and education—should be suffering from hunger and disease and ignorance. Then you see that what we call progress has been spotty. What we have that is good is spread in pretty thick gobs for special crowds in special countries. Despite all the preaching and teaching, those who have the good things have given little thought to the have-nots. What we lack is not wealth or knowledge or skill. It is the will to help other people.

And that brings us spang against the thought of war. For war is the chief obstacle to human improvement. It consumes both our wealth and our energy. If it could be abolished, the good things like health and education could be rapidly diffused. And here we are in this mid-twentieth century world—driving full tilt into the most horrible war of all.

This line of thought forced me to undertake a relentless review of the policies of the *New Leader*. For years we have been busy telling the world the truth about Communist Russia. We have told more of it and have told it faster and sooner than any other paper in the world. We have been the Paul Reveres of this age. Our plea has been that the threat of war is decreased by open-eyed facing of the facts. Because for years we have been giving America evidence of Stalin's and Khrushchev's plans, we have been called warmongers. Now the news peddled everywhere proves that we were right five years ago, ten years ago.

But as I lay there gazing at the ceiling and reviewing recent history, I got little satisfaction out of all our scoops in the field of Russian relations. We have done a lot to warn America about what lies ahead. But we have done mighty little to head off what lies ahead. We have told a lot about Russia and China, but we have told it to the wrong people. We should have told it to the Russians and the Chinese. They are the most deceived and abused people on earth.

I refuse to believe that the iron curtain is impenetrable. If we

Americans were to devote no more than a slight fraction of our money and our brains to the task, we could pierce it with a barrage of facts. The *New Leader* has no way of reaching these people, but the Voice of America can do it. That sort of action is the only sort of positive policy looking toward the prevention of World War III. ∎

The undeserted village

∎ Isabel Bryan started it all. Some weeks ago I wrote a row of rapturous paragraphs about how wonderful life used to be in my old Ohio village. At that time it didn't happen to occur to me that I am living in a village now just as truly as ever I did. And I have worked and played in this present village of mine, which we call Greenwich Village, longer than I have ever remained anywhere else in my life. For years it has been my legal and voting residence—not to mention short snatches of life in it going back as far as 1910.

When I maundered on for a page or two about that Ohio town, I was pointing with justifiable pride to the fact that out there and in those days Negroes and whites lived along together and didn't think much about the difference in color. Well, Greenwich Village deserves praise for the very same virtue. Every now and then I eat in some restaurant—perhaps on West Tenth Street or West Eighth, and there I see men and women of varying hues eating together in perfect peace and contentment. The nice thing about this circumstance is that nobody pays the least attention to it. The Negroes are not big-heartedly tolerated. They are there just the same as anyone else. They belong there because they like the food and have money enough to pay for it. So—speaking of villages—I now pay tribute to this one that lies west of Fifth Avenue and south of Fourteenth Street.

Isabel Bryan jarred me into making this tardy motion in the direction of justice by publishing *The Greenwich Village Guide.* For the expenditure of a small sum you may escape untold trouble.

Everyone has heard about the chap who, having had a bit too much to drink, hunted helplessly for an address on Gay Street and when, finally, he came to the place where Fourth Street runs into Fourteenth, he began to foam lightly at the lips. From there, of course, his troubles were ended by his being carried off to Bellevue. Since the Bryan guide includes a beautiful map, it is precisely designed to save you from this sad fate and to lessen the population of our largest hospital.

This Bryan lady knows her neighbors. If you don't believe it, send for a copy of her weekly, the *Villager*. There you will learn that Mr. and Mrs. So-and-So celebrated their fifteenth or their fiftieth wedding anniversary and that Mrs. Flibbertigibbet entertained last Tuesday with cards and tea. And don't think for a moment that we dislike this sort of reporting. That is the way we are. When I stroll down West Twelfth Street on the way to my breakfast, I am sure to exchange greetings with old friends. Charlie and Phil and John and Anita live in my block and on my side of the street. On the other side, along with the New School of Social Research with Uncle Dan living at the top of it, are Fred and Vincent and a lot of others. And if you who read this happen to live in Kansas or Vermont, forget about the notion that these people are different from you and your neighbors. They are not one bit different—just as hearty, just as decent, just as friendly. The butchers and bakers and grocers are just businessmen trying to make a living. They know us and our families. We know them and their families. It really is a village. Often enough on my way to my office I see the rubberneck bus making its rounds and can hear the driver broadcasting about the house that Mark Twain lived in. I feel like shouting to all the good out-of-town people in the bus, "You have come a long way to see exactly what you could have seen at home."

I should explain that nowadays I live on the edge of the Village, not far from the *New Leader* offices. My colleagues are much too vigilant to let me get away with anything like an imitation of William Dean Howells' wisecrack about the coast of Bohemia, but that is about the size of it. Formerly, I was at home in the very center of the warm and beating heart of things, down on Christopher Street. So, under the inspiration of the *Guide*, last night I went on a tour of exploration into things long past. Mrs. Bryan's excellent map was

quite unnecessary. That is a funny thing. The streets of this crazy
wonderland go every which way, and I would find it impossible to
tell anyone how to find any house or street or corner or place. But
myself, all I have to do is to set my feet in motion and they carry
me just where I want to go.

First I visited the courtyard of my old home. You go in through
a gate in a low archway. Instantly you are in another world, an older,
more charming, more carefree world. Narrow paths, deep-shaded under boxwoods, conduct you to a pool with water splashing forever in
and out. All around are quaint old houses, and to the west are the
wide windows of my old apartment. Many a night there near to the
very center of Manhattan I went to sleep to the music of that
splashing pool, hardly knowing whether I was deep in the greatest of
cities or far out in the country beside some sequestered brook.

Upon my return from this excursion into the past I eased the
shock to my sensibilities by hunting out *The Greenwich Village
Poetry Anthology*, a fine little collection compiled some years ago by
that charmingly shy and elusive fellow Martin Bernfeld. The introduction, by John Rose Gildea, opens with these words: "The poetry
of Greenwich Village is the poetry of revolt, and Village poets who
remove from the Village often become static—as did Le Gallienne,
Seeger and Kilmer."

It is an engaging theory, but one hardly borne out by the text
that follows. There comes e. e. cummings's sonnet beginning, "Little
Joe Gould has lost his teeth." And the bird-eyed and alertly peering
Joe Gould is himself represented by a masterpiece on the barricades
that happen to be "the prissy sidewalk hedges in front of the
Brevoort" behind which "the comrades die of overeating." Floyd
Dell writes of romance at 11 Christopher Street as if love and
laughter had been his private discovery and he is quite sure that all
other pairs who follow him and his girl in finer houses along that
thoroughfare will be such dull bourgeois that the delights of love
will be practically thrown away on them.

Poe and Whitman must have written better things in our Village,
but in last night's mood these rhymed, or at least metered, things
gave me real pleasure. My perusal of them, however, increased my
doubts as to whether the Village stands for revolt. I recalled the art
fair that had been held around Washington Square only a couple of

weeks before. In the galleries along Fifty-seventh Street modernism may puzzle the country visitor with strange forms. On Washington Square he would feel at home. Among the artists who exhibit there every cow, ship, tree, or sunset is indubitably just what it sets out to be. It may be good or bad, but art of revolt and change it is not.

I may be wrong, but last evening's wanderings left me with the impression that the Village in general is less restless than it used to be. My meditations on the bench by the pool below my old apartment led me to the notion of dining at Lee Chumley's. What a place that used to be! What smoking, what drinking, what singing, what arguments far into the night! What crowds of people coming from parties or going to parties! But now, as I soon found, only the name is left. It is a quiet and respectable place for the consumption of inexpensive food—and patronized chiefly by young married couples. All this makes for the preservation of the race but hardly for revolt.

■

I join the aristocracy

■ In this country we have only one genuinely aristocratic class. It is made up of invalids. I gained my place in it inadvertently, in fact, unwillingly. As long as possible I struggled against recognition of the fact that something was wrong with my insides. But once my resistance was broken down, my eyes were opened to an amazing fact. The moment you acknowledge that you are no longer an ordinary human being but an invalid, you achieve superior status. It was a discovery worth some little inconvenience.

From the moment of acknowledged invalidity I moved into a strange new world. My health and comfort became the central point in the thinking of the entire household. My slightest wish was instantly attended to. I must not rise, not move, not even think. I was stethoscoped and X-rayed. My temperature became a matter of grave importance. There were a few disadvantages. The thermometer seemed to be left under my tongue for unconscionable periods. I had lost my taste for tobacco—so there was no point in smoking, but attractive young ladies kept running into my room bearing offerings on trays. And, like all the chaps who have had their various dreams of heaven, I just settled down and took life as it came.

That was a couple of days ago. Since then I have spent many quiet hours in bed with magazines and newspapers. And plenty of hours I have spent just lying there. My thoughts, I confess, have for the most part just wandered aimlessly. But aimless thoughts are not necessarily futile. They may wander and finally find a mark. So it happened with me. I naturally got to thinking about this cult of invalidism. Among primitive tribes a fellow smitten by disease is in disgrace. He is ashamed of himself and looked down upon by his fellows. It is a social pattern easy to understand. Most sick persons are disgusting. There is reason enough for keeping them out of sight. Why, among us, have manners gone the other way? Why does a fellow who counted for nothing practically all of his life become the center of attention the moment he gets some fool disease?

My case is, of course, not an especially striking one. You can easily imagine a better one. We have great and elaborately equipped hospitals here in New York that cater partly or exclusively to charity patients. Picture to yourself a poor chap living in any one of our numerous slum sections. He was never trained for a good job. He has never had a regular income. No one ever took the trouble to teach him how to take care of himself. He has been and is just one of those countless little fellows who work when they can and get along as well as they can. Only two things can center the attention of society upon this unimportant chap and bring its vast and expensive machinery to play upon him. If he commits a misdemeanor the police and the courts take the little fellow up in a big way. The other possibility is an accident that brings the long-neglected little fellow to a hospital.

Picture the scene as O. Henry might have sketched it. This chap who has never been anything, never had anything, for whom nobody has ever done anything, has the right of way as the siren raucously cleaves the traffic. Within the hospital, interns and nurses quickly install him in such a spotless bed as he has never before beheld.

From here on, all the resources of our city's hospital services are at his disposal. The most elaborate and expensive mechanisms are at hand with which to probe and picture every corner of his anatomy. Any sort of operation, any special treatment, any approved medication is at hand to fit his need. The cost does not matter. As a sick man our hero has a right to all that modern medicine and surgery can do for him. An hour or two ago, before the little man had his accident, he was nothing. Now, through misfortune, he has become a person of importance.

My room faces south. The earliest morning sunbeams would regularly spatter the west wall of it with gold. And all through the day, as the golden splotches moved along the north wall toward the east, I would lie there and think of human beings and what they have done in the twenty-five thousand years or so during which they have been making what we call history. I thought especially of men and women who have tried to make things better and often enough have made them worse.

I thought, too, about nations. There are the Russians with their all-inclusive plan to make everyone happy in spite of himself. There are the British with their gradual and reasonable Socialism. And here are we Americans. In Parliament the other day we were set down as a crassly capitalist and backward lot. Impatient young Labourites feared that the British might be corrupted by association with us. Perhaps these men are not to be blamed. They may have been deceived by the Pleistocene pronouncements of some of our Republican statesmen.

But if such good friends as British Labourites are deceived, there must be something puzzling about us. We are big and successful and rambunctious and, except for our industry, pretty much unorganized. So contrary are our various trends that a man may go far in our public life without understanding very much of what he observes. The flustered Labourites in Parliament may take for granted that Republican (or southern Democratic) congressmen who make such backward-looking speeches will be able to turn our public in the direction of their troglodyte thoughts.

The world that all good Utopians have in mind consists of many things. Everybody is to have enough to eat and to wear, good housing, the best of education, plenty of recreation, the finest of health

care, and so on. And, of course, liberty. I almost forgot that. The
Bolsheviks wanted to get all these things at one crack by introducing
their sort of Communism, but all that they have got in thirty years
is increasing misery for an increasing number of people. The British
are going after these same things under more difficult circumstances
in their careful way—with their minds set on liberty at every step of
the way. For they have an old-fashioned idea, which Americans
fully share, that without liberty those other things are hardly worth
having.

In comparison with either the Russians or the British, we Americans seem to be a strange people. Our system can be more or less
truthfully described as capitalistic, laissez faire, free enterprise. But
all these words came into use long before any such mixture of planning and go-as-you-please had come into existence. There is no word
for this system except the one so recently and so happily applied to
it: *mixed*. Mixed it is—and with the proportions of the ingredients
constantly changing. The British constantly and purposely pursue a
policy of gradualism. We are inadvertently gradual. When this
country is nine-tenths Socialist we shall still be pretending that we
are capitalist. That's the sort of people we are. Let members of
Parliament take note.

I seem to have wandered from my subject, but actually I am
right on the beam. Thinking, there in my bedroom while the sun
was creeping round the walls, it occurred to me that our development
has been extremely uneven. Take, for example, the resources that
are placed at the disposal of the average citizen. After my slight
tussle with illness I naturally thought of the medical attention available to everyone in New York. But a man who falls ill down in the
mountains of Tennessee or Arkansas will have nothing of the sort.
He may die without even the most elementary care. With regard to
this feature of life, obviously our progress is uneven.

We have developed our various services in response to uncertain
and rather wayward attention. This applies even to public defense.
The Army and the Navy have by no means had consistent and even
support. It applies to education, to which traditionally we have
pledged the deepest devotion. After these two sections of public activity, the next one in the popular mind is health. We are not yet
ready to see to it that every citizen has a good job with good pay.

We are pretty slow about providing that each one shall have a decent house. But the cult of health and the cult of education have taken a firm hold on the public mind. We can develop these two and work back from them.

I have been encouraged by a news item in the morning's paper: The Department of Agriculture has on hand thousands of carloads of potatoes. They are being sent out *free* to become a part of school lunches all over the country. We do not believe in seeing to it that all the people are well fed. We do believe in seeing that they are well educated. But educators find that children learn better if they have good lunches. So—all right—we feed them. It's a part of education.

And so this other cult of care for invalids may have social significance. The notion that a fellow should have extra privileges when he is ill seems silly. But it is something to build on. Everybody seems to be excited about illness. It is but a short step to interest in health and whatever it is that produces and preserves health. The physicians themselves are beginning to protest against the slums that produce so much of the illness. You will understand, of course, that all this has nothing to do with Socialism or Communism or any other sort of ism. It is pure and practical Americanism. It is, in fact, right in line with Republican doctrine. It is a move in the direction of economy. Health is far more economical than illness. Republicans cannot escape being for it. ∎

ANNALS OF THE INNOCENTS

An American masterpiece

■ Remember the days of the horrendous confessions. You might call them the cloak-and-dagger days of the ex-Communists. Louis Budenz is only the last of a long line of those who came up puffing and heaving from the political underworld to astonish the simple natives with accounts of their former misdeeds. Their tales of lying, theft, and conspiracy made the whodunnit products of the pulp industry seem stale and dry. Glamour encompassed them as they strode, dripping mystery and revelation, into the literary arena.

The eminence of these bright brands plucked from the burning naturally rouses something like envy among simple and ordinary folks whose biographies contain no high lights of horror with which to hold an audience or brighten the counters of the bookstores. I am reminded of the revival services that during my youth annually relieved the tedium of village life in Ohio. The star performers among the converts were the ones whom the clergy pulled from deepest down in the gutter. Either those—or the others who were blessed with the most creative imaginations. To play a glittering part it was necessary either to have committed great sins or to be able to imagine and recount them. Many a time I have seen an honest, decent citizen sit back and envy such a one his moment of greatness.

These meditations result—as so many of my notions do—from office conversations. The boys keep saying to me: "Look! All these Communists hit the headlines by revealing what goes on behind the iron curtain that rings the building on Thirteenth Street. Why don't you write the confessions of a Socialist? You might call it 'I Chose Freedom from the Start,' or something like that. Anyway, tell what went on in the early Socialist movement."

Nice boys, but little do they realize what they are asking. Socialists don't know anything about who killed Leon Trotsky or Carlo Tresca. All that they can do is to ask the prosecuting attorney to make an investigation. They never even forged a passport! When they wanted to go to Europe they just asked for passports and bought tickets like anyone else. And not one of them ever sported an alias. If a member of the Socialist party had a father named Adams or O'Malley or Plotsky, he just remained Adams or O'Malley or Plotsky to his dying day. He had nothing to hide, and one name was enough for him. What is there interesting about such ordinary folks?

But in the end my protests are always talked down. Disabused and deflated as my young friends may be, they will say, hopefully, "Well, you can at least tell how you first heard of Socialism." This part of my story dates back more than half a century—so it has at least the flavor of old, far-off things and battles long ago.

It was not from Gene Debs or Karl Marx that I first received intimations of the economic interpretation of history. It was, rather, from a sturdy plumber named Dietrickson or Erickson or something like that. It was in Columbus, Ohio, where I was a student at the state university. My brother and I, having come from the country, were filled with a great yearning for varieties of experience. I recall that we visited every sort of church that we could find in the town. That round of exploration resulted in some curious adventures, but I refuse to be deflected. The doughty plumber, who represented in our university town the theories that were later interpreted by Lenin and Stalin into the foundations of the Soviet state, held forth on a soapbox near the state capitol. Imagine, then, the two ingenuous youths filling in the gaps in education as offered by their professors as they listened to this street-corner instructor.

He resembled not at all the anemic revolutionary orators whom writers and artists have made familiar. His great head, mighty shoulders, and resounding voice would have commanded attention in any assemblage. The soapbox platform was hardly required to enable him to tower commandingly above the crowd. He would start something like this: "I am a plumber. Now, you students, you businessmen, you slick and well-dressed people, don't walk away just because I am a man of a necessary occupation, one whom you will call quickly in a moment of need but from whom you would scorn to take instruction on the great matters of politics and history.

"Who is there better fitted to speak than the necessary man who can fix the things which are mysteries to you and who may, before he has finished, enlighten you more than the professors in their classrooms or the preachers in the pulpits? What is the greatest thing that America has produced? Is it our pictures? Europe laughs at them. Is it our literature? It is but in its infancy. Is it our government? Don't make me laugh. America has produced but one masterpiece which is the wonder of the world. It is the American bathroom. Wherever you go it is held in highest respect. The artists who produced it are regarded as the master craftsmen of the age. Behold, then, this chamber of marble splendors, this symbol of cleanliness and health! With our cunning of hand and brain my helpers and I have produced it. The deep and gleaming tub awaits my lady's pleasure. The hot and cold water, at the touch of her dainty finger, gush to caress her limbs.

"But who is it who sits upon the gleaming throne which is the central glory of this prime product of American genius? Is it I, the man whose cunning produced it? No!" And I wish there were some typographical way of reproducing that explosive and reverberating syllable. It was the high point of this oration. From this point on, the speaker attained his effect by contrasting pianissimo. With the growing audience completely in his power, he would let his voice sink to a hoarse whisper. "Listen," he would say, "I will tell you who sits there taking his ease. It is the capitalist. Not one secret of the pipes does he know. Not one single shining tile could he lay. He toils not, neither does he spin, but Solomon in all his glory never sat on such a throne.

"I am but a plain man. I have never attended the classes at your university to have my mind destroyed by what is called economics. But this I know: between the man who builds the throne and the one who takes his ease upon it there is a great gulf fixed, and any true and good system of economics would aim to bridge that gulf. We speak of equality. It says something about it in the Declaration of Independence. But true equality we shall not have until the worker enjoys the product of his labor and every man has the right to sit upon the throne of his own creation."

From this point it was but a short step to the invitation to join the Socialist party, which in those days was the Socialist Labor party. What would now be called the commercial filled more time than it does on any radio program. It was a two-pronged appeal. The missionary had to sell the party and what was grandiosely described as "literature." He would have considered his oration a failure had it not led to the signing of a number of membership applications and the purchase by listeners of numerous pamphlets or subscriptions to papers.

My plumber was typical of the sturdy, native advocates who laid the foundations of the party that made so deep an impression on American life between 1900 and 1920. A collection of their speeches and writings would be as folklorish as Carl Sandburg's *Songbag*. There was nothing foreign or subversive about them. They smelled of the soil. In Michigan we had a state secretary who could entertain an audience for an entire evening with a discourse on bedbugs—and it was easy to see that his sources of information were not second-hand or merely literary. In Toledo, Ohio, lived the apostle who couched his Socialist message in the form of a fable about men and mules—the conclusion being that if men had the sense that mules are born with they would soon end their troubles by turning to Socialism. And in New Jersey, the leading advocate of reform based his canticle on the cruel sufferings caused by the alarm clock.   ∎

The tenth beatitude

∎ Looking back I can see that our Midwestern brand of revolution was eclectic, not to say irregular and unorthodox. Some had ideas that stemmed from Henry George, and in many a meeting I have thought I heard the voice of sockless Jerry Simpson. More than once a comrade with a red card in his pocket denounced Karl Marx as a foreigner who might be O.K. for old Europe but who had little to teach democratic America. And nothing happened to these heretics. We wanted to do away with exploitation, but we were skeptical of blueprints.

In relation to New York, however, we had a lamentable inferiority complex. It was, therefore, with exaggerated excitement that my brother Frank prepared for his first trip to the Metropolis. He had been elected delegate to a national Socialist convention. It must have been about the year 1900. This representative of improvised grass-roots revolution was to sit with the elders, men who had known Karl Marx and who were authorized to expound the scriptures.

This must have happened during the summer vacation, for I recall that I was loafing and reading under the trees during the time that Frank was away on this epoch-making pilgrimage to the Orient. This was in the town of four hundred inhabitants in which I spent my boyhood. When I returned later and saw the house, I realized it was an exact reproduction of those that settlers had left in New England. It had the same homey and gracious lines you can still observe in Vermont or New Hampshire, and sat back, like its eastern prototypes, deep among the trees in a wide lawn.

It recalled its New England antecedents, too, in other ways. Dirt-detesting cleanliness began at the fences and hedges that ringed it round and increased the rigidity of its regime as it penetrated inward. A little wickedness now and then might not matter much, but to be unclean—that just didn't happen. My mother was a gentle and easygoing mistress of the establishment. It was sister Bertha who served as the goddess of antisepsis. Don't get the idea that I am saying anything against her. She was a wonderful cook—and the things she could do for a fellow could not be counted up on any adding machine. All that she asked in return was our cooperation in the interest of constant and complete cleanliness.

Our town came nearer to being a classless society than anything that I have seen since. Some had more money than others, but richest and poorest sat piously together in the church pews or leaned cheek by jowl over the bars of the three or four well-patronized saloons. We went to different churches, Methodist, Congregational, and Catholic. There was a large group of Irish, and we had one Negro family. But the fact that people were different didn't make any difference. We had no interracial or interreligious conference or council or commission to sponsor programs and big words. No one had ever taught us that we ought not get along—and so we just got along. As I look back from the vantage point of 1961 and all its hates, that town looks wonderful.

Mention of that one colored family suggests that there was, after all, one slight rift. But it was not along the color line. Those Negroes, father, mother, and daughter, were as respectable as anyone. The daughter had a fine voice and sang among the best in the Methodist choir. When she got married we all attended the wedding. But it was not her musical gift that placed her among the elect. I recall hearing the other women say, "She's as neat as a pin." That was what counted. She was colored but she was clean—so she belonged to the upper class.

Well do I recall that when as a child I was taken anywhere among such crowds as we could muster—fifty persons made a crowd —there were a few who were avoided or looked down upon. But the people who did not quite make the grade were not the poor. They were the ones whose persons or clothes showed lack of washing. I feel sure that if the women of our town had written the Beatitudes, one of them would have been: Blessed are the immaculate, for they are already in the kingdom of heaven. I should add that the most dreaded and despised symbol of uncleanliness and disgrace in this Spotless Town was a certain widespread but seldom-mentioned insect. To be in any way associated with this biological species did definitely place one beyond the pale.

From this town, then, my brother departed to attend the convention of big-time Socialists in New York. He returned tired, excited, and full of strange tales. To our astonishment we learned that he had been received with honor among the bearded elders. It took whole days and nights for him to describe what he had seen and elucidate what he had learned. But sister Bertha took no part in all this. She went about her accustomed tasks with more than her usual vigor and austerity as she conspicuously reserved her judgment.

After two or three days of this, we returned one day from the riverbank where we had pleasantly continued our discussion to find our whole establishment in an uproar. Furniture, carpets, and utensils of all sorts were being dragged out of doors by all hands that could be pressed into service. Bertha was sternly in command, and before we knew what was up, we too were busy emptying the house of all its furnishings. There was no time to satisfy our curiosity. Out everything went. And then the house from top to bottom had to be cleansed. It took days. For weeks there was the smell of turpentine and paint and other cleansing agents.

We learned the cause of it all from Bertha's ejaculations. She would tug at a bed or a carpet and say: "This is what your Socialism amounts to. . . . Can't stay at home. . . . Have to go gallivanting about the country. . . . Want to save the world, do you? . . . And what do you get? . . . Does anybody thank you? . . . Do you make things better? . . . No. . . . Bedbugs—that's all you get. Want to make everybody equal! . . . The bugs will make 'em all equal."

It was—indubitably—a setback for the cause of world revolution. It never has prospered in that town. Later on we could go to other places and deliver the message of the class struggle. But inside our town, Gus Greeley was the only man who listened with sympathy and understanding. But Gus was not the sort of follower to give strength and prestige to a struggling cause. In that citadel of cleanliness, Socialism got away to a poor start. ∎

An introduction to Socialism

∎ My first appearance at a real and regular official Socialist meeting came about fortuitously. In those days I was living a carefree life as an instructor at the University of Michigan. Ann Arbor is still a charming place in which to live, but it cannot possibly be as gay and uninhibited as it was during the days of Fielding H. Yost. Mr. Yost and I arrived on the campus at the beginning of the same year, but I must confess that his advent aroused more interest than mine.

The status of what is called an "instructor" is a peculiarly happy one. Why this peculiar title was ever dreamed up for him I never tried to make out. He instructs very little. I am sure I learned more from my students than they learned from me. In those days we had many serious and mature students in a place like the University of Michigan. Men and women would save up money all their lives to get a college education, and by the time they got round to realizing their dream their hair might be streaked with gray. But the "instructors" were all young and gay. Everything was done to free us of responsibility. We were expected to attend faculty meetings, but had no vote. The lack of money bothered us not at all. Days and nights were long and we had fun. The teaching had as little as possible to do with what was happening outside.

There came a letter asking me to go to the big city to address a meeting on unemployment. It was an invitation I could hardly refuse. The letterhead was that of the Detroit "section" of the Socialist Labor party, but that name meant little to me at that time. I felt sure that Socialists of any sort would be seriously concerned about what was happening. Talk with them would, at least, be more satisfactory than the cool and distant theorizing of our Department of Economics. So I promised to go, and I set about preparing my address.

I wish I had the manuscript of what I intended to say. It was elaborately ponderous. Not only was I prepared to give exact references to all my authorities: I also carried with me a stack of books, mostly history. If I was challenged on any point, I intended to be able to establish my facts out of the mouths of scribes from the time of the Greeks on down. So furnished for intellectual battle, I set forth on the journey to the city where Henry Ford was at that time just beginning to establish his mighty empire.

Someone should somewhere and at some time do justice to the rooms, the "halls," the places where Socialism has been incubated. We have heard a lot about the country store, the shoemaker's shop or the barbershop as a forum of democracy. Schools, churches, social settlements have all been celebrated as grassroots parliaments. But from one end of this country to the other, Socialist meetings have been held in a particular sort of place with a special sort of atmosphere. Out of these meetings has gone an influence that men such as Franklin D. Roosevelt have recognized as potent. But I cannot recall ever having come across a reference to the peculiar qualities of the places where they have been held.

On that Sunday afternoon away back there near the beginning of this century for the first time I climbed the dark and redolent stairway that led to a meeting place of the radicals. The second floor offered only closed doors bearing the strange names of foreign societies or business concerns. So I braced myself for a second climb. As I gained altitude I noted that the atmosphere gained density, the wallpaper lost adhesiveness, the dirt and darkness deepened. When at last I reached the "hall," I found that a number of persons had already proved themselves possessed of the hardihood necessary to qualify as partakers of whatever stimulus was to be on tap.

Far over to one side, and near a dirty window that furnished a dim light just sufficient for his purposes, there sat a big man laboriously reading. Accustomed as I was to all the devices whereby my university attempted either to lure or force the students to read, I watched this huge fellow with fascination. The chairman had received me with appropriate solemnity and introduced me quaintly to comrade this and comrade that. But these workingmen in their Sunday best soon realized that the person I really wanted to know was the man who read. They referred to him as Big John and explained that he was a Great Lakes sailor who could be with them only when his ship happened to be in port.

As we approached him, one great finger was slowly traveling along the lines while his mouth slowly moved as he silently formed the words he was perusing. I noted that the part of the book that had been read was dull gray from dirt, and the page that at that moment occupied Big John's attention was dirty exactly down to the point he had reached. So intense was his concentration that he was surprised and somewhat disconcerted when we finally broke in upon him. To my eager question as to what it was that so held his eyes and mind, he answered in the heavy accent of the North of England: "It's the first book of Kar-rl Mar-rx that I'm r-readin! An' tough goin' it is for a wor-rkin' man like me. But I'll r-read it through if it kills me."

That was my introduction to the organized Socialist movement. In a dark and smelly "hall" a little group of earnest men who would read Karl Marx if it killed them.   ∎

Camp-meeting Socialism

∎ In my last chapter of these simple annals I may have given a false impression. It must be understood that I was writing, not about the Socialist movement of America, but about the Socialist Labor party—

which was something quite different. I soon began to realize what an "un-American" organization I was dealing with. In New York sat Daniel De Leon and in Detroit sat the obedient and conscientious Herman Richter, and what the Prophet Daniel said went. When I made my first trip to New York I understood why. I was taken to see three of the city's wonders: the Flatiron Building, then the highest in the town; the Stock Exchange, and Daniel, dictator of the oldest branch of Socialism on these shores. I am quite willing to believe that Lenin learned from De Leon. The methods of purging his organization, of destroying those whom he could not control, and especially of making war by lying, slander, and defamation—all these tricks that we now associate with the Communists, Daniel had developed to a high stage of perfection back in the first decade of this century.

But I soon learned of another—and different—organization known as the Socialist party. My first information about it came by way of the columns of the *Weekly People*, the vigorous and vituperative organ of the SLPers. My first inkling of the fact that there were such persons as Morris Hillquit, Eugene V. Debs, and Victor Berger came to me in the form of epithets, mostly from the animal kingdom, hurled at them by the denunciatory De Leon. But soon came an invitation from the Socialist party group in Detroit, and I discovered that there was a brand of undictated Socialism gathering followers throughout the country.

It is practically impossible to make today's young people realize what sort of spirit was abroad in this country during those days—say, from 1903 to 1910. I had no contact with what might be called official Socialism. I attended no conventions, held no offices, and, excepting for speaking at meetings now and then with Gene Debs, I did not meet any of the party bigwigs. In all the surrounding states, Ohio, Indiana, Illinois, Wisconsin, there were influential Socialist leaders. In Michigan there were no leaders and mighty few speakers. Our state secretary was a Grand Rapids furniture worker who had lost his job when "mission" furniture came in and furniture carving went out. He had sacrificed most of the fingers of his right hand to a buzzsaw—and I shall never forget the dramatic impression he made when he pleaded for the Socialist utopia with bad grammar but shining face, and tried to pluck the better world down out of the air with that mutilated hand.

In those days—at least in that state—the word *Socialism* was a fighting word, a word to conjure with. In every town and in many places out in the country there would be a little band of working people—not an intellectual in sight. They were humble people, but so genuine, so earnest, so idealistic that it was a privilege to live in the same world with them, to do any little thing to carry forward the movement in which they so devoutly believed. These little people, with no cleverness, no influence, no tricks of publicity, with nothing but their faith for motive power, would hire the biggest hall or theater in their town and invite whatever out-of-town speaker they could get. Such meetings were usually held on Saturday evenings or Sunday afternoons. What impresses me as I look back is that every Socialist gathering of this sort would be crowded. In the smaller towns every-one of importance would be there: the city officials, judges, clergy, the trade-union leaders. The Socialist party was small. As I recall it, we got only about 400,000 votes throughout the nation in 1904 and not many more in 1908. But the idea of Socialism was abroad in the land. People were hot either for it or against it. The question-and-answer sessions after an address were prolonged, impassioned, and fruitful.

Probably most of the sophisticated readers of the *New Leader* have nothing more than sketchy ideas of camp meetings. Telling you that they were packed and concentrated religious orgies that supplied drama-hungry rural America with sufficient summer emotion to last through the year will probably furnish but slight assistance to an understanding. Our early western Socialist organizers soon discovered the showmanship value of the camp-meeting environment and routine. Only once did I have the opportunity to function at this sort of gathering, but the occasion is a bright part of my pageant of the past.

Up in the northern part of the Southern Peninsula of Michigan the farmers had been summoned to three days of meetings in a circus tent. There was a brass band that would give us its limited repertory at any hour of the day or night. Tents for families had been erected under the trees, and long tables dispelled any fear of starvation that the wild aspect of the scenery may have wakened. And when the farm families began to pile out of their buggies and wag-ons, the bulging baskets they brought promised days and nights of plenty. There may have been a lack of the sort of hysteria that characterized the more or less similar religious occasions, but from the culinary point of view the Socialist farmers continued an ancient and splendid tradition.

That wildwood assembly lasted for three days, and I delivered six lectures. I fear they were pretty long and more serious than necessary. I covered the history of capitalism, imperialism, agriculture, the rise of the working class, and the promise of the future. And not only those farmers, but their wives and children, packing that tent to its last rows, sat and listened with a seriousness and attention that would have warmed any speaker's heart. The band was a help, it must be confessed, for there was always the promise of brassy music at the finish.

Perhaps there was something appropriate in our stealing the ways of primitive evangelism. As I look back now, I am conscious of the fact that the sort of Socialism all these people believed in had a good deal of myth about it. They thought that soon—very soon— we would get a majority; then we would "have Socialism"; then— immediately—everything would be all right. I recall being asked again and again, along about 1907 or 1908, "Do you think we will make it in 1912? Do you?" Men and women in this naïve state were poorly prepared for the long pragmatic pull necessary to transform a complicated society.

In Detroit we had as Secretary of the Socialist party, a traveling salesman, and of his sort of Socialism he was a very effective salesman indeed. He was, by the way, thoroughly convinced that we would usher in a full-blown Socialist regime by the year 1912. He was deeply devoted to his wife, and the only shadow that ever crossed his normally cheerful face came when he confided to me that she suffered from tuberculosis and he feared that she would not last till the great day of triumph. In an effort to restore her health he took her to Texas, but soon returned with the sad news that she had passed away. In trying to comfort him I drew from him more of an account of her last days than I really wanted to hear. What I learned was that he had solaced her final hours with readings from Marx's *Das Kapital*. And the last words he said to me about her end were these: "I am afraid, comrade, I am dreadfully afraid, that she passed away without quite understanding the theory of surplus value." ∎

Revolutionaries on the rods

■ There is one feature of the early days of American Socialism that, as far as I know, has escaped attention. I refer to the relation between the mendicant and the Marxist, the rider-of-the-rods and the revolutionist. It would never occur to an innocent historian that a tie would develop between social idealists and the bums who are from time to time thrown into jail under suspicion of chicken theft. And it took me a long time to discover that there was any sort of link between them.

Picture me, then, between 1901 and 1910, living a carefree life in an idyllic college town. For the young instructors at the University of Michigan, Ann Arbor offered a wide variety of good things. We lived in pleasant wide-porched houses ranged in deep yards along tree-lined streets. Our own golf course lay less than a mile from the campus among rolling hills. Off in the other direction curved the Huron, one of the most charming and many-mooded of streams.

There was an agreeable balance of interests and activities. In the clubs of faculty and graduate students there was a pleasant hum of intellectual life. The topics of debate might seem remote, but to us the interest in them was real. To the young instructors, leading an amphibious existence between professors and students, contacts and activities were richly varied. On one evening we might be attending a reception in white tie and tails, and on the next we might be singing rowdy songs with a gang of undergraduates high on a hill above the Huron.

The sour critics of these 1947 days might say that our whole life was an escape from reality. There are fellows who would scorn puppies or kittens for having a good time. At any rate, my academic paradise was soon invaded—and not by a tempting and romantic serpent. We had on the campus a small and devoted band of Socialists who satisfied some inner urge by holding sober discussion meetings. The authorities failed to interfere with us for the very good reason that they had never heard of us. The depression and unemployment of 1908 roused some of our consciences, but not sufficiently to lead to any unseemly or sensation-seeking activity. I was, however, sufficiently aroused to start writing. The first contributions went to the *International Socialist Review*, published by Charles H. Kerr & Co., Chicago. In between golf games and canoe trips I would send off to Chicago my thoughts on the causes of unemployment. As an escape valve for a conscience beginning to warm up toward a boil, this worked pretty well. I carried in my mind a picture of the sturdy workers with whom I was establishing a link by means of easy and agreeable activity.

During this period I lived at the Churchwardens Club, with a group of twelve carefree chaps whose long clay pipes suggested the eighteenth century and furnished the symbol of their sodality. What fun we had, what meals, what talks, what drinks! But this is not what I am leading up to.

Soon a strange and disturbing thing began to happen. Queer-looking fellows began coming up to our door. They would look around furtively at the unaccustomed surroundings and then ask for me. When I came to the door, they would invariably grasp my hand in a generous and dirty grip, the while addressing me volubly as "comrade." Any Churchwardens who happened to be lounging near listened with eyes, and possibly mouths, wide open. Soon they became so accustomed to the performance that at first sight of one of these seeking wayfarers they would shout loudly to me: "Hey, Bill, here is one of your comrades!" Month after month and year after year this stream of roving radicals continued. It was not until years later that Dr. Ben Reitman made the whole business clear to me. Hoboing, he explained, is a highly skilled profession. The real professional is as clever as any salesman in the matter of arranging his connections, picking his victims, and preparing his approach. These men got my name from the *International Socialist Review*, shared their knowledge for reciprocal favor with various of their fellows, and then started the procession to my door.

The conversation would begin with a sharing of thoughts about the voraciousness of the rich and the undeserved suffering of the poor. For good measure praise of my last article might be thrown in. I was given the impression that there was wide rejoicing among the downtrodden and abused over the fact that an instructor in a great institution devoted to the nurture of the offspring of the rich had cast his lot with them and would cooperate with them in the overthrow of the bloodsucker system that had reduced such valiant citizens to peripatetic beggary. But, having begun on this high level, the dialogue would soon descend to a more practical plane. From the economic interpretation of history we would turn to the depression, to the sufferings of the poor and, finally, to the empty stomach of the particular representative of the suffering poor who stood before me. The allurements of ham and eggs might be alluded to, or the desirability of a dollar.

As time passed, I thought I noted a propagandist tilt to the conversations of these radicals of the road. They were concerned about me, worried lest I be seduced and debauched by my bourgeois environment. They wanted it understood that they and all true proletarians stood firmly grouped on the extreme left. In those days William D. Haywood was the symbol of root-and-branch revolution, while Morris Hillquit and Victor Berger stood for gradualist and political change. They wanted no half-baked Hillquit and Berger stuff. Haywood was their man. And, they assured me, when the great day of revolution came, the knights of the road with Big Bill as their head would make a clean sweep. And unless I watched my step, even a Socialist college man like me might be suspect. ■

The fringe

■ Not long ago I stumbled into an incident that carried my mind back many years. Strolling along Broadway somewhere on the Upper West Side, I chanced upon a street meeting. These open-air forums have always had for me an irresistible lure. There is some magic in the tossing about of words and ideas under the open sky and amidst the tantalizing sounds of surging crowds. The whole thing is like a laboratory of public opinion with the roof removed and all its inner workings revealed. So I stopped to listen and observe. The meeting was being held by a group of Socialists, and they had a respectful and attentive audience.

Not far away, across an intersection, a street salesman was doing business with an equally large and responsive audience. I don't know precisely what he was selling. It may have been a can-opener or a knife-sharpener or some sort of medicine. While I stood there watching curiously as strollers paused and went on or became sufficiently intrigued to linger, I noted that the neighboring pitchman was closing up shop. Perhaps he had sold out his stock, or had made enough money and was ready to call it a day. Some of his listeners wandered over to the Socialist meeting, and soon I looked around to find that the salesman himself, with his little collapsible platform in his hand, was standing beside me.

Of all the listeners, he was the most alert and intelligent. With a professional eye he took in all the arrangements, and his criticism of the techniques showed real acumen. What interested him most, as he put it, was that "these guys don't pay nothin' for what they sell." As he turned this thought over in his mind, I could see that an idea was being born. "This spiel ain't hard to learn," he confided. "In a coupla weeks I could take this crowd right away from that guy."

We people of the University of Michigan had only casual—chiefly commercial—relations with the town of Ann Arbor. In those days there was a good deal of the traditional feud between town and gown. I was told that in the whole history of the place only one sturdy businessman-citizen had ever crossed the barriers and been received as an equal in academic circles.

I soon discovered that being known as a Socialist involved a pass that carried me across the class lines of the college town. Suddenly I found myself in close contact with an eager group of townsmen ready to band themselves together into what was called a "local" of the Socialist party. All that was needed was assurance that I would help them, and the thing was done. We formed the "local," obtained a charter from Chicago, and proudly affixed it to the wall of a meeting place that we rented.

The meetings we held in our little room, called "the hall," contained in essence the whole story of the rise and fall of the Socialist party in the United States. We had our superrevolutionist, who was, naturally, one of the richest men in the organization. He was tall, soft-spoken, elegant—and he believed in every comma and exclamation point in Karl Marx's theology. He was, I should interject, clean-shaven. At the other end of the scale we had Comrade Hodge. Hodge was bearded, not precisely like the pard, but with a long and luxuriant gray appendage sweeping from his chin. He could be depended upon to open almost any meeting with an attack upon Karl Marx's beard. And then the clean-shaven revolutionist and the bountifully bearded gradualist would go to it, with the Marxian beard inextricably intertwined with Marxian doctrines.

The thing was funny, but as I look back upon it, I can now perceive a tragic significance. This man Hodge was a plain, old-fashioned American farmer. In his looks, his speech, all his ways of thinking and acting, he symbolized our native life. He used to talk about cooperation, a thing that had been developed on the old frontier. He insisted that if we continued to follow a foreign guide and use a vocabulary alien to our people, we would fail. Subsequent events proved that he was right.

Nothing could have been more loose and bungling than the Socialist party of the State of Michigan during those years. Our little group was practically cut off from the world. We carried on our campaign to save mankind in our way and with whatever resources happened to offer. Among these were the itinerant evangelists, especially those who turned from patent medicine to what they thought was Marxism. We read in the Socialist papers about street meetings—so we naturally relied on them as the accepted method of spreading our ideas. For speakers we depended upon the four winds.

Our secretary was a young butcher, eager, handsome, full of energy. When he came up to the university to consult about our common interests, he always inspired me with visions of what the world could be. If a butcher boy could see visions that were closed to the professors, well, there was hope. He and I would pass judgment on the would-be street speakers who made application for our support.

I recall one particular fellow who had ridden the rods into town. He told tales of his prowess in other places. He would guarantee success if we would call a street meeting and give him the privilege of taking up a collection. The butcher boy appeared in dubious mood. This man had Socialist pamphlets to sell, and he seemed all right. "But," said the secretary, "I don't know. He might be all right in a hall, but I'm afraid to put him up on the street." This seemed queer to me, but the perplexed secretary continued his explanation: "He looks all right in front. But on the street the crowd can get around behind a man. And his pants look kind of funny behind." There was a difficulty. The itinerant was raring to go, but his pants were unreliable in the rear. The problem was solved by the hurried gathering of a purse. We raised four dollars and bought our orator a pair of breeches, and, inspired by our generosity, he turned in an extra-brilliant performance.

Practically every sort of quack was represented among those who turned to the propagation of Socialism. Every now and then, even today, I get a letter from some good comrade out West who has his ideas of social reform all intertwined with some panacea for disease. The hydropaths, naturopaths, and every other sort of *paths*, along with vegetarians and raw-fooders, were sure to come our way. The practice of medicine by regular physicians was, of course, a part of the wicked capitalist system. The way to circumvent these robbers was to turn for cure to this or that perfectly sure method that was being concealed from the people by the grasping capitalists. At the top of the Socialist movement we had some of the greatest idealists and most distinguished scientists of this country. At the other end we had a lot of panhandlers and faddists—the lunatic fringe. It was, all in all, a gay and gaudy outfit. ■

Areopagitica

■ It is with mixed feelings that a man looks back and considers circumstances that grabbed him by the scruff of the neck, jerked him out of one way of life, and chucked him down in another. Every time I see a college professor with his comfortable little salary and his freedom to spend endless time with books and young people, I say, "There, but for the grudge of the devil, go I." From my very earliest days on the farm I dreamed of spending my life with books. As if the whole thing were decreed in advance, I went steadily along from class to class and degree to degree until, at the age of twenty-three, I found myself teaching university classes.

Everyone acquainted with academic ways knows that, once you are in, all you have to do is to behave yourself with moderate discretion and display a minimum of intelligence and energy. If a fellow quietly plays the game along with the others, nothing less than an earthquake can throw him out. Many a chap has lost his place for some moral or intellectual irregularity. I can hardly recall one who lost it because of lack of brains or initiative.

I was exceptionally happy and contented in the university environment. When I think back to the classes, the clubs, the parties, the football games—even the concerts and lectures—Ann Arbor seems to me in retrospect a heavenly place. I recall with special delight a certain alcove in the library. After achieving my doctorate I saw beyond that in my imagination a series of books, one every year or two down through the pleasant years that were to be the future. Nobody else ever came to this particular corner. I was working on the literary criticism of the seventeenth century, and the plays, the poetry, and prose of that period filled the shelves all about me. I knew the lives of the two Johns who covered the century, John Milton and John Dryden, almost from day to day. I would get immersed in some old play or diary and forget about my classes. Then I would learn that in my absence the students had organized and gone on with their work. I wonder if students still do such things.

It is difficult to designate in retrospect the stages through which I passed in growing discontented with the agreeable existence. During the depression years of 1907 and 1908 I had a mounting feeling that life was passing me by, that the important things were happening elsewhere. Over the platform of our auditorium we had some of the fine words written by Jefferson in the original statute setting up the Northwest Territory. In student assemblies President Angell and other dignitaries often stressed the importance of the university to the people of the state. But the things that we were teaching in what we called the Arts College seemed to me irrelevant to the public welfare. In the College of Engineering and that of Medicine we had leaders in those fields definitely helping to solve important public problems. There was eager and vital activity on the part of students and faculty. In the Arts College—so it seemed to me—we were daydreaming.

Take the Department of Economics, for example. We were a state institution. A lot of the citizens were unemployed. If there was a health problem, the College of Medicine helped to solve it. If there were railways to be built, the Department of Civil Engineering took a hand. Why should not the Department of Economics, supported by taxpayers, have something to say that would help send the citizens back to work? It did, as it happened, have something to say, but not on the helpful side.

The head of our Department of Economics was in Washington busily at work setting up the Interstate Commerce Commission. We were all proud of his prominence. Left at home to run the department in his absence was a certain Frederick Taylor, always referred to by the students as Freddie. A student asked Freddie in class what he thought about the unemployed who were tramping the streets of Detroit in search of jobs. According to reports Freddie answered, "It's a good thing they are out of work." A student reporter for a Detroit paper grabbed this story and it got a big play in his paper.

That was something in the nature of a cyclone. A nice, decent little university professor in the metropolitan headlines—and in headlines with a vicious twist to them! Something must be done— and quick. The wickedly intruding world of industrial strife must be pushed back. The academic quiet must be restored. The trial of that reporter before the Sanhedrin of the faculty must still be vividly recalled by many. It was really Professor Taylor's system of economics that was on trial.

That boy facing the wide circle of professorial faces insisted that he had reported the truth, that the professor had actually said it was a good thing that people were out of work. Then the professor, choking with rage, desperately explained to his colleagues that what he meant had been something quite different. That affirmation was but a part of the economic theory he was endeavoring to make clear. His intention had been to use the perils of the unemployed to demonstrate the relentless and, in the long run, beneficent nature of the business cycle. The low swing was an essential feature of the rhythm of production and employment—so unemployment and the resultant suffering were inevitable. To deplore them or get excited about them was as ridiculous as to go berserk over the variations of the weather.

The boy who put the professor in the headlines was thrown out of school. It probably did him no harm. His experience at that trial must have been worth a couple of university courses to him. I record the incident merely to show the sort of "economics" that was taught in American universities while William Howard Taft was running for the Presidency. It was during that campaign that this particular Taft, father of a later aspirant to the Presidency, dramatically summed up the inutility of this whole theoretic system. Asked in Cooper Union what an unemployed man should do or where he should turn, the distinguished jurist honestly blurted out, "God knows; I don't." Those words summed up an age and a theory. I had had enough of it.

There I sat in my alcove reading seventeenth century poetry and criticism while outside the unemployed pounded the pavement. I could not but connect the surging words of Milton's *Areopagitica* with the smug silence that was maintained about me. And with increasing urgency there came to me calls from Detroit, from Grand Rapids, from Lansing—even from the rural districts of the great State of Michigan. My alcove seemed more and more barren. Real life seemed to be out there calling to me.　■

The fortunate martyrs

■ As I enter upon this tale of the events that led to my separation from the academic life, it occurs to me that I owe an explanation to my younger readers. It is now many years since I have heard of anyone who was ousted from a university or college position because of his profession of Socialism. On the contrary, I know a goodly number of men well known to be Socialists who occupy high positions in various institutions of higher learning. There has been a great change in the world of teaching and learning since the days of which I write, away back in 1901–10.

I hope that no one will rise to remark that it is the Socialists who have changed rather than the world about them. Communists will naturally say that the Socialists are now accepted because they are no longer dangerous. Their revolutionary ardor, some will maintain, has been so cooled off that they are hardly distinguishable from the despised bourgeoisie. And—such persons will assert—it is the Communists who are now fired from academic posts—which is supposed to prove that it is the Communists who are now the genuine and dangerous representatives of a different and better world.

I have followed with a good deal of care the cases of Communists who have been discharged from positions as college teachers. In every case that has come to my attention, the men who have been dropped did not lose their posts because they entertained any revolutionary economic or social doctrine. They were sent into the outer world either because they hatched conspiracies against their fellow instructors or the students or because they were guilty of perjury in court. The men who in that former age were fired from universities because of their Socialism were, as far as my recollection goes, all decent, honorable persons. The Communists, who in rare cases are now being dropped, are fellows who have been proved unfit to have anything to do with the training of youth. They rouse opposition because they are liars and dishonest connivers—and agents of a foreign power.

It is with a good deal of amusement that I think back upon the list of those who were dropped from teaching positions because of their Socialism. There was always a good deal of dramatic commotion connected with their cases. Some decent, conscientious young fellow teaching economics or history would become discontented with the superficial notions he was supposed to believe and impart. He would feel impelled to speak out about low wages or unemployment or slums. If, after being gently spoken to by president or dean, he persisted in his unorthodox ways, he would find himself in trouble.

From this point on, practically all cases ran identical courses. Presidents would say impressively that the matter had nothing to do with free speech. The newspapers, always happy to unearth something scandalous connected with an institution that usually furnished only the most colorless of stories, would play the fracas up in flaming and unacademic terms. From being nobody at all, the young deviator from orthodoxy would find himself living a hectic life on the front pages. If he had any taste for publicity, he would luxuriate in it. The college bigwigs, hating this sort of indecent exposure, squirmed under it.

The august machinery of the board of trustees would run its course. In the end the young man would find his status changed, with a speed that left him dizzy. From being an unknown little chap inside a great institution, he would find himself turned into a well-publicized man-about-the-front-pages. All that he had to pay for hundreds of thousands of dollars' worth of advertising was his security. And if he worked things right, he was a hero. He had stood up for his convictions against the higher powers. He had sacrificed his position and his career. Standing high on his tower of publicity, he faced the great outside world.

I have always had the feeling that the central figures in these successive dramas were improperly represented as martyrs. Actually, they should have given thanks to the presidents and boards that chucked them out of their comfortable seats into the exciting hurly-burly of the world. They were better men for having gone through a shaking-up.

In some cases the only authority and prominence these men ever attained they owed to this disturbing experience. Now and then a young chap who had been put through this academic chute-the-chutes would quickly attain in wide circles greater regard than would have resulted from the awarding of the most exalted degree from the most respected of universities. His martyrization instantly conferred upon him a license to speak on the most varied matters of economics or history. Once you become a hero, your word is accepted on any subject you deign to discuss. Teachers fired from university posts for their opinions should give thanks to the presidents, deans, and boards who, thinking to punish them, rescued them from lives of comfortable obscurity.

The ejection of unorthodox young men from teaching positions was good for the young fellows, but for the school it was bad. Think of the effect on the faculty members who were left behind. This kind of thing is in part responsible for the docility of the teaching profession, which is so often discussed as its chief fault. Instructors who keep their mouths shut because they fear to lose their jobs are not fit to teach young Americans. A job that you can lose that way isn't worth having. But a teacher who pussyfoots because he is afraid of losing it is even more worthless.

The basic root of the whole evil lay in the crude ignorance of many of the men who occupied positions of authority. On the governing boards of both public and private educational institutions were men who knew no more about education than any chap you would pick up on a subway train or on the street. They got their appointments because they had money or political influence. Whatever stupid notions they had in their heads became the law. Now and then you would find a college president who ranked not much higher in intellectual attainments. Most of them, however, had sufficient sense and idealism to realize that this sort of thing was bad. But they were overpowered by the weight of trustees and wealthy alumni.

I don't believe I have many illusions about our educational system. An editor gets plentiful evidence of its faults. But I think I am right in saying that during the past forty years we have made some progress. We now get better men on boards of trustees and in authoritative positions.   ∎

The parting of the ways

∎ As I look back on things I did and things that happened to me from 1907 to 1910, I realize that they have a certain significance as proofs of the progress our society has made since then. But at the time I was not interested in any such cool and distant point of view. It is hard to reconstruct the mood of a time so far away. In your backward-looking view you seem a stranger to yourself. The young chap who did this or said that had your name and some of your idiosyncrasies. But he was, it seems to you now, strangely gay and irresponsible about the consequences of his deeds. He was serious about his views and frivolous about his fate.

I was under thirty when actions that seemed to me perfectly simple and well intentioned brought me in conflict with the directing authorities of the university that had been for a generation the most distinguished educational center of the West. Its halls, though conspicuously lacking in beauty, had to our western eyes the dignity that goes with age and hallowed associations. Distinguished men had lectured in its classrooms. Our faculty even in my time contained many men of widely recognized scholarship. Though I had attended a number of other colleges and universities, the University of Michigan had all my loyalty. The other day I happened to hear "Hail, Hail, Michigan" played on some radio program, and I came near rising right up out of the chair to cheer for the team. You would think that a young fellow like me, loving the place and my work as I did, would have done anything within reason to stay where he was and pursue the life that so eminently suited his tastes and ideals.

You would think, on the other hand, that such a university would remain undisturbed by the doings of a young fellow who quietly pursued his way as a Socialist and whose most violent flings into radical activity were the writing of an occasional article and the taking of weekend speechmaking trips. It is only fair to say that it was not, properly speaking, the university that made trouble for me. A university consists of the faculty and the students. I had plenty of evidence that most of the teachers and students who were aware of the fuss that was kicked up about my case were on my side. It was not the university that objected to my being at once an active Socialist and an instructor. It was the Board of Regents.

The university was a state institution. Most of its support came from appropriations made by the state legislature, and the regents were appointed by the governor. We instructors had the privilege of seeing these regents once in a while, and we always viewed them with a good deal of well-concealed amusement. They were just the sort of fellows you would expect them to be. Some were young politicians on their way up. Others were older politicians on their way out. But most of them were prosperous businessmen from whom the governor expected substantial favors in return for the formal dignity he had bestowed. Whether any of them ever knew or cared anything about education was something no man was ever able to discover. The impression they gave on their visits to the campus was that if we had a good football team everything was O.K. During my time, and that of the famous coach Point-a-Minute Yost, the team swept all before it, the legislature was generous, and the regents were happy.

The point that was important to me—and that is, too, of chief significance in connection with the development of American education—is that the members of the faculty had little to say about what went on at the university. A group of men whose interest was elsewhere and who made but fleeting visits to the campus set the policies and made the decisions. Professors were only professors. Men who had no more than a slight fraction of their mental grasp could make them tremble in their academic chairs. It was in a collision with the regents, not, properly speaking, with the university itself, that my career as college teacher was wrecked.

I remarked some weeks ago that it seems to me things on the campus go better nowadays. A wide latitude is permitted to members of many faculties. In many of our institutions of higher learning professors far out in front in their social thinking are not merely secure in their positions but are regarded as the principal ornaments of their schools. Among them are some who are well known for their Socialist views—and no one looks at them askance. Yes, there has been a change.

Looking back, I can see that I was caught in the backwash of the age of the robber barons. At the end of the Civil War, thirty or forty years before my time, Michigan was covered with forests. The men who founded the University of Michigan came from the East, from Harvard and Yale. But the men who ran the state legislature and, too, the great state school, were the same men who ruthlessly ripped down the forests to turn them heedlessly into fortunes. They were the first generation of post-Civil War capitalists. In my time there were still some of these lords of lumber on the Board of Regents, where their interest was conspicuously centered in athletic prowess. Some of the others were, of course, the predecessors of Henry Ford. But all of them were businessmen in the raw, fellows in a hurry to whom learning meant nothing and quick success meant everything. To them, of course, the way things were going was perfect. They had succeeded, hadn't they? Why couldn't everybody succeed?

Without any idea of what I was doing, I ran afoul of this set of men. I went out and made speeches about poverty, about unemployment, about inequality of opportunity. These men quickly heard of what was going on. Their reaction sent me out into the wide, wide world.

My separation from the serene and easygoing academic ranks—when the slow-moving anti-Socialist forces finally got into action—was surprisingly friendly and painless. Certain aspects were even amusing. Since the moving forces were among the regents and influential alumni rather than among the professors and students, my relations with my associates remained normal. Action to rid the university of the instructor who had come in some circles to be regarded as a danger to the great State of Michigan was up to no less a person than the university president himself.

The incident occurred at the moment of a change of administrations. James Angell, the distinguished diplomat who had led the university to the position of prominence which it has occupied ever since, was finally being relieved of duties he had for some years sought to lay down. He had long since in subtle and diplomatic ways expressed his disapproval of my mixing in the vexatious social messes outside our halls of learning. I was left under no misapprehension as to what would eventually happen to me under his regime or that of anyone like him.

But, as things turned out, the retirement of President Angell had no influence at all upon my fate. When the old captain stepped down, the regents did a characteristic thing. Instead of looking about and selecting a leader from among the distinguished educators who were available, they chose for his successor the one among their own employees who looked and acted most like a college president. His name was Harry Hutchins, and he had served for some years as Dean of the Law School. During his first years as head of the institution I became well acquainted with him, and, strange to say, I think of him now with real affection.

But during the numerous and protracted conferences with this college president I could not get out of my head the sense of puzzlement over the process by which such a man had become head of a great educational institution. He looked precisely like one of Peter Arno's stuffed shirts. He had been for years a conventional teacher of law and had become Dean of the Law School because he looked like a dean. Because of his looks and, too, because he had never, never done or said an improper thing, he became, in due course, president. But in all my talks with him—and they ranged over wide fields—I never heard him utter a word that might suggest the idea that he knew what a university should mean to a state or nation. He just knew what a university should mean to a state or nation. He just did and said what he was supposed to do and say. As far as he was concerned, the great institution simply marked time. Since Fielding H. Yost, the football coach, was a far more imaginative and enterprising person, and the football team continued to shed glory on all of us, the regents were, I suppose, satisfied with what was going on. There would be little use in recording these observations were it not for the fact that many American universities still have the sort of trustees who select this sort of man for president.

How it happens that I recall such a stiff and conventional official with amused affection remains to be explained. When I was first called to the inner sanctum of this man who held my immediate fate in his hands, I was slowly, kindly, and with dignity informed of the charges against me. The blow was softened by general commendation of my academic record. With warm approval President Hutchins attested the fact that I had not used my university position to instill into my students the virus of Socialism. You would have thought from the way in which this dignitary approached the subject that I was about to receive a medal or a promotion.

I was, naturally, forewarned by some inner sense that something quite different was to follow. Slowly and portentously the President drew from his desk a thick file of letters. "Look," he said. "All of these have come from alumni scattered all over the state. Some, even, are from distant outside points."

I wish I had that file now. There were hot letters from every town in which I had lectured. For the past year or two I had spent most of my weekends visiting the scattered industrial cities of Michigan to lecture upon the problems of the day from the Socialist point of view. In many places I had had in my audiences mayors, legislators, and business leaders. Often I had been asked questions by these men and had entered into arguments with them. Before my eyes I saw evidence that most of these hecklers were influential alumni of the university—and that they knew how to bring pressure to bear where it would count.

President Hutchins sat wearily watching me as I leafed through these exhibits. When I had finished he spoke sadly, like a man who is caught in a painful dilemma: "What can I do? I don't want to drive you out. But these men are leaders in their communities. We depend upon them for gifts to the university. Some of them are members of the legislature, and it is from the legislature that we get our appropriations. No matter what my feelings, I cannot disregard them."

This was only the first of many conferences. In the kindness of his heart President Hutchins clung to the last to the thought that I might be induced to change my ways and save him from the inconvenience of being forced to go contrary to his natural impulses. Why couldn't I just be a good boy and spend my Saturdays and Sundays having a good time? Surely I needed leisure for recreation. I could safely and comfortably remain a Socialist to the end of my days if only I would not go shouting about it where influential alumni and legislators would hear me. It sounded persuasively reasonable. But I was young.

In trying to recapture the scenes and emotions connected with events that separated me from the academic world back in years from 1907 to 1910, I now approach the climax—or what would have been the climax if the whole affair had been more important to me. My interviews with President Hutchins, who unwillingly was forced to represent the will of the regents and alumni, mounted in emotional tension. But the strain was on the president's feelings rather than on mine.

The last time that I saw the good man he exhibited many signs of discomfort. I was not at all surprised when he finally looked at me fixedly and exclaimed: "Young man, do you realize what I have been going through? Many a night recently I have not been able to sleep because I was so worried about whether I am doing the right thing in your case." I really felt sympathetic, and tried as best I could to administer comfort. By this time I had become genuinely fond of the man. He had one of the kindest of hearts. I said to him something like this: "Don't take this so hard. I know perfectly well that you would not willingly hurt me or anyone. You are simply doing what you are forced to do by powerful groups that are behind you and behind the university. I shall leave without the least feeling of resentment against you."

By this time it was known on all hands that I had accepted a position in a New York school that would give me the benefit of a salary considerably larger than the one with which I had had to content myself at the University of Michigan. In justice to President Hutchins I must record the fact that this change in the situation afforded him little comfort. He had a feeling that a wrong was being done, and his sense of justice was sufficiently strong to prevent him from taking solace to himself on the basis of any external circumstance.

By this time, of course, news of what was happening had leaked out about the campus and had even reached the Detroit papers. Until the official announcement was made, my friends seemed rather shy about discussing the matter. But sooner or later they all gave me signs of their understanding. Many of them, in fact, seemed more concerned about it than I was myself. To me it was an illuminating experience. To them it was a plain case of injustice.

The comedy that relieved the situation was furnished by the Detroit reporters. Detroit was, of course, our metropolis. It was there that we went for escape from the small-town limitations of Ann Arbor. There we saw plays and attended parties with a free-and-easy metropolitan atmosphere. Some of the more stiff and academic instructors even made the journey thither to enjoy the educational advantages of the red-light district. It was, for most of us, a big and glamorous place.

I shall not seek to deny that it gave me a thrill to have sundry reporters from the newspapers of this roaring city seek me out in my quiet quarters in order to get my side of what was for our quiet college town a scandalous affair. The young writing men came to my study—and my first impression was of their astonishment at seeing so many books. They were looking for the works of Marx, but what they found were those of John Milton and his contemporaries. I tried to interest them in the *Areopagitica*, telling them it was far more revolutionary than anything by the bearded Karl, but I got nowhere.

What they wanted to dig up was some dirt either about me or about the university. They inquired in all directions, but without any satisfactory results. They seemed so disappointed that I felt sorry for them, felt that their long trip had been for naught. But when I saw what they made of their meager interviews with me my sympathy was changed to admiration. Dressed up with shots of me and of my study, there were long stories that made the case seem far more important than it actually was.

The final scene of this simple drama, however, is one that pulls hard at my emotions even after all these years. The newspaper stories informed the student body of what was taking place. Students at a great state university are, apparently, a carefree and self-centered lot of young human animals. It had never occurred to me that the displacement of a comparatively unknown instructor would be much noted by them. And then one evening, while I was going on with my usual work, I heard a great murmuring and mounting clamor out on the lawn before my house. When I went out to investigate I found a crowd of students there. In a completely unorganized way they expressed their understanding and sympathy. At the end I stood on the porch and said something to them. Fortunately, I have forgotten every word of that speech—else I might be tempted to turn it into print at this late day.

And then occurred the final touch. When all the rest had turned lingeringly away, Don Henry remained and followed me into the house. Don was a freshman from Kentucky and a student in one of my classes, a queer, inward-turned, and overemotional lad. With face dark and lips trembling, he restlessly strolled about my study. Finally he burst out: "Look, Doc. You can't fool me. Someone is doing you dirt. There is someone in this town who has it in for you. Now, down in my country we have ways of dealing with such fellows. Don't get scared. I won't get you into anything. But you're my friend, see? And in Kentucky that means something. You don't need to do anything." At this point he pulled a revolver from his pocket. "You don't have to tell me a thing. But after a while as we go on talking you just bring that fellow's name into the conversation. I'll go out, and tomorrow morning that guy won't be around to bother you or anybody else." ∎

POLITICS AND LABOR

The American system

■ For a long time I have had at the tips of my fingers a little essay on this so-called free enterprise system of ours. The idea came to me on reading a release about Freedom's Foundation, Inc., a conclave of business big boys headed by a group of advertising men. This is an obviously well-heeled outfit put together for the purpose of granting annual awards for outstanding contributions to the better understanding of the American way of life.

The men who have planned this scheme of awards are opposed to Communism—and this is well. The prospect of having something like a hundred awards handed out each year to persons active in letters, arts, journalism, education, and business is also pleasant. The effect of these upon our national life, it is suggested, may be comparable with that of the Nobel prizes on international thinking.

I hope that I am not ignobly suspicious, but I confess that this whole project looks to me unpleasantly propagandistic. In its charter the organization is said to have been set up "to build and create an understanding of the spirit and philosophy of the Constitution and the Bill of Rights and our 'bundle' of indivisible political and economic freedoms inherent in the American way of life." Perhaps it is this picture of this indivisible bundle that rubbed me the wrong way. In human history and sociology nothing is indivisible. Without divisibility, in fact, there can be no progress. All through our happy college commencement season this notion about the fixity of the American system has been drummed into the hopeful graduates. I don't know why it is, but the finest philosophers, soldiers, statesmen and business leaders become pompous asses when they stand up to give advice to the youngsters who are saying farewell to their alma mater. Judging by newspaper reports, this year's crop of academic orations has been especially depressing. One of the minor sins of Communism has been the effect it has had upon American thinking and oratory. We have come to the point where all that an aspirant

243

to oratorical preeminence need do is denounce the Soviets, loudly laud the American system, and his speech is made. The implication is that most systems, the American and the Russian, are fixed and indivisible and the only distinction between them is that one is good and the other is bad. But the American spokesman is as much opposed to any change as anybody in Russia. He may shout for the "American system" of society, but he has unconsciously accepted the main feature of the Russian system of thought.

Now, all this is especially unfortunate at the present time. One of our prime difficulties in finding ways of cooperation with Western Europe is the wide misunderstanding of what the American system really is. In a very thoughtful column Marquis Childs recently summarized an editorial by Count Giuseppe Dalla Torre, editor-in-chief of *Osservatore Romano*, the official paper of the Vatican. According to Childs, the Italian editor "went so far as to say that the church would almost prefer Communism to capitalism if it were not for the atheism and materialism of the former." The count explained that the Communist notion of dividing all of the world's goods among "all of the world's inhabitants has much more in common with Christianity than a system which seeks to concentrate the major part of the goods in the hands of a few men."

American politicians ought to get through their heads the fact that this intelligent European has been taught by us that our system, the capitalist system, the free enterprise system, is a scheme permanently organized to "concentrate the major part of the world's goods in the hands of a few men." It is about time that we began to let the world know what goes on here.

Actually, there has never been a more flexible system than ours. Viewing the old plantation system of the South, the individualistic enterprise system of early New England, the great scheme of public-land division that underlay the development of the West or, finally, the wide range of projects whereby our business is now carried on, any onlooker would soon see that ours is not one system but a great maze of meshing and constantly changing systems.

It works. It works very well. Not perfectly, of course. Its blessings are unevenly distributed both in time and in space. There are some who are too rich while others are obviously too poor. The ups and downs of the business cycle are a trial that Congress does not yet take seriously enough. But the system is flexible. We have changed it. We are changing it. We shall continue to change it. That is why it works and will continue to work.   ∎

The lesson of Israel

∎ The United States was greatest when it was small and—theoretically, at least—weak. It was great because its people had nerve and imagination. All the experts of the day, all the realists, would have advised them to keep quiet, to knuckle under, to make the best terms they could. But they did none of these sensible things. They shouted something crazy about liberty or death and went in and won.

This age in which we live has been notable for official and public cowardice. It is doubtful whether there have ever been in the world at any one time so many cowards as during the past decade. I mean that there have been more people who didn't think what they believed in was worth fighting for. Or perhaps they just didn't believe in anything to start with. Think of all the countries that submitted to Hitler without putting up a fight. Except for a few valiant countries like Poland, Yugoslavia, Finland, and Greece, it was just taken for granted when the dictators began their march that little countries had no recourse but to lie down and be trampled over. In the Balkans great populations first accepted the Germans and then the Russians as conquerors. A correspondent reported: "The Czechs have a good deal of Micawberism in their make-up and a Schweik-like capacity to adapt themselves to almost everything." This Schweik-like capacity is the prime curse of our time. One wonders what existence under a tyranny can possibly hold that makes it so desirable.

To all people who have given up, given in, knuckled under, the example of Israel must come as a trumpet blast from a half-forgotten world of faith and courage. What these men and women have done is in the great tradition. We have seen played before our eyes a heroic epic. The reports in the press have had all the glamour of legend. David and Goliath, St. George and the Dragon have been enacted before our eyes in realistic terms.

There were, I suppose, something like 750,000 of these Jewish settlers. They had a reputation for cleverness, for intellectualism, for artistic talent. They were, moreover, famous for individualism. It was taken for granted that they would sliver into factions, that they could never organize in a big way. The Arabs, on the other hand, were supposed to number 40,000,000. They were known as men mighty in the ways of battle.

When it became evident that the Israelis intended to go through with their resolution to defend themselves, practically all of us thought that this would be another case in which a great power would calmly and ruthlessly march over a little one. We admired the courage of Chaim Weizmann's young fighting men and women, but we took for granted that their entry into battle was nothing more than a magnificent gesture. Millions of sympathetic persons must have had the thought that it would have been more reasonable, more realistic, to give in and acknowledge Arab rule.

But these people were not wise, reasonable, or realistic. They were of a surprising breed. They did not imitate the little nations in the path of Hitler. They acted like the British under Churchill, like the Americans under Washington. They stood up. And then a miracle happened! When men stand up instead of lying down, miracles have a chance to happen. David beat Goliath. St. George conquered the Dragon. I suspect that all the time Goliath had a weak heart and the dragon was nothing but a showpiece out of Macy's Thanksgiving parade. A breath of authentic courage was enough to do for both of them. And authentic courage was what those Israeli boys and girls had plenty of.

It may be that these Jewish fighters have done a much greater thing than to found a homeland for their few millions of people. Perhaps their deeds will waken the world from this miserable period of complacency and compromise. It may be that we are entering upon a new time when heroism will not appear foolish. It is only fear that makes tyranny possible. One bright example of courage may illuminate the world.

I intended to write of quite other things, of the Israelis as farmers and gardeners and planters of trees. Basically they are not fighting men. They are planting men and planning men. And that, too, serves as a tie between them and us. We have every reason to stand by them and be proud of them. ∎

Manhattan merry-go-round

∎ I first saw the island of Manhattan in 1903. I have lived on it since 1910. That is a long time, from William Howard Taft to John F. Kennedy. But in all that time I had not, until last week, taken the Circle Line trip around this fabulous outcropping of granite. Last Saturday this blank spot in my experience was filled in.

The journey down the Hudson and around the nose of the island, up along the busy East River, around through the Harlem, and then down the Hudson to complete the circle—it was all richly educational. I learned that in addition to having the tallest building in the whole world, we have the fastest elevators, the largest number of tunnels, the most expensive real estate, the richest university, and the largest cathedral of Gothic design.

All this information—and much more—was imparted over a loud-speaker system by an ingratiating and intelligent young gentleman. To do him justice, I should mention that he did point out one or two of the great city's disadvantages. He took pains to emphasize that in Harlem 4,500 people live in one block. He remarked that as many as 12,000 pupils are crowded into one school and that many school buildings serve for double sessions.

The fact that a spieler on an excursion boat spread such items for the attention of sightseers seemed to indicate some slight progress in the direction of intelligence. And along with the Empire State Building and the Chrysler Building, the city's housing projects were pointed out and explained.

Our bright little yacht carried about a hundred passengers. We had not proceeded far from our pier when I became conscious of the fact that I was participating in something of importance. The *Queen Mary* was sailing that day and we made a special detour to have a good look at her and her passengers. The young spieler explained that if she were upended beside the RCA building she would extend fifteen stories above the skyscraper. A man sitting next to me exclaimed, "This is the first time in my life that I have seen a boat bigger than a rowboat."

On one side of me sat a group of men from Caracas: a doctor, a lawyer, a student. On the other side I soon got acquainted with two young couples from South Dakota. They told me, to my surprise, that their summer's work is about finished this early in the season. In mid-summer their oats and corn are in and their fall plowing is done. So, about a week ago, the four of them had set out in a car, had come through Canada and seen Niagara Falls—and here they were looking at the *Queen Mary* and the New York skyline.

After a little shifting about I fell in with a man and two women from St. Clairsville, Ohio. The man is a bookkeeper for a coal-mining company; the ladies were his wife and a friend. These three have set themselves the task of seeing America. Last year they covered 5,700 miles of the West in eighteen days. This year they have been to Florida. They have now visited all but eleven of our fifty states. Others with whom I chatted are from Canada and Kentucky.

All these travelers had come to New York in their own cars. They were footloose and carefree. They were out to see the world and extract the best from it as they went. I tried, naturally, to dig down to their motives, to find what they were up to when they spent their money for cars, tires, and gasoline.

From the social point of view, it seems to me that the picture of millions of citizens on the road has terrific significance. Our nationalism is on the defensive. In these days you can't, on the basis of appearances, distinguish between a farmer and a city man. I should like to have photographs of my two young couples from South Dakota to prove my point. These four young people who finished their fall plowing early in order to see the world are bright, eager, and well dressed. In no crowd of people anywhere would you pick them out as having come from the country. The hicks have been quietly buried. Perhaps the old cliché-cushioned prejudices may, in the course of time fade away—both in town and country.

My bookkeeper friend from southern Ohio gave me my best lead as to what goes on in the minds of our out-of-town guests. He and his ladies were especially interested in the Bowery, the bright lights of Times Square, and seeing a broadcast—and the preceding evening they had had the great pleasure of being present, seeing how the show is put together, and sent out. So, I discovered, radio and TV play an important part in tying up city and country. The man playing the lead, I was told, had made the folks from Ohio very much at home in Megalopolis.

I sat watching my new acquaintance and wondering what question I could ask that would open him up, when suddenly he murmured, "I guess I'm just lucky."

"Why?" I asked.

"Oh," he went on, "I was thinking about those men we saw down in the Bowery. They rent rooms for thirty-five cents a night. I wonder what the rooms are like."

I tried to describe the accommodations in a flophouse. Then the bookkeeper went on: "Last spring we saw things just as bad down in Georgia—and right out in the country."

"Oh!" I prompted, "two kinds of slums. Country slums and city slums."

"Yes," he came back, "I guess that's right. But you seem to be doing something about yours. We saw those Alfred E. Smith Houses. But I couldn't see that they were doing much to change things in Georgia."

I let matters rest there. My amateur sociologist had traveled and seen and reached an important conclusion. ∎

A visit to the House of Commons

■ To me the Houses of Parliament are just about the most thrilling spot on earth. When I enter the dark old building, past the statues of Cromwell, Hampden, and Pitt, I feel that I am on sacred soil. It is here that our own first battles for political liberty were fought and the techniques of democratic government were perfected.

You enter the House of Commons through a great round nineteenth-century-style Gothic chamber called the Central Lobby. To get in touch with a friend in the House you send in a "green card." While you wait for your man to appear, you watch the members of Parliament hurrying past or coming out to greet constituents. It is a scene that is paralleled every day in Washington when our Senate and House are in session. The only difference is the wide margin that separates a British M.P. from an American congressman. The Britisher is not so obviously a politician. When he comes out to greet a constituent in the lobby, he does not prance or smirk or overwork his facial muscles in the effort to appear ingratiating. He acts and speaks soberly.

The first full-dress debate I attended during the final week of the last session of the British House was on the subject of home defense. It was a revelation of the parliamentary temperament and method. The House Office Under-Secretary outlined the plans of the government. When the opposition rose to speak, I thought that surely the sparks would fly. I had in mind, of course, our own Republicans trying to make hash of anything the Democrats have done or proposed. But practically nothing happened. Neither one tried to make out that the other was a horse thief. The critic emphasized that the opposition backed up the government 100 per cent in its support of general military affairs. He thought that the measures taken by the Home Office were very good. The public might have been made more alert to the dangers and more could have been done in the way of enlisting recruits, but on the whole the government had done rather well.

Now that is the way of British debate. I like it. It is reasonable, decent, intellectually honest. It is, moreover, the sort of discussion that is likely to lead to a useful conclusion.

That evening a Member invited me to dinner at his club. When I gave him my impression of the debate that I had heard, we soon found ourselves in the midst of a debate. He regretted the dullness, the flatness, the lack of fire. I praised the calmness, the even tenor, the broad fairness. In the end, I yielded sufficiently to remark: "I should think that these cool, fair-minded Britishers would be very unsatisfactory lovers. Imagine one of them remarking to his lady-love: 'I am not at all sure about this, but my opinion of you seems to be not at all derogatory. Don't you think that it is about time for us to consider a matrimonial relationship?' "

Later that evening I went to a party and there fell in with a pert and pretty girl from Yorkshire. I told her about my debate with the Member, concluding with my imaginary declaration of love. My lively young lady burst into laughter far beyond what seemed demanded by the occasion. When she regained her composure she explained: "That is exactly what happened to me. A young man, not yet a Member of the House, was in love with me. But when I had on an extra pretty gown he would say only that I didn't look too bad. And when he finally got to the point of making a declaration, he said: 'I think we could make a go of it. What do you say to our having a try?' "

I said to her: "Now, look. This young man was obviously honest and sincere. He would make a husband on whom you could depend, a husband for life." "That," replied the lively lass, "is precisely the trouble. For a little while one could endure him, but not for life. I'd rather go back to Yorkshire—or there is always America." ■

Instead of a political meeting

■ This afternoon, I received a rather smudgy postcard inviting me to attend what will doubtless be a rather stuffy political meeting. Animated by some streak of perversity, I straightway began to think of all the other things I could do with a wide-open afternoon before me.

This is perfect summer weather—bright sun, cool air, soft breezes. What I would like most would be to lie prone under a tree giving my eyes time to explore the myriad designs into which the blue sky is etched by the green leaves. Since they are forever changing with the movement of the sun, they keep me steadily employed. And since this tree is doubtless in my own garden, my birds are there taking deep drinks or splashing luxuriously in the pool—and singing, of course, just for me. That tirelessly tuneful mockingbird starts me thinking of how my flying friends have changed their migration habits. Then I look at the big gum tree and speculate on how this part of the world looked when it was planted. There is much to consider lying under a tree.

Or, instead of attending a meeting, I would like to sit with a pretty girl at a small table in a restaurant. She would make all sorts of alluring small arrangements as she sinks into her seat. There would be an inconsequential bag to be laughingly disposed of, a bonnet to be shoved ever so slightly this way or that, perhaps a touch of lipstick to be surreptitiously added. And then the grave question of drinks. The little lady drinks, of course, but daintily, selectively. A Manhattan, perhaps, or an Old Fashioned or a Whisky Sour. No long drink—no bourbon or Scotch. An air of intimacy is added when I, after careful consideration, choose the same. Selection of food leads us through the same sorts of tantalizing turns—seafood or steak or chops—or just a salad. The lady wants the mere suggestion of nourishment. As for dessert, she has definitely foresworn it. I see my evening coming to an end and unconsciously begin to scheme ways of prolonging it.

A ball game, of course, is not a meeting—even if it is attended by fifty or sixty thousand people. I am not bound to look or listen. The fact that these thousands of my fellow citizens are simultaneously having a good time merely adds to my pleasure. I can sit in the bleachers or in a box up at the Yankee Stadium or over at Ebbets Field. The sun streams down on that heavenly quadrangle of gleaming green grass, the members of the home team disperse to the stations where they will later perform deeds of heroism—and I pinch myself from pure happiness.

Or, while I am turning over in my mind the advisability of

attending that meeting, I recall some of the concerts which I have enjoyed at Lewisohn Stadium. In the first cool of the evening after a hot day, I have gone up in a bus or have rolled up in our own car. First, the thousands of boys and girls trooping up the hill give me a lift. Once I am seated in that wide semicircle of youth, perhaps under a full moon, I look about me. How beautiful they are—these quiet-speaking youths and maidens. I wonder if all that they say about juvenile delinquency can be true in a world which produces such wonderful people. And when the waiting crowd is stilled and the music bursts from the central shell, it is as if a window from heaven had opened.

Or my mind wanders to all the mountains in the world, to all those I have climbed and to all of the much greater ones I have left unclimbed. While people are sitting indoors listening to speeches in steadily worsening air, they could be in the open making a great discovery. What is revealed while a man is climbing a mountain is that the world looks different from different levels. It is not merely that trees and shrubbery grow less abundant and finally disappear. It is that the angle of vision is constantly changing. More and more a chap looks down on towns and streams and lakes. The air grows more rare. The circulation is correspondingly speeded up. Within limits, until you are finally put out of working order, you can think faster than you did at sea level. The tops of mountains are for inspiration, the lower levels of earth for rest, meditation, restoration.

Or, instead of going to a political meeting, I will start on an automobile journey. For full enjoyment, there will be at least two of us—perhaps three or four. I can never go through this experience without a thought of Charles Dickens. How he loved the stagecoaches and the roads. How the whips did crack! How the horses did go! What towns they passed! What cries echoed back and forth!

It is a thousand pities the old boy cannot be with us now. How he would love to glide along in one of our sports models with the wind catching at his long hair. What jokes he would crack with filling-station attendants! And instead of creeping a few miles along the crooked roads of nineteenth century England, he could glide hundreds of miles on the smooth highways of America.

Come to think about it, I shall not attend that meeting. ∎

Twelve times around the world

■ Many years ago I made my home in a green and mountainous corner of New Jersey and rattled into New York five days a week on a Delaware and Lackawanna train. One of the pleasantest features of this journey was crossing the lovely, lively Hudson River twice a day. Our time-saving tunnels now rob us of the thrills that accompanied this passage in the old ferryboat days.

One experience lingers in my memory. A schoolteacher friend of mine appeared one bright morning in a state of exultation. Instantly he exclaimed for all to hear, "I've gone around the world on a Hudson River ferry!" What he meant, of course, was that all of his tiny journeys by water, added together, would amount to 25,000 miles. When I asked what he had learned during his long composite journey, he seemed nonplused.

It was about forty-five years ago that this slight incident took place, but I am still a commuter. For twenty-six years I have journeyed almost every week from Delaware to New York and back. According to my timetable, this journey covers 118 miles—each week, 236 miles. In a year this adds up to nearly 12,000 miles, and in twenty-six years more than 300,000—or enough to carry a fellow more than twelve times about this planet of ours.

I am hesitant about putting to myself the question with which I embarrassed my friend so long ago. How much I have learned during the long tale of miles I dare not try to estimate. But one thing I dare say: The oft-repeated journeys have constantly increased in interest.

Coming to New York, I always read the *Times*. On the way home, I invariably relax over the *New Yorker*. Both of these weighty and important journals leave me plenty of time to observe both the landscape flashing past the windows and the manners and temperaments of my fellow passengers.

Modern engineering has robbed me of my view of the Hudson. We approach the metropolis, of course, through the inevitable tunnel. But the deprivation is compensated for by a seven- or eight-mile journey beside the lordly Delaware. With the passing of the years, the waterborne traffic on this great stream has steadily increased. Every time I slide along beside it, I see three or four boats plying up or down. It is like catching a breath of ocean air in the midst of routine, landbound occupations. Vessels bearing oil from Texas or Venezuela or untold things from Asia or Europe symbolize the wide, wide world.

During these twenty-six years I have observed the redistribution of industry along the mighty Pennsylvania's right-of-way. Great concerns like the Baldwin Locomotive Works, the Bethlehem Steel Company, the principal automobile plants, and many of New Jersey's well-known chemical concerns have moved from the cities to roomy sites out in the rural districts. Some of the most beautiful buildings that we have in this country were constructed to house these transplanted industries. And every now and then I glance up from my paper and catch glimpses of the University of Pennsylvania, Princeton, or Rutgers.

As we approach Philadelphia, my mind invariably plays a trick on me. The tower that rises from City Hall bears a mighty leaden statue of William Penn, the city's founder and patron saint. Ever since I have known the town, he has patiently stood there under his wide Quaker hat, keeping watch over his people. Whether I approach from the north or the south, I have seen that figure standing high with its authoritative air. Then I say to myself: "Old William is still there; his city is still safe."

Every Monday morning as my train pulls out of Newark, I see the towers of our metropolis rising into the blue. Our amazing complex of railways and highways begins to concentrate. The New Jersey Turnpike, the Garden State Parkway, the Pulaski Skyway, and half-a-dozen other systems all swerve toward a point to deliver their burdens of traffic to the little island of Manhattan. As I come rolling in each Monday morning, I see New York as the terminus of a mighty web of activity, and the realization of our physical achievement leaves me wrapped in silent wonder.

But I have not mentioned the most important feature of a commuter's life: his fellow passengers. I would be ungrateful if I failed to do justice to the conversationalists I have met between Delaware and New York. For they have poured into my ears the materials for many a column.

Most people are lonesome. Practically all of them yearn to be understood—and if you will listen, they will talk. Sitting there on the red plush cushion of the trains, I have had many a really exciting conversation. Once I even found a friend. We clicked while the train was still standing in the New York station, and we talked incessantly until I dismounted at Wilmington. This is one of the most important possibilities of a commuting career. When you sit down beside a fellow human being, you never know what will happen. ∎

Another War Between the States

∎ We in the North are constantly being urged to understand the feelings of our southern neighbors in connection with the Negroes. I, for one, have spent a good deal of time in the South. I have a deep appreciation of the graces of upper-class life in the southern states.

Now I want to tell my friends in Virginia and North Carolina that we northerners also have feelings and traditions. And we are the vast majority. When the chips are down, it will be our feelings and opinions rather than theirs that will prevail. This is one country, and the majority will rule. I have tried hard to understand the southerners. Now I want to give them a chance to understand me.

When I was a boy, between 1880 and 1890, the most exciting event in our family life was the occasional visit of my older brothers who had fought as northern soldiers in the long and dragging years of what we called the Civil War. My father had come to this country from Germany because of the failure of the Revolution of 1848. He had brought with him six lively and lusty boys as well as a couple of girls. That was in 1852. When the war started, nine years later, the oldest of these sons was eighteen and the second was sixteen.

The story of what happened in our house when Lincoln sent out his first call for volunteers is a moving one—and, I suspect, not unrepresentative of what happened all over the North. According to the tradition, Father called the oldest of his sons into solemn conference and said to them: "My sons, when we sold our farm in the old country and made the long and dangerous journey across the water, we had no intention of becoming citizens of a slave country. And I, for one, have not changed my mind. One member of this family must volunteer and fight for the Union. I am a little old for soldiering. I hope that one of you will go. But if you prefer to remain at home and run the farm, I will put on a uniform and try to play my part in the struggle for liberation."

As things turned out, both the eighteen-year-old and the sixteen-year-old volunteered and fought through the entire four years. The second one of the pair, my brother Chris, was seriously wounded in the fighting around Gettysburg, was captured, and spent a painful time in Libby Prison. When he would come to visit us, my younger brother and I were thrilled by the scars that crisscrossed his shiny bald skull. We would force him to tell over and over again the tale of how his horse was shot out from under him and he was forced to meet on foot the attack of mounted cavalrymen.

One of our veteran brothers lived in Wisconsin, the other in Florida. They visited our old home in Ohio only when the Grand Army of the Republic met in Cleveland or some other nearby city. Then there would be long evenings of talk. My brother and I would be overawed, but my father would proudly insist that the old stories of battle and imprisonment be retold. We would hear again how the Union had been preserved and the slaves set free.

That war, which we are now learning to call the War Between the States, was the worst conflict that had taken place in the world up to that time. And the boys who bore the brunt of the suffering on the northern side had no doubt about what it was fought for. Despite all the strange things that we are now hearing, there is no doubt about the fact that the forces in favor of liberation and union won the war.

The Thirteenth, Fourteenth, and Fifteenth amendments were immediately written and ratified. The privileges and immunities of citizens were not to be abridged as the result of laws passed by any of the states. The right of any citizen to vote was not to be denied. When the Supreme Court decreed that white people and black people shall have the right to attend the same public schools, it was obviously carrying out the intentions of the postwar Congress and of the soldiers who fought and won the great war. Anyone who opposes the application of the Court's decision is trying to wipe out the war, to reverse an important chapter in our history.

I should like to remind the citizens of the six or seven recalcitrant states of the Deep South that they cannot win in 1961 any more than they could in 1861. At that time the South had brave soldiers, clever officers, and a deeply emotional conviction that their cause was just. But they were a minority of the states and of the population. They simply could not win. The segregationists are now in a similar position. Already they have been deserted by five or six border states. In the end no more than seven or eight states will be left fighting the Court's decision.

We are entering upon the centenary of the great nineteenth century struggle. All of us had hoped that this would be a time of good feeling and reunion. Now some of the leading citizens of the segregationist states are acting precisely as their ancestors did a century ago. With deep emotion they are driving themselves into the support of a hopeless cause. If this thing continues to develop as it is going now, the anniversary celebration will be nothing but a postscript to the old war.   ∎

The beauty of change

∎ More and more of my friends are fleeing to Florida or California to escape our northern winter. And oftener and oftener they spend their postage money to send me invitations. Why am I so stubborn? Everyone else escapes from the snow and rain and deep-diving thermometer. What fun we could have rolling on the wide winter beaches! Am I wedded forever to my snow shovel?

No. What I am in love with is the rhythm of the seasons that has furnished the framework of my life for all of these long years. Florida and California are wonderful summer lands in wintertime. Long before the steam engine and airplane made rapid and easy travel possible, the English, the Germans, and the Scandinavians dreamed of Italy. Goethe, Shelley, Ibsen—what poetry they wrote about the lure of the sun and the South! *Kennst du das Land?* Even in slow and clumsy coaches the eighteenth century northern Europeans lumbered over the mountains in search of Italian peace and rest. This thing is deep in our mores. I don't expect to change the habits of our race. I aim merely to explain myself, to give my friends a chance to understand why I do not join their numerous procession.

The fact that I love winter is only a minor point. People who have never savored our northern season of snow and ice really don't know much of outdoor fun. In the first place, when the trees are stripped of leaves and the earth is covered with snow, the world has a compelling beauty that is like nothing else in human experience. At dusk, the sharp blue or purple shadows of the tree forms on the pink snow are really something to rave about. And when birds fly over, creating a moving picture of their lovely motion on the gleaming carpet below, they give me a thrill that I would not exchange for anything Italy or Florida or California has to offer. I recall that long ago I wrote of gliding that mile to the little red schoolhouse snugly tucked under a buffalo robe in a highly decorated sleigh with the horses prancing high. Winter is beauty. Winter is fun.

But this is not really what I want to write about. What I set out to say is that it is the changing of the seasons that makes life lively and good. This year has been wonderful, and I have been closer to the moods of Nature than ever before. In fine weather, we have been reading and writing and taking our afternoon drinks under the trees or out on the sunny lawn. We have made closer observations than usual, have been nearer to all the growing, living, shining things.

The seasons have been late and cool and better watered than usual. The trees have kept their deep green color right through the summer. The roses have bloomed on and on as if June were lasting forever. Even now, in October and November, the great blossoms are bursting as if it were spring. All the flowering trees and shrubs have come later than usual and have remained bright and colorful for longer periods. The birds, too, have entered into the spirit of the thing. If we were to have eternal spring, they were willing to go along with the gag and stay with us longer than is provided by the expert ornithologists and sing their mating songs when usually they have gone silent.

Now we are having autumn—and what an autumn! One of our

lawns is surrounded by a rough stone wall that maintains at an upper level my diminishing attempt to raise vegetables. In midsummer we planted along this wall and above it generous quantities of marigolds and zinnias, and now we are enjoying our reward. There are floods of golden beauty pushing from below the rough stones and falling down from over them. Here and there these billows of gold are broken by cliffs of pyrocantha with their masses of deep red berries. In such an environment it is practically impossible to write an unfavorable book review or to think deprecatingly of anyone or anything. Life is treating us too well.

It seems to me that all the seasons have come up to an extra high standard this year. Spring has been richer, summer longer, and now autumn has maintained the standard by being particularly rich and fine. And there is one sort of beauty that has been important to me all my life and that has been particularly wonderful throughout this season. I am thinking of the effect produced by the low-slanted rays of the afternoon sun striking across the rich and even verdure of the lawns. As the day grows mellow and evening comes on, they produce a green-gold that is the liveliest experience reported to the human eye. Anyone who has the opportunity to look on as the afternoon sun adds golden liveliness to the deep green of the grass has enjoyed one of nature's most precious privileges. It seems to me that this year this supreme effect has been offered more often than usual and developed to a more exquisite degree.

What I started out to say is that the changing seasons of this Temperate Zone are what keep life lively and good. Someone should publish an anthology of the changing seasons. A good editor could probably find as much poetry—and as good—about the changing beauties of the North as has been poured into the lap of the luscious South by Goethe and Shelley and the other seekers-of-the-sun. As for me, in very simple prose, I hail our northern life of change and chance and all the varied experiences of heat and cold with all the liveliness that they inspire.   ∎

Ring a bell for Christmas

■ It was a couple of thousand years too soon for bombs or rockets as Mary and Joseph plodded along that dusty road on the way to Jerusalem. Israel was a mere colony instead of a proud, young, independent nation. Bethlehem was a mere hamlet where there wasn't even a motel or a diner. It was located, moreover, in dreary desert country, with not a tree or a decent bush anywhere about.

The so-called Wise Men were, of course, better off than the other folks. That is the proof of their wisdom. The shepherds came gawking after that wanton, wandering star, but they had brought nothing—not even a lock of wool to keep the baby warm or a measure of milk to stay his hunger. And the Wise Men—after all, they were not so all-fired smart. To a just-born baby they brought "gold, incense and myrrh." The whole thing, the plot, the dialogue, the symbolism, was Oriental from start to finish. It is a good thing for us to recall.

Christmas is a strange sort of celebration to grow out of Christianity. In fact, the whole history of this European-American religion is a strange one when looked at from the point of view of ceremony, custom, and costume. I take for granted that during their first three centuries the humble, outcast Christians lived sparsely and had their eyes firmly fixed on the gorgeous life they would savor in the other world. Then the Emperor Constantine took over, and under the new manager the show took on a different tone. The mass was performed with gorgeous costumes not at all suggestive of Mary and Joseph squatting there on that flinty road. If they had any relation to the Christian tradition, they were probably like the robes of the Wise Men who were smart enough to be rich in the midst of the desert. Anyway, Christianity became bright and colorful, even gay. In northern Europe it took over the heathen Druid celebration of the winter equinox, the glad time when the days slowly began to lengthen. It was the time of returning light—hence the candles, which really have nothing to do with the Christian tradition.

And then came Protestantism. An old Reformationist like me cannot pretend that it was bad. But it had this peculiarity—at least at first: Its followers were so sternly bent on forcing religion back to its original meaning that they leaned over all the way toward the stiff and sorrowful side. There had been too many holidays. That was one reason why the Industrial Revolutionists were against the old religion. But now, like most real revolutionists, these tough old changers of things abolished entirely the seasons that had been set aside for fun. Until they invented our rather solemn Thanksgiving Day, our New Englanders, whom we praise so much, had no provision in their calendar for so much as the cracking of a smile. To celebrate the Yuletide was a crime punishable by law. Since those days Protestantism has been working its way back toward some of the things it condemned and abolished in the overenthusiasm of its early days. Now the sternest religionists decorate trees and squander their money on gifts.

We are now told by legions of perfectionists that the sacred holiday has gone too far, that it has become commercialized, that it is nothing but an orgy of advertising and selling. There are so many things to buy, pack, carry, and send that many of us are driven frantic, and the love and pleasure are driven out of a celebration that formerly was meaningful and beautiful. But I say, "Down with all such picayune complainers!" In the first place, what sight is more gladdening than hosts of people in great stores spending their money buying gifts for other folks—especially for children?

As a matter of fact, the holiday season is a sort of vacation from the practice of what are considered the standard virtues of a commercial society. For the time we do not buy just what we need or with any purpose of making a profit or acquire it necessarily at the lowest price or wrap it and send it in the cheapest way. It is a fine, generous, outgoing time. We shall receive gifts, but that is not what occupies our thoughts. Our minds are set rather on giving—especially to the young. That may be good in countless ways. It will do more than evoke the longed-for smile that gives so much pleasure to the adoring adult. It may even give a boy or girl the idea that the human race has virtues that overbalance its vices. It may plant solidly in some youthful mind a bracing faith in humanity that will stand him in good stead in time of need.

In my part of Delaware, a lively campaign is going on, centered about the slogan, "Put Christ in Christmas." I am a little suspicious of the persons who are paying for this effort, but within limits I am willing to go along with them. Teachings of Jesus, judiciously selected and wisely put into practice, would guide the human race out of many of its troubles. Love rather than hate, cooperation instead of enmity, understanding rather than blank individualism—surely in that direction lie healing and help. If all the "Christians" who pretend to believe in these things would live up to their creeds, we could do some plain speaking to the Mohammedans and Buddhists and other neighbors to the East.   ■

My eighty-first birthday

■ I expected to slip past this birth date without paying it any mind. But people have been sending me letters and cards—even from 'way across the ocean and the continent. If a chap has been fed and clothed and sheltered all these years, I suppose he owes the world some sort of answer to its questions.

Physically, socially, and psychologically the world I had about me as a boy was quite different from the one I look upon now. In those days of the 1880's I attended a one-room schoolhouse with some twenty-five other children. On our way to this simple institution we walked a mile past isolated farmhouses, gathering our procession of fellow learners as we went. In the winter we were warmed during our studies by a big-bellied wood-stove. In summer we spent our leisure periods running wild in the deep woods where the pawpaws and the hickory nuts grew. At home, with Father and Mother as teachers, we learned the basic arts of life on the farm. It was a simple life, but a good one. I am ready to maintain against all comers that the education imparted to us was as good as any that is now available anywhere.

We had, of course, no automobiles, no telephones, no gas or electricity (except in the form of lightning), no radio, no television, and no Sputniks. We read, we talked, and we sang. Of a winter evening there would be a bowl of apples and a plate of cookies on the table, and the family would be gathered round—Father with his paper and Mother and children with their books or handiwork. Or perhaps we would form a circle about the fire and Father would tell stories of his boyhood in Germany—perhaps going over our favorite tale about the German Revolution of 1848. The other possibility was that Father and Mother would be singing. I can assure you that when they started an old song no one felt the need of entertainment piped in from Hollywood or New York.

If one of my older brothers happened to drop in on a journey from the West, where they were laying low the forests and opening up the frontier, the only tolerable subject would be the Civil War. Then only fifteen or twenty years in the past, it still lay like a great shadow over the land. The recent world wars have been more terrible in some ways, but in their profound effects upon the people they were not comparable with the horrible struggle between American brothers. What I recall most vividly in connection with these conversations with veterans about the war is the cheerful assurance of all concerned that the race problem was forever settled. We had won the war, and the amendments to the Constitution had been adopted. The Negroes were the equals of anyone. There was nothing more to be done. It was these easy assumptions that led to the tragedies now being reported in our papers.

I came just in time to witness the great transformation from hand tools to power machines on the American farm. The mowing machine was coming into use during my boyhood. But now and then I did see a field cut by hand, and my father prided himself on his expertize with the ancient scythe. I recall the first reaper that came into our neighborhood. It had a long cutting-knife with a wide platform behind it, and the grain was pushed over and ejected by great fans that revolved as the horses plodded along. Then the binder followed with bands made of long rye straw that had been made limber and tough by being soaked in the brook during the past night. It took three men and a pair of horses to do a very slow job.

I recall how proud I was when for the first time I was allowed to help with the binding. Several times I wielded a flail with the men as we threshed oats or wheat precisely as the patriarchs did in Israel three thousand years ago. Four or five of us would throw bundles of grain in the middle of the threshing floor and then form a circle about them and bring the heads of our flails down in rhythmic rotation till the grain was all beaten out of the heads. The first threshing machines that came during my early days were operated by horsepower. The animals went mechanically in a circle like a merry-go-round—and so furnished the required power.

Within my time we have come from manpower and horsepower to steampower, to internal combustion power, electric power, and atomic power. The population of the United States has catapulted from 50 millions to 170 millions. And, to crown it all, this busy, booming nation has been tied in with a busy, booming world. In my boyhood we had no United Nations and no need of one.

I recall a day when President Garfield, driving past our house in his top-buggy, stopped his horse to exchange a few friendly words with my father. And then there was that night when a neighbor, lumbering by in his wagon on his way from town, shouted over our gate, "Cleveland has been elected!" And I have even more reason to recall Father's deep-toned response: "Thank God! At last we have an honest President." The tools we use grow better and better, but the men we send to Washington seem to remain about the same.

■

Those good old days

■ A long time ago—in fact, away back in the 1880's—my brother and I were given some intimation of the better things of life by reading a weekly journal called the *Youth's Companion*. This high-class publication was sent out from Boston and carried by train, canalboat, stagecoach, and pony express to the farthest and wildest points of the frontier. I vividly recall what a fresh element it brought into our life on the farm out in Ohio when some neighbor who had come past the post office at the "center" threw the tightly wrapped little parcel over our front gate. How carefully we would cut the wrapper to avoid tearing any of the pictures or paragraphs of the reading matter! There were stories of the West and stories of the East, stories of adventure and little essays on morals. In those days there were no movies, no television, no radio, very little travel. Every printed word seemed wonderful.

This paper for young people began publication on April 16, 1827, during the regime of John Quincy Adams, and sent out its last number while New England's Calvin Coolidge was sitting quietly in the White House. For the last ten days, my leisure time has been spent in reading a book called *Youth's Companion*. Four former editors of the good old paper have selected for republication what they consider the most representative stories, poems, essays, and illustrations published during that exciting century. What they have saved from oblivion fills 1,140 pages. As a chapter in American history, it is priceless.

The *Youth's Companion* was always very much of a New England product. Yankee authors were played up, and one usually found them taking a quiet and refined pleasure in the superiority of their part of the country. A traveler relating her experiences in passing through Pennsylvania acknowledges that the streets of Philadelphia were surprisingly clean, but goes on to relate that the young people of Pennsylvania were growing up in "ignorance and sin." Writing to a Massachusetts Sunday-school class, she exclaimed, "Think of the privileges you enjoy!" This appeared in the era of Andrew Jackson.

During the early years, at least up to the Civil War, the *Companion* paid a good deal of attention to sundry reforms. There are articles and sharply slanted stories against war, slavery, tobacco and, especially, the demon rum. Snuff taking is also referred to in derogatory terms, and every now and then there is a crack at the spittoon. This vessel, so necessary for the protection and preservation of rugs and floors, was obviously regarded as a symbol of the bad habits of the lower classes.

But what fascinates me most about this series of stories and articles reaching from 1827 to 1927 is the light they throw upon our own much discussed subject of juvenile delinquency. The young people who read the *Companion* were expected, of course, to be models of behavior. But during the early days, let us say from 1827 to about the time of the Civil War, the young men of the lower classes were the objects of grave concern—even as they are today.

On June 28, 1849, the *Companion* published a short editorial entitled "Juvenile Incendiaries." It dealt, of course, with what was going on about the highly cultured city of Boston. "The burning of Mr. Bemis's barn in Watertown," begins this piece of adult wisdom, "which has been found to have been purposely set on fire by boys, and the detection of a fire in Park Street Church in Boston has led me to think that if boys were better instructed in the consequences of such conduct they would not dare to commit such wickedness and expose themselves to imprisonment or death."

The second young scamp whose vile deeds have been recorded for the edification of succeeding generations was a New Yorker, and we owe the account of his escapades to a story in the highly respectable New York *Post* that was reprinted in the *Companion* of February 24, 1859:

"Here is a specimen of the kind of boys that are not infrequently found in the low streets of such cities as New York and Boston. Most of these owe their wickedness to drunken, swearing, desperate parents, and to young companions who are old in vice and crime. The boy whose history is given below was arrested by a New York police officer for some misdemeanor. He was called Little Johnny, and although he had just commenced his course of crime, his history even thus far is a fearful one." The account that follows fully justifies this ominous introduction. Johnny was able to assemble a gang that beat up the police. In prison he was so actively vicious that the officers were glad to get rid of him.

What people said about young rascals like this one was very much like what similar people are saying about good-for-nothings today: There has been a loosening of old rules. Strange people have come in from strange parts of the world. There has been a backwash from the ill-regulated frontier. What else can you expect in such a changing and unsettled time? What we seem to have discovered is that what we call juvenile delinquency is pretty much a static affair and worldwide affair. ∎

The new world of the big snow

■ The long season from Thanksgiving to Easter may be rather dull or even plain unpleasant. There can be fog and rain and sleet and the sort of cold that goes with the damp. But the end of 1957 and the beginning of 1958 has been the opposite of all of this. It is sharp, fine, brilliant, inspiring. Even if the fugitives from north of the Mason-Dixon line had found in the semitropical South what they had paid their good money to secure, they would have made a bad bargain. For what they have deserted is so lovely and inspiring that words seem pale and feeble when one tries to describe it.

A real blanket of snow like this one of ours—ten inches here in Delaware—transforms the world. You wake in the morning and see the land an unbroken stretch of smooth and gleaming white. Sometimes after a fall of snow the trees are outlined in feathery softness by the clinging crystals. But this time the air was cold. The temperature was almost zero. The snow was fine and light and constantly swirled into changing drifts by the restless wind. None of it adhered to the trees or shrubs. The design of every limb or branch or twig was sharply outlined in black against the endless stretch of shining white. It was as if suddenly, without benefit of airplane or train, we had been whisked away to a different sort of universe—different earth, different planets—yes, even a different sky.

I have spoken of this new and astonishing world as white. But this description does it less than justice. All day as the sun swings round his mighty orbit the colors of the bright earth blanket are changing. Just after sunrise and immediately before sunset, the onlooker is furnished his most exquisite prismatic experience. As the sun's rays slant at sharp angles early and late, each tiny crystal acts as a kaleidoscope, and the vast expanse we conventionally refer to as white turns to the gaudiest display of dainty hues. Instead of being simple white, the snow is pink, rose, blue, purple, yellow—all these shades and others for which I have no names are blended in endless variations. How can a man—or especially a woman—spend good money to go to Florida and miss such an indescribably exquisite show?

When I see the children rolling and tumbling and shouting with glee over their caves and forts and snowfights and snowmen, I realize that the winter transformation affords a psychological release. Because the world looks so different, feels so different, induces such new sensations, we are cleansed of our routine sets of reactions. Young people now miss the fun my generation had with horses and sleighs. But now they have all the delights that stem from skiing. Gains and losses seem to be pretty well even.

This great fall of snow has seemed to bring us unusually close to the birds and squirrels and other little beasts. The Wildlife Commission of the State has called upon the people everywhere to set out food where it can be easily found and eaten by the little wild creatures of various sorts. Our regular feeding station has never been so popular. The starlings, the sparrows, the cardinals, the junkos, the titmice, and nuthatches come crowding round the moment the grain or suet or breadcrumbs are put out for them. We feel as if they belonged to the family—as if they were our semidependent livestock.

The extreme cold has made us especially sympathetic with the little wild things. We have placed in the trees a number of birdhouses that are intended to furnish protection for some of them. But thus far they have scorned our well-meant endeavors. Flocks of sparrows and starlings spend their nights in some forsythia bushes over against the vegetable garden. The only help they want is the box full of the right sort of food. That they do appreciate; and by furnishing it, we are to a limited extent entering into their lives.

Edith has long yearned to be snowbound, and this time she has nearly had her dream come true. For a couple of days automobile traffic, except for scrapers, snowplows, and police cars, came to an end. Church services, dinners, card parties, all sorts of routine engagements were abrogated by common consent. The chief use of the telephone was to seek release from social bargains.

Under these circumstances we have had an experience that may suggest a lesson appropriate to these feverish times. For two days no one came to visit us and we visited no one. And those particular days were among the most satisfactory we have ever experienced. Since we had no newspapers, we read books. I turned back to the essays of Robert Louis Stevenson, which I read with my students many years ago. What beautiful, beautiful writing! What gentle wisdom! In this quiet room it all came back to me.

And then Edith happened to ask a question about a painting by Reynolds—and so we pulled down from its shelf an old book of reproductions that we had forgotten. There was, too, the recording of Beethoven's Ninth by Toscanini and a really fine performance of *Rigoletto* on television. Being cut off from outside disturbance gave a special depth to all these experiences.   ∎

The 20-20 vision of Elmer Davis

∎ In the course of a long life I have said farewell to many a good man. One of these made a habit of saying to his friends: "There is no one who cannot be replaced. No matter how good a man is, someone will be found who will do his job better." Generally I have found this to be true. No matter how efficient or how useful a man has been, after he was gone the world has wagged on. One of life's useful lessons is that no one is irreplaceable.

If ever there was an exception to this rule, if ever there was a man for whom no substitute can be found, it was Elmer Davis. As writer, radio and television broadcaster, news analyst and interpreter of current history, he functioned with a special sort of integrity. It was as if the very tones of his voice carried his guarantee. His choice of words constituted a running interpretation. His looks, stance, manner, tone gave assurance of complete honesty and profound understanding.

Elmer Davis came from the American heartland. His father was a banker in a small Indiana town. He spent his youth among the Midwestern common people and attended a little Midwestern college. You have the feeling through all his writing and broadcasting that he has faith in the ordinary folks from whom he sprang. His constant return to the Founding Fathers is the result of an early bent. In his youth, and in his part of the country, the writers of the

Constitution seemed very near. Elmer Davis, and Abraham Lincoln came from the same wide valley and had the same deep faith in the American people's ultimate devotion to liberty.

One fine thing about this man was that he spoke with a sense of power. You felt as you listened that in the end he would be on the winning side. There were times during the McCarthy era when un-American reactionaries swarmed about the Capitol and even the President of the United States seemed cowed by their clamor. But when you listened to the sharp, countrified accents of Elmer Davis, your faith rushed back. This man's calm analysis gave you reassurance.

Too little has been made of Elmer Davis's scholarship. In general, the antilibertarians are ignorant fellows. They use the names of our great men, but have no idea of what these men thought and no understanding of what they did. Mr. Davis led a busy newsman's life. He worked for The New York *Times* and for two of the great broadcasting systems. During the war he had charge of the three thousand employees of the Office of War Information. He was a busy and successful man at the very hottest spots in the world of news reporting. In his book *But We Were Born Free*, however, he showed a profound insight not only into American and British history but also into the affairs of the ancient world. He might have been one of our greatest historians, but he chose rather to fill a worrisome and difficult spot in one of our history's greatest struggles.

The notion that many people have that McCarthyism is dead and buried is deceptive and dangerous. It is true that in the form given it by the late junior senator from Wisconsin it has been defeated, and for help in this defeat we owe a debt of gratitude to the great newscaster who has so recently gone from us. But McCarthy did not stand alone. He had rich and influential backers. In the Senate he was supported by men who, because they were more moderate and decent than their leader, will, in the end, be more influential. McCarthy is gone, but Walter and other companions have inherited a good part of his mantle. The know-nothing attack on the Supreme Court seems to gather strength from strange sectors of our population. We need, as desperately as ever, men like Elmer Davis.

Reasonable men devoted to good sense and moderation have

always been at a disadvantage in public debate. Their arguments generally lack the lightning flash that often gives the thrusts of the totalitarians their flash and their bite. In his book Elmer Davis quoted an article he wrote twenty years ago: "To admit that there are questions which even our so impressive intelligence is unable to answer, and at the same time not to despair of ability of the human race to find, eventually, better answers than we can reach as yet—to recognize that there is nothing to do but keep on trying as well as we can, and to be as content as we can with the small gains that in the course of ages amount to something—that requires some courage and some balance."

This book was written in the shadow of McCarthyism. With cowardice so disgracefully common in the press, in the government, even in some of the universities, he called for courage. On his last page he went back to the battle of the Philistines as reported in the Book of Samuel. Facing what seemed an unconquerable foe, the followers of the Lord cried out: "Who shall deliver us out of the hand of these mighty Gods?" And then, realizing that outside help was unavailable, they braced themselves and said to one another, "Be strong, and quit yourselves like men."   ■

Washington and Lincoln

■ At first glance, these two February heroes of ours seem as different as two men could be. Washington was an aristocrat. He was born, of course, an Englishman and was bred from his youth up as a member of the British ruling class. He had the mind and manners of the Virginia elite. With these went the sense of responsibility that was characteristic of the British landed aristocracy. He and others like him were charged with guarding the church, the state, the educational system and the welfare of the common people. Anyone who reads his life must be struck by the amount of time and energy he regularly devoted to public affairs. And in his personal relations, not only did he look after the welfare of his slaves; he was also concerned about the fortunes of many neighbors and acquaintances who had a hard time getting started in the new country. This was not mere charity. As an upper-class man, Washington felt bound to take the lead in his part of the colony and to see to it that things went well in the lives of his friends.

Lincoln, of course, was born in a different sort of place and was acted upon by a sharply contrasted set of ideas and influences. I hope that no one will go away with the notion that our Civil War leader was a lower-class sort of fellow. He was far from that. The Lincolns of Massachusetts were of the best Puritan stock. The branch that produced the northern leader happened to wander down to Virginia, up to Kentucky, across Indiana, and into Illinois. But it never lost its quality.

When Washington was twenty-one, he enlarged his estate by the purchase of 552 acres. Before the end of the same year, he was appointed by the governor and the Provincial Council as adjutant with authority over one-fourth of the territory of the colony. The governor and the council agreed on "the great advantage of an Adjutant in this country instructing the officers and soldiers in the use and exercise of their arms, in bringing the militia to a more regular discipline, and fitting it for service, besides polishing and improving the meaner people."

When he was twenty-one, Lincoln trudged with his father and his stepmother from Indiana into Illinois. There he helped build the log cabin that was to serve as their home and split enough rails to fence a ten-acre plot. Soon afterward he hired himself out at $12 a month and produced the timber required to build a boat. In 1832, when our hero was twenty-three, a frontier army was raised to protect the settlers against the Indian Chief, Black Hawk. In the army, described by William Cullen Bryant as "a hard-looking set of men, unkempt and unshaved," young Abraham Lincoln, without ever having had any sort of military training, was elected captain of his company. He was given this honor not merely because he was the tallest man in the lot and could lick any of his comrades, but because the others had faith in his fairness and friendliness.

These two men, so different in origin, environment, and training, both turned out to be genuinely great. They were tested in great wars that came near to wrecking their country. The parts they played happened to be opposite. Washington was at the head of the army in the field, and pushed through to victory despite all the failings of the civilian authorities who were in control at the capital. Lincoln, on the contrary, sat in the capital and tried desperately to counterbalance the failings of his generals. In the end, both won by the display of enormous will power, intelligence, and skill in the management of people.

There was something very similar in the devotion with which these two were rewarded by the common people. When Washington journeyed from Mount Vernon to New York for his first inauguration, great crowds of shouting, singing, flag-waving citizens met him at every stop. When Lincoln's corpse was transported by train from Washington to Illinois, practically the whole population stood weeping by the way.

As the years have gone by, there has come about a sharp contrast in the popular attitude toward these two heroes. Washington has taken his place as a supreme military strategist and a statesman of notable wisdom, but a rather cool and distant leader. If he has had a failing, it has been merely in the control of words. There was more dignity than warmth in his speaking and writing. Lincoln, on the contrary, probably excelled any other statesman in his mastery of speech. With the gifts of a poet, he was able to interpret his sense of democracy in terms that went to the hearts of the common people around the world. If today someone were to take an opinion poll on the matter, I feel sure that our Civil War President would stand higher than the Revolutionary General. It seems to me that there is an injustice involved in this popular judgment. In the course of time, more knowledge and deeper understanding may swing the balance the other way so that these two really great men will stand even in popular estimation.   ∎

Coexistence on a railroad train

■ For six months I have been hearing about a neat little bargain agreed upon between the U.S.A. and the U.S.S.R. Once a month we publish in Moscow 50,000 copies of a magazine about our country called *America*. It is said that the copies are grabbed from the newsstands within a few minutes after they have been placed on sale. The Russians avail themselves of their reciprocal privilege by sending out from Washington 50,000 copies of an English-language monthly called *USSR*. I have occasionally seen a copy of *America*— and I must say that our boys are doing a first-class job of editing and printing. But up to this week I had not seen a copy of *USSR*.

Every now and then I fill this space with tales of my experiences as a commuter. On my weekly journeys between New York and Delaware astonishing things keep happening. What occurred last week was one of the most charming incidents of the lot. I had made myself at home in the rather crowded train in the Pennsylvania Station when a tall, slender, well-dressed, and altogether elegant young gentleman came along and asked in a pleasant foreign accent whether he might occupy the seat beside me.

Naturally, I invited the youth to dispose of his rather spiffy baggage and make himself comfortable. I was reading an extra good story in my *New Yorker* and was not, therefore, inclined to pay attention to my seatmate. As the train slid along toward Newark, I noticed that he was carefully examining some of our more splurgy and popular weeklies—*Saturday Evening Post, Life, Look,* and some others. A young man reading *Life* or *Look* is nothing special. So I read my *New Yorker* and left the stranger to his own devices.

As we approached Philadelphia, I finished my tale and began to look at my companion. It dawned on me that there was something peculiar about him. He was obviously an intellectual. He had the clothes, the looks, the manners—everything. And I began to see that he was not really reading his popular picture journals. He was examining them from a technical point of view. He was looking at the captions, the arrangement of photographs, the make-up in general. He was obviously a journalist.

While the train was standing in the Thirtieth Street Station, Philadelphia, I finally was pushed by curiosity into opening a conversation. There were only a few minutes left. It was necessary to work fast. And my friend was shy, reticent, backward. When I spoke to him he blushed as a girl is supposed to blush but doesn't. Finally I got from him the confession that he was the editor of a magazine. Then came the information that it was published in Washington. Next followed the item that it has a circulation of 50,000. Finally the youth capitulated: the journal was called *USSR!*

I blurted out: "But I am the editor of the *New Leader!* Look! This is dramatic. We are enemies. You represent Communism and we are against it." And I reached over and grasped the hand of my enemy. It seemed wonderful that we should be there together in that railway seat and talking quietly in that friendly way. But to the young Russian there was nothing wonderful about it. When I took his hand he seemed to shudder—as if I had had some sort of disease.

Next I reached into my suitcase for a copy of the last number of the *New Leader,* and said: "Here. Take this. There are a number of interesting things in it. You will find it at least as exciting as the *Saturday Evening Post.* For a moment he took our magazine (with David Ben-Gurion's picture on the cover) and held it gingerly in his hand. Then something seemed to happen inside him. Trembling, he held the paper toward me and said: "Please take it away. I don't want it."

That is about all there is to this incident. The conductor was calling out, "Wilmington!" The young Russian had given me his name and told me that I could get a copy of his publication at any American News Company stand. Then he remarked, "You live out in the country?"

I said, "Yes, my wife will meet me with the car and we will go 'way out in the country."

He looked envious as he murmured, "That will be very nice." I wished that I could take him with me.

Just one more note. My young man seemed worried for fear I should take his picture magazines as an index of his taste. In the few words that he said about the *New Yorker* he proved his point.

That is the tragedy of this little tale. When I returned to New York, I found *USSR* on the first newsstand I came to. It was full of gorgeous pictures—even like *Life* and *Look*. But the literary text—except for some sports notes—is unbelievably naïve. I could not shake off the feeling that I had read something like this before. At last I picked out the recollection. The English—or American—style of these Russians is like that of the children's books published in this country about a century ago. And my friend, this man of taste and discrimination, must spend his days and nights over it. ∎

The tired and the nontired

∎ All this was started in my old head when I surrendered my foothold in New York and moved out to live in a corner of my Delaware garden. For twenty-six years I have had an apartment on West Twelfth Street just a step from Fifth Avenue. Union Square, the *New Leader* office, Washington Square, and all the Greenwich Village eating places were no more than a few blocks away. On any street along which I might wander I would meet friendly neighbors. It was a charmingly comfortable and convenient place to live. It had all the advantages of a great metropolis combined with many of those usually associated with country living. Every Monday morning I rolled up to the great city and every Thursday afternoon I commuted back to my garden.

Nothing can last forever. For a long time argumentative termites had been gnawing at my beautiful existence. Life would be so much easier, so much more convenient, if I would stay in my garden, forget about the trains, the subways, the taxis, the endless telephone calls. So I gave in, blinked a few times, and ordered a moving man to go into action. I have now spent a couple of weeks in the country. And—perhaps prematurely and inadvisedly—I am drawing conclusions about the change.

The first conclusion I have reached as a result of my initial period of hard labor is that we must revise our theory of the division into classes. The basic distinction—the one that marks the difference between those who rule and those who are ruled—is not the line between the rich and poor but between the tired and the nontired.

I am speaking, of course, from experience. In the course of a couple of weeks, I have moved from one class to another. During my first days on the land I happened to tackle a couple of rather tough jobs. First there was a big willow tree to chop down and chop up. The work was made harder by the fact that my tools consisted of a hatchet, an ax, a handsaw, and a spade. Digging out the roots took me back to tales of the frontier. Next the lawn had to be rolled with a rather substantial cement roller, and three truckloads of mushroom soil had to be scattered far and wide. All this, of course, is precisely the activity I like. It is what I was born and bred for. I should never have left the farm. I never belonged in the city. Work that strains the muscles and makes the skin tingle is the best sort of fun.

But there is another side to this tale. The first day after my work on that willow tree, I was sleepy. The next morning I was stiff. And at the end of my second day, I found that my tastes and desires were rapidly being transformed. Among books and magazines I now instinctively turned to the lightest and least improving. I had hardly the energy to hold thirteen cards in my hand and hardly the brainpower to play them. There was, for a man in this condition, no thought of having an idea, engaging in an argument, or writing a column.

I began, then, to think about the working people I knew when I was a boy. They were naturally thoughtful and able men. Some of them had a good deal of native talent. But they were held down by their hard labor in the open air. Neighbors would come to our house to spend the evening or I would be taken by my parents up or down the country road to pay a visit. My father would sit there with the other farmers. They would talk in short, slow, widely spaced sentences about crops or weather or some neighborhood event—but always slowly, as if their brains were tired. I remember hearing them discuss how Garfield was shot, but it was merely as they might have mourned a similar misfortune of any other neighbor. They never discussed public affairs. They seldom laughed, and if they told a story it would be the narrative of some simple incident involving a hired man or a farm animal.

In the city the distinction between those who do hard physical labor and those who don't is just as sharp. Nothing made a deeper impression upon me during my years at the Rand School and the *New Leader*. The trade-union officials—no matter how conscientious —could hardly avoid acting like members of a class different from that of their members. The oppressively class-conscious Industrial Workers of the World tried hard to bridge the gulf by making rules. They would decree that officials were to receive no higher pay than workers at the bench or down in the mine, or that the trade-union snob was to be sent back to his proletarian job at the end of a certain turn in the more aristocratic office. But this Utopian mechanism never produced the hoped-for results. Unions that were run in this way soon went out of existence.

As a *New Leader* columnist I have received a good many letters. I have always wanted, most of all, to hear from wage earners and farmers. I know pretty well what intellectuals think. I have lived with them these many years. There is just one farmer who writes to me—and that is at long intervals. It would please me no end if he would write a comment on this piece. I wonder what he will think of this notion of mine. ∎

History does not always repeat

∎ This morning I heard the first robin of the season. Those rich bubbling notes came to me while I was looking over the perennial bed. At just about the same moment my ears announced the return of the birds, my eyes attested that the daffodils and hyacinths were well up out of the ground and on their way to break the dull scheme of winter with flashes of spring. In this crazy world the basic arrangements have not been altered. This northern region is again turning its face to the sun. The birds return as they have done each spring for thousands of years, and the plants push their way into the light in response to the ancient law.

In the Temperate Zone, the rhythm of nature—hot, cold, hot, cold—is the very basis of human psychology. We have the notion that everything passes. One extreme turns into the other—with pleasant periods of compromise in between. Youth comes like spring and old age like winter. Prosperity shines upon us for a while—to be followed—inevitably—by depression. The Democrats may manage things for a time, but it is taken for granted, as night follows day, that the Republicans will return. Nothing, no matter how much we may like or dislike it, is permanent. As spring follows winter, so a period of good will take the place of a time of evil.

The American optimism that Europeans find so superficial and objectionable is based on the faith that this chain of evil and good will continue forever. It has been continuous from the time of our colonial beginnings—and we are able to persuade ourselves that each new good period has been a little bigger and better than the last. The Civil War period may be regarded as a break, but it disturbed the traditional pattern for only one section of the country and for a minority of the people. For the most part, Americans still think that everything will go on forever just about as it always has.

The First World War hardly produced a ripple on the calm surface of our assumptions. Europe had gone haywire, and we were forced to send troops over there to straighten things out. That was all there was to it. After the neighborly job had been attended to we could go peacefully on our way, with prosperity following depression, but on the whole continuing to grow richer.

The rise of Hitler troubled the daydreams of many of us. But it took the sharp concussion of Pearl Harbor to rouse the majority of Americans. Stress on Nazi and Fascist philosophies was a necessary part of the war propaganda. But they seemed to have few advocates here, and as our great war machine began to roll a good many of us felt reassured. After all, our civilization seemed to be sound. It could, at least, produce tanks and planes and ships. In the end it proved its soundness by producing that miracle of scientific and industrial cooperation the atom bomb.

At the end of the war, which inevitably ended with a victory for our side, we were again pretty well fortified with self-satisfaction— all except the dead, of course. We had spent money by the hundreds of billions, but by God we had won! We had shown the world. Our land was still unravaged, still ready to produce all the trappings of luxury and comfort.

I have just been reading, a bit late, Victor Serge's book *The Long Dusk*. It is called a novel, but it is not. It gives a cross section of bleeding and bewildered France during the days of annihilation. People, from poets to prostitutes, quiver before us as they show the inner workings of their consciousness. It is a shattering thing to experience. Here is an entire people really flat. Their faith in themselves, their system of ideas, the framework of their society have been torn apart. Like men on a desert plain, they are forced to rebuild from the bottom up.

André Malraux recently faced up to the question "Is Europe dead?" His answer is: "We are not in the shadow of death. We are rather at the focal point . . . where nothing is left but intelligence and energy." Europe is a continent where men, stripped naked of pretenses and of the comfortable faith in routine, face the fates barehanded.

Until recently, even England stood outside the circle where destruction has reduced men to first principles. Even while the bombs crashed on London Englishmen put out the flames, buried their dead, and took for granted that the old British system of things would go on indefinitely. But I have a feeling that what could not be accomplished by bombs and rockets is being brought about by the bitter experience of this winter with freezing cold and low production of all the things that make life possible. British confidence in traditional patterns is shaken at last. Stiff and stoic men on that tight little island are, like the French, the Germans, the Poles, up against the tough realities of existence.

I have a notion that the bell has also tolled for optimistic and self-satisfied America. After we won the war against Nazism and Fascism, more of the world was enslaved than before the war began. There were more men being starved and beaten down in concentration camps and more little countries robbed of their independence. In the face of this situation the President of the United States said: "I believe that it must be the policy of the United States to support free peoples who are resisting attempted subjugation by armed minorities or by outside pressures."

This hardly sounds like a clarion call to battle. Roosevelt would have put it into more resounding terms. Part of its impressiveness results from the unimpressive quality of the language, the occasion, and the speaker. Harry Truman is a common little man who happens to be President of the United States. Henry A. Wallace and the so-called liberal writers talk a lot about the common man. But Harry Truman really is one. When he spoke as he did, it was proof that many of the American people had made up their minds about the conflict that divides the world.

When we fought the First World War we took for granted that when we had beaten the Kaiser everything would be O.K. During the Second World War the idea was that when we had beaten Hitler and Hirohito "the peace-loving nations" would fix everything up in a satisfactory way. We were fighting symbols. We took for granted that when the symbols were removed the realities would also vanish. It failed to happen.

Harry Truman's call is not for the destruction of any foreign monarch or state. It is a call for struggle against an idea, a system. The enemies mentioned are "totalitarian regimes, coercion and intimidation." We are called upon to use our power in favor of "free institutions, representative government, free elections, guarantees of individual liberty, freedom of speech and religion and freedom from political oppression."

This struggle cannot be localized. It may start in Greece. But our objectives have been stated in terms that include China, Italy, France, Poland, Austria, and so on. It is amusing to see editorial writers like Max Lerner jump to the conclusion that this means atombomb war. Truman says that we must help people to be free, and the nimble Max scents a declaration of war on Moscow. The implication is, of course, that the rulers in Moscow are against freedom, that they are so desperately against it that we must fight them with atom bombs. Whether they are as irreconcilable as Mr. Lerner makes them out is something we shall discover in due time.

It may come to war. Last night I was talking to my nephew Dick. He has just returned from serving his time in Korea. Next fall he will enter college. We were talking about his experiences away off there and how happy he should be to have his army days behind him. Dick took it all very calmly and finally pulled us up by remarking: "Don't go so fast. In about five years I'll be back there again—or in some other place just like it." You will hear similar remarks from a lot of the boys home from the war. They do not expect everything to go on forever just as it always has.

We are lining up in a world-wide struggle the end of which no man can see. No matter what action we take now, in the end we cannot side-step it. The President's initiative has the advantage of taking us in before another Pearl Harbor lands on our heads. But the conflict, whatever form it takes, will be longer and more important in its results than any other in which we have participated. We are now directing our course into the central current of world affairs. Never again can a conscientious American citizen be a simple, satisfied, naïve, and serene denizen of a wide and prosperous Ruritania. From now on, each of us is a responsible citizen of a troubled and dangerous world.   ■

What do liberals really want?

■ In my recent report on the Army-McCarthy conflict, I mentioned meeting two charming young ladies from Minneapolis who had hurriedly flown down to the hearings because they thought their hero, the junior senator from Wisconsin, was not being fairly treated by the unsympathetic East. They felt that he needed support, and they came prepared to give it with hands, lungs, and letters to the press.

You would have said in advance that we had small grounds for friendship, but you would have been wrong. From the start, we had wonderful times, eager conversation, tumultuous give-and-take. They really wanted to know what I thought, how it was that a man could be opposed to their shining hero. And I was bent on discovering how two bright gals could join the procession behind a man like McCarthy.

Naturally, this cheerful process of give-and-take has not been allowed to lapse. The young ladies read the *New Leader*, and now and then an exchange of letters keeps our discussion alive. This brings me at last to my point, which is a question contained in a letter that arrived this morning. After referring in a rather derogatory manner to some of our contributors, my correspondent says: "I do enjoy your articles, and I feel so fair reading both sides. The Catholic *Tablet* arrives the same day as the *New Leader*. I am afraid that it more eloquently expresses my convictions, and I can understand it so much better. In the *New Leader* I read and re-read sentences and then decide it's all over my Irish head! What I want to know is: What kind of world do the liberals really want?"

Here is a challenge. I feel that, if this Irish girl and I had the time and patience and could find the right words, we would discover that we believe practically the same things. Generally, people don't try to express themselves clearly, and they don't listen carefully. So each remains stuck in his sect—and that is one of the things that is wrong with the world. I am going to spend the rest of this page trying to break through the wall by telling what we liberals "really want."

I might begin by saying that we want for the people of this country—and of all countries, for that matter—enough good food, good shelter and clothing. But that would be starting at the wrong end. What we are after is a good life for everyone, and the things which make up a good life cannot be handed to people—they must be won by thought and work. To begin with, however, the people must have freedom. Solomon is credited with saying that "wisdom is the principal thing." He may not have been far off the mark. But if they are to be effective, the people who have achieved wisdom must have freedom to think, to learn, to speak, to organize, to operate.

We have had a fine row of prophets in this country: Franklin, Madison, Jefferson, Lincoln. It would be possible to make a wonderful Old Testament out of their sayings. These men had a very clear picture of the world both as it was and as they wanted it to be. Much of their wisdom has been interpreted and condensed in our Constitution. The basis of their thinking was the idea that, if people are free and have access to knowledge, they will gradually build a world closer to their hearts' desire.

We are constantly being told how many people are hungry or

ill-clothed or ill-housed. These are terrible facts that shame us, but we should constantly recall that freedom is the basis of a progressive civilization—more basic than a full belly or a warm body. If we Americans are to go on as we have in the past, producing more and better goods, distributing them more and more equitably, encouraging learning and the arts, improving our country and having fun living together in it, the main thing is to keep it free in all the areas of work and play.

In the schools, we must remain free to learn and teach. In the churches, the worship must be that which satisfies the individual. Newspapers, radio, television and all other media of communication must be so conducted that the whole populace will have access to accurate information. In industry, we must do our best to keep ourselves free from cartels and every other coercive form of organization; workers, managers and investors must be able to operate wherever and however they can get the best results. In politics, there must be open and enlightened discussion so that the best men can get to the top and, having reached there, be free to legislate and administer for the public good. What we have in mind is no set form like that of the Communists or that pictured by the philosophers of the Middle Ages. We picture, rather, a constantly improving setup going forward under the drive of its citizens.

To this I wish to add two remarks. It is because Senator McCarthy always seems to be pointed toward a coercive world rather than a free one that I am opposed to him. I am envious of the Catholic *Tablet* because my correspondent can understand it better than she can the *New Leader*. ∎